Voices of Innovation – AI

Innovation in healthcare has been both fast and slow.

As an industry, we have clearly made great technological advancements, and yet we find ourselves behind peer industries when it comes to innovation with patient care, customer experience, augmented intelligence, virtual care, and cybersecurity. One reason for the lack of innovation velocity is the need for a universally adopted model or best practice framework. The time has come for *Voices of Innovation – AI*. Artificial intelligence is what some call the fourth transformative revolution in human history. Healthcare is among the many industries with significant opportunities for the use of AI and machine learning, as the convergence of technology and healthcare will result in significant innovation. This book is both practical and inspirational. Using the HIMSS model for innovation as the structural framework, *Voices of Innovation – AI* will showcase the great AI innovations being implemented across healthcare globally.

With contributions from leading authorities in this field, this book will become the de facto resource for any organization seeking to leverage AI effectively. Loaded with numerous case studies and stories of successful innovation projects, this book helps the reader understand how to leverage AI to help fulfill the promise of technology in enabling superior business and clinical outcomes.

Voices of Innovation in Healthcare
Series Editor: Edward W. Marx

Everyone talks about innovation, and we can all point to random examples of innovation inside of healthcare information technology, but few repeatable processes exist that make innovation more routine than happenstance. How do you create and sustain a culture of innovation? What are the best practices you can refine and embed as part of your organization's DNA? What are the potential outcomes for robust healthcare transformation when we get this innovation mystery solved? Through timely essays from leading experts, the first edition showcased the widely adopted healthcare innovation model from HIMSS and how providers could leverage to increase their velocity of digital transformation. Regardless of its promise, innovation has been slow in healthcare.

Voices of Innovation – AI leverages the same framework and construct but zeroes in on artificial intelligence to include large language models, voice and robotic process automation.

Voices of Innovation: Fulfilling the Promise of Information Technology in Healthcare, 2nd Edition
Edited by Edward W. Marx

Voices of Innovation – Payers: Opportunities for Creating Solutions to Improve Member Experience and Health
Edited by Edward W. Marx and Sakshika Dhingra

Voices of Innovation – AI: Fulfilling the Promise of AI in Healthcare
Edited by Edward W. Marx, Sakshika Dhingra, Dr. Frank Papay, and Dr. Piyush Mathur

Voices of Innovation – AI
Fulfilling the Promise of AI in Healthcare

Edited by
Edward W. Marx, Sakshika Dhingra,
Frank Papay, MD, and Piyush Mathur, MD

Routledge
Taylor & Francis Group

A PRODUCTIVITY PRESS BOOK

Designed cover image: Shutterstock

First published 2025
by Routledge
605 Third Avenue, New York, NY 10158

and by Routledge
4 Park Square, Milton Park, Abingdon, Oxon, OX14 4RN

Routledge is an imprint of the Taylor & Francis Group, an informa business

© 2025 Edward W. Marx, Sakshika Dhingra, Frank Papay, and Piyush Mathur

ISBN: 978-1-032-71512-4 (hbk)
ISBN: 978-1-032-71510-0 (pbk)
ISBN: 978-1-032-71515-5 (ebk)

DOI: 10.4324/9781032715155

Typeset in Garamond
by SPi Technologies India Pvt Ltd (Straive)

Contents

Foreword

I have known Edward W. Marx for more than 15 years. When Ed asked me to write the Foreword for *Voices of Innovation – AI*, I was both flattered and elated! I said YES, sign me up! I read Ed's previous books in the *Voices of Innovation in Healthcare* series and have featured him as a keynote speaker in several of our "Beckers" conferences. As a big fan, writing the Foreword is like being asked by Jay-Z to do a music collaboration (ft. S. Becker). Jesting aside, what you hold in your hands is a practical book that teaches how to innovate with impact, and specifically, AI adoption and execution. A dose of theory yet full of real examples that stand the test of time. Something we will all benefit from.

The Editors

Ed is not alone as an editor. He is joined by Sakshika Dhingra, a Payer executive who previously partnered with him on *Voices of Innovation - Payers*. To strengthen the clinical connection, Cleveland Clinic physician leaders Dr. Frank Papay and Dr. Piyush Mathur also helped. Together, the four of them oversaw the process where they collected best practices from around the world to ensure representation from organizations small and large, community-based and local. There are examples in this book all of us will relate to.

With the proven innovation construct developed by HIMSS, this book inspires and provides practical guidance on how to enable digital transformation via AI.

Why this Book

In today's landscape of healthcare, innovation is not just a buzzword; it is a critical imperative. Innovation stands as a beacon of hope and progress, guiding us toward a brighter and more effective future enabling improved clinician and patient experiences. The challenges we face in providing accessible, affordable, and high-quality healthcare to our communities demand innovative solutions. As leaders in healthcare, it is us who must drive this change and make a positive impact on the lives of those we serve.

I am delighted to introduce this groundbreaking book on AI innovation, a comprehensive guide for leaders like you. This book brings together a wealth of knowledge, insights, and strategies that will help you navigate the complex and dynamic landscape of healthcare and the myriad of areas it entails. It delves into the intricacies of transforming the way we interact with different entities and, most importantly, the members, patients, and clinicians.

The chapters explore a wide range of AI applicability. Transforming our capabilities to cure cancer, improve productivity, and enable improved experiences for patients and clinicians. Importantly, the first chapter tackles an important prerequisite. Governance and ethics of artificial intelligence. We need to get this right before embarking too far down the road on our AI journeys. You will read perspectives from physicians and nursing leaders, which set the tone for the remaining chapters.

Why Now

The journey of healthcare innovation is no longer an option; it is a necessity. With the rising costs of care, an aging population, and the ever-present need for efficient and effective healthcare services, we must adapt and innovate. *Voices of Innovation – AI* is designed to be your compass in this uncharted territory, providing you with the tools and ideas to foster and execute AI-related innovation in your organization. Survival of the Digitalist.

I encourage you to use this book as a resource, a source of inspiration, and a catalyst for change within your healthcare enterprise. The transformation of healthcare is a collective effort, and by fostering AI innovation in your organization, you can be a driving force in improving the health and well-being of countless individuals.

I applaud Ed, Sakshika, Frank, Piyush, and all the contributors for their dedication to advancing AI innovation. I thank you, the reader, for your commitment to making a difference. Together, we can ensure that healthcare remains a force for good, delivering better outcomes and experiences for all.

Let this book be your guide, your inspiration, and your call to action. The future of healthcare awaits, and with innovation as our compass, we can shape it into something remarkable.

Scott Becker
Founder and Publisher Beckers Healthcare,
Partner and Former Chair HealthCare Department,
Board Member, McGuireWoods,
July 2024

Acknowledgments

I dedicate this book to my Dad, Herbert Marx. A Holocaust survivor and concentration camp escapee, Dad eventually made his way to Switzerland. First, he spent several years hidden from Nazis by Catholic nuns in a French convent. Second, he spent several years as an orphan in Geneva before the Red Cross sent him to New York to assimilate with the only known surviving family member. Drafted into the US Army post-high school, Dad spent 20 years as a soldier, followed by 20 years as a civil servant. With Mom, he raised seven children and now enjoys life with 30+ grand and great-grandchildren. At age 90, he continues to share his story of hope, forgiveness, and love. Central to his life story is resilience, something he passed on to me. Dad, thank you for giving me life and being my biggest cheerleader next to Mom. I am proud to call you Daddy.

I am also thankful for my co-editor, Sakshika Dhingra. We met a couple of years ago via an introduction from the CEO of Tech Mahindra. While I served as her mentor for one year, I learned as much from her. An innovator herself, she did much of the heavy lifting for this book you are holding.

Thank you to additional co-editors, Dr. Frank Papay and Dr. Piyush Mathur. When we served together at Cleveland Clinic, you both stood out as innovators, especially with all things AI. The global BrainX community you developed is an inspiration for many.

Edward W. Marx

I dedicate this book to my oh-so-graceful mother, Smt Kamal Dhingra, and my loving husband, Vivesh Sharma. Two individuals who have been my constant source of unwavering love, support, and encouragement.

Oldest of five siblings, my mother started playing the role of the head of the household at an early age, since my grandfather was in the Indian Navy and used to be away for long periods of time, and my grandmother, one of the wisest people I've personally known, never went to school. She was and continues to be the problem solver of the family. Her journey has not been easy, and no matter what the setback was, she was always smiling and teaching my sister and me reasons to be grateful. Her sacrifices and endless support have allowed me to pursue my dreams, and her belief in me has given me the courage to face the toughest challenges.

One of the core values that defines her is "resilience". At 70, staying true to her nature, she is relearning life after my dad's demise. Any value that I can create in this lifetime, including this book, is a testament to the values and the "always keep going" attitude she has instilled in me and the foundation she has built for my life.

Vivesh, your belief in me and my work sustains me through the ups and downs of life. Thank you for being my partner in every sense of the word. This is for you.

I would like to express my deepest gratitude to my co-author, Edward W. Marx. His ability to rethink routine and his zest for life are an inspiration to me and many others, and I consider myself fortunate to have had the opportunity to collaborate and work closely with him on a topic we both are passionate about – Healthcare Innovation.

Sakshika Dhingra

This book, "Voices of Innovation: AI Strategies in Healthcare", is a heartfelt dedication to what we believe will be the most transformative technology in the history of healthcare: artificial intelligence. Its potential to revolutionize medical practices, improve patient outcomes, and transform the delivery of care is unparalleled.

To my family: thank you for putting up with me and my unyielding passion for innovation, science, and the pursuit of the next big thing. Your unwavering support has been my foundation, and this book stands as a testament to the legacy we can leave for future generations. If we can implement AI to create a more equitable and efficient healthcare system, we will not only advance medical science but also improve the healthspan of generations to come.

I extend my deepest gratitude to my mentors and collaborative co-authors and partners—Dr. Piyush Mathur, Sakshika, and Ed—who have paved the way for this groundbreaking literary work. Your wisdom, guidance, and pioneering efforts have been instrumental in shaping our understanding and approach to integrating AI into healthcare. Your legacy of innovation and excellence continues to inspire us.

To the younger staff embarking on this journey, this book is equally dedicated to you. Your energy, creativity, and commitment to a more equitable healthcare system are more vital than ever. You are the torchbearers of this transformative era, tasked with improving access, eliminating biases, curtailing unnecessary costs, and enhancing personalized patient care rather than "sick care" throughout one's lifelong healthcare journey.

Together, let us embrace this technological revolution, honoring the past while forging a future where AI enables a more efficient, inclusive, and compassionate healthcare system for all. This book is a tribute to both the trailblazers and the innovators, united in our mission to advance healthcare through the power of artificial intelligence.

Dr. Frank Papay

This book is dedicated to many clinicians, data scientists, and information technology experts, from across the world who are researching and innovating tirelessly to bring data-driven solutions to solve some of the biggest challenges in healthcare. We formed BrainX, an AI in healthcare company, to investigate opportunities to apply artificial intelligence solutions to healthcare. I would like to acknowledge the dedication of this team, which has persevered to advance not just science, but also create a community around us with many partners, interns, and consultants joining us. Thanks, Edward W. Marx, for leading this effort and being part of our team. You are always inspiring us to do more, do better, and do faster.

Special credit goes to Raghav and Shreya, our technology leads at BrainX, who have worked hard to understand the clinical needs, educate many, and research solutions that are likely to transform healthcare. Frank, Kamal, Jacek, and Ashish, who started BrainX, are the true voices of innovation in AI, selflessly dedicating their time and efforts to create a better future for all of us with one goal – machine learning in healthcare for good.

Hope this book inspires many to think differently. From where I personally started, my goal of innovation in healthcare remains the same. Apply advanced technologies and data-driven science to improve quality and patient safety.

Dr. Piyush Mathur

*****

All author royalties for this book go to Mayo Clinic Foundation to help cure cancer in their names.

We think of you Herbert, Kamal, Vivesh, and the BrainX community.

About the Editors

Edward W. Marx is CEO of Marx Advisory, a consultancy aimed at improving the marketplace experience for vendors and providers. A healthcare best-selling author of multiple books around innovation, transformation, and experience, all his royalties are donated toward the eradication of cancer. His writings reflect his deep expertise gained while serving as CIO of the global Cleveland Clinic and NYC Health and Hospitals. He is an advisor for start-ups and multinational companies and sits on the boards of multiple health systems. He advises governments on digital transformation strategies. When not working, Ed competes internationally for TeamUSA Triathlon and is on pace to climb the Seven Summits. Ed is married to Dr. Simran Marx, and they share 5 children and 5 grandchildren.

Sakshika Dhingra is a director with Humana, currently focused on strategic and operational planning to serve their Medicaid membership. She has spent most of her career serving different population groups while working for multiple leading Payer organizations across the country. She is a results-oriented healthcare strategist with a passion for developing and implementing innovative solutions and frameworks centered around sustainability and scalability. Sakshika, a doting Mom, lives with her loving husband Vivesh Sharma and her affectionate and curious six-year-old son Aveer.

Dr. Piyush Mathur, MD, FCCM, FASA, FAMIA, is a staff anesthesiologist and critical care physician at Cleveland Clinic, Ohio with more than 20 years of clinician experience. He served in the role of the Quality Improvement Officer and chair of the compliance committee at the Anesthesiology Institute, Cleveland Clinic, between 2011 and 2024 and has recently transitioned to lead innovation at the department. He is the co-founder of

BrainX, an AI in healthcare company focused on translational aspects of AI in healthcare. He has also co-founded one of the largest online groups for machine learning in healthcare, BrainXCommunity.

Dr. Frank Papay, MD, DSc(hon), FACS, FAAP, is a distinguished health-care executive, pioneering surgeon, and innovator with an impressive track record of leadership and groundbreaking contributions to medicine. Based at the Cleveland Clinic, Dr. Papay currently serves as Chairman of the Plastic Surgery Institute at the Cleveland Clinic. His leadership has driven the Plastic Surgery Department to nearly triple in size and revenue through strategic regional and international expansion, the creation of new service lines, and a 34% enhancement in clinical efficiency. His distinguished career is underpinned by a robust educational foundation, including a master's in biomedical engineering from Case Western Reserve University and double board certifications in Otolaryngology and Plastic and Reconstructive Surgery from the Cleveland Clinic. Dr. Papay's extensive expertise and leadership continue to drive significant advancements in healthcare, making him a respected and influential figure in the medical community.

About the Contributors

Merrill Anovick: 25m Health. Merrill is the co-founder and President of 25m Health. He helped launch 25m Health in partnership with Apollo, Lifepoint Health, and Scion in November 2021. He sits on the 25m Health Investment Committee and oversees both the investing and incubation strategies where he has co-founded Kouper Health, Gratia, and Ladder Health and invested in M7, Keragon, Midi Health, and Thrive Mobile.

Dr. Gregory Ator, MD, FACS, FAMIA, Chief Medical Informatics Officer, KU Medical Center: Dr. Ator is a board-certified informatician and serves as the CMIO for Kansas University. He has an electrical engineering degree and practices as an otolaryngologist with a subspeciality interest in Otology – Neurotology and Skull Base Surgery.

Raghav Awasthi: Experienced Researcher in policy modeling for Public Health with a demonstrated history of working in the higher education industry. Skilled in Causal analysis, Counterfactual modeling, Machine Learning, NLP, Linear Algebra, Research, C (programming language), R, and Python (programming language). Strong research professional with a Doctor of Philosophy – PhD focused in Computational Biology from Indraprastha Institute of Information Technology, Delhi.

Thom Bales: Principal at Strategy and PwC US Health Services Sector Lead. Tom has 20+ years in consulting with PwC Strategy and (formerly Booz & Company) focused on health operations, technology strategy, and transformation. He leads PwC's Health Services Sector and San Francisco Strategy and teams. Other past experiences include strategy setting and financial analysis in financial services, automotive, consumer products, chemicals, and energy.

Dr. Susana Bowling, MD, FAHA, FNCS, FAAN, ACC: Dr. Bowling serves as Medical Director for Summa Health's Neuroscience Institute and Akron City Hospital Comprehensive Stroke Center. She is board certified in Neurology as well as Neurocritical Care and Vascular Neurology. She is a Fellow of the American Academy of Neurology (FAAN), American Heart Association (FAHA), Fellow Neurocritical Care Society (FNCS), and Associate Certified Coach (ACC). She earned her MD and Fellowship in Vascular Neurology and Neurocritical Care (Medicine) from the University of Alabama. She worked at Beth Israel Hospital in NYC as an associate professor and later Director of the Neurocritical Care program at the Alabama Neurological Institute before coming to Summa Health System in 2008.

Casey Bryson: Casey Bryson currently serves as the Vice President of Solution Consulting at Abridge. After graduating from the University of Missouri with a focus on business administration and economics, he began his 20-year career in healthcare information technology. In his role at Abridge, Casey is able to show the world what is possible through conversational AI and bring joy to the people that take care of all of us, our clinicians. Prior to Abridge, Casey held the roles of Vice President of IT at The University of Kansas Health System, Chief Information and Innovation Officer at Hurley Medical Center, Chief Strategy Officer at Datica, and Implementation Executive at Epic Systems Corporation.

Dr. Harvey Castro, MD: Helpp.ai and Medical Intelligence Ops. Dr. Harvey Castro is an ER physician and the Chief Medical AI Officer at Helpp.ai, focusing on AI-driven fall prevention and workflow automation in healthcare. He is also the CEO of Medical Intelligence Ops, where he integrates Large Language Models into healthcare systems. With over 20 years of experience in emergency medicine, Dr. Castro is recognized for his pioneering work in AI and healthcare, authoring multiple books and developing innovative AI solutions. He serves on various advisory boards, including the Singapore Ministry of Health and the American Board of Artificial Intelligence in Medicine. Dr. Castro's expertise spans practical AI applications in healthcare, personalized medicine, and ethical AI integration.

Paul Brian Contino, CPHIMS, FHIMSS, is a highly accomplished technology leader with over 25 years of experience in healthcare, biomedical research, and academic medicine. At the forefront of digital transformation, Paul has been involved in the development and implementation of sophisticated IT systems including EHR platforms, analytics and artificial intelligence, cyber-security, and cloud computing to enhance and advance patient care and operational efficiency. Paul has held senior leadership roles at The Guthrie Clinic, NYC Health + Hospitals, and Mount Sinai Medical Center. Currently, as the Chief Information Officer at University Hospital in New Jersey, he shapes the hospital's IT vision and strategy, leveraging technology to enhance patient care and experience, streamline operations, secure information systems, and improve overall health system performance. As a nationally recognized thought leader in healthcare technology, Paul's contributions have made him a respected voice in the industry.

Grace Currie: Grace is a clinician researcher and Senior Program Manager at the Sydney Children's Hospitals Network and the University of Sydney. A leader in digital health transformation, Grace's research and hospital role focuses on operationalizing learning health systems by understanding the enablers for healthcare-embedded research technology. Grace is leading the Learning Health Initiative at the Sydney Children's Hospitals Network, which aims to transform the hospital network into a learning health system by utilizing routinely captured data for quality improvement, research, and predictive analytics.

Kieran Donaldson: Kieran Donaldson is a highly accomplished engineering leader with a strong background in artificial intelligence, mobile, and gaming technologies. As the Vice President of Engineering at Iconic AI and technical advisor to Medigram, his expertise spans critical and innovative areas in tech. Ranked in the top 5% of tech professionals, his Oxford training, experience in regulated technology, and successful startup exit make him an invaluable part of an ideal team to partner with healthcare leaders seeking cutting-edge solutions.

Dr. Arthur Douville: Dr. Arthur Douville, CMO at Medigram and a practicing neurologist is recognized among the top 5% of physician executives, renowned for his leadership in medical administration and healthcare innovation. As a repeat health system enterprise CMO, Dr. Douville has consistently championed the integration of advanced technologies in clinical settings to improve patient care and operational efficiency. His insights and strategic vision have made significant impacts on healthcare systems.

Sherri Douville: Sherri Douville is the CEO of Medigram, Founder and Chair of the Trustworthy Technology and Innovation Consortium (TTIC), and co-chair of the Trust SG for IEEE/UL 2933. She leads at the intersection of AI, Cybersecurity, mobility, and healthcare, setting new standards that place her among the top 1% of tech executives worldwide. Sherri's visionary leadership and strategic acumen have earned her the recognition and trust of industry leaders and policymakers, driving industry-wide advancements and shaping the future of healthcare technology.

Deborah Gash: Deborah Gash, CHCHIO - is a senior healthcare technology expert, who accelerates digital strategies, business transformation, and innovation. She is known as a forward-thinking champion for innovation and spearheads HIT solutions for a health system of 16 hospitals and 13K employees. She leverages her profound understanding of the healthcare business to develop and implement practical technology solutions to empower and enhance the health and well-being of patients, staff, and community while improving operational efficiency.

Alex Goryachev: Alex is a globally recognized AI and Innovation Leader and a Keynote Speaker, bringing a wealth of experience in formulating and executing forward-thinking digital strategies in complex environments. His tenure at global companies, such as Dell, Amgen, IBM, Pfizer, and Cisco, where he led Global Innovation Centers across 14 countries, increased revenue and accelerated the industry's digital transformation through pioneering artificial intelligence, IoT, and other digital solutions.

Debra Graves – Commonwealth Care Alliance: Debra is a Medical Claims Senior Product Owner for Commonwealth Care Alliance. She has worked in the healthcare Industry for a little more than 4 years after switching industries from finance. She has her master's in health informatics from Northeastern University in Boston and is a Certified Scrum Product Owner (CSPO).

Deepak Goyal: Partner at PwC Strategy, Deepak is a seasoned healthcare technology professional with over 19 years of experience across the payer and provider sectors. Deepak currently leads the Healthcare Technology Strategy practice as part of PwC Strategy and is focused on providing IT strategy, IT transformation, Digital, Analytics, and M&A-related advisory to many national and regional healthcare providers and payers. In his role as the healthcare Technology Strategy leader, Deepak is responsible for business development, team building, capability and offering development, and managing C-suite client relationships at several healthcare clients. Deepak is a thought leader in the healthcare sector who regularly publishes his thinking and is a regular speaker at leading industry conferences.

Raouf Hajji: International Medical Community (IMC) Raouf Hajji is a co-founder and Medical Lead of the International Medical Community (IMC), an Innovative HelatTech Hub serves as a connector and resource-sharing hub for stakeholders ranging from academics to scientists to regulators. He has over 12 years of experience working in the healthcare sector, academia, biomedical research, and HealthTech innovations. He is the author, reviewer, and editor of many peer-reviewed medical journal articles and book chapters. He is also an assistant professor of Internal medicine at the Medicine Faculty of Sousse, Tunisia. He supports and mentors teams and individuals worldwide in biomedtech innovations, research, and development. He focuses on integrating cutting-edge technologies and fostering partnerships that drive progress and innovations in medical practice, biomedical research, and academia.

Lyndsay Hercule: International Medical Community (IMC). Lyndsay Hercule is a co-founder and the Director of the International Medical Community (IMC). She advises technology startups across multiple jurisdictions. Utilizing my years of experience in International Business and Corporate Strategy, I assist in developing entrepreneurial operations in intellectual property, data security, and trade, covering various industries globally. She holds a Masters in International Business from Hult International Business School and was admitted to the Supreme Court of Brisbane, Australia, as a Solicitor.

Karen Marie Joswick, MHA, is the Founder and President of Benevolence Health. With over 20 years in healthcare, including system executive leadership roles, she is a recognized thought leader in payment innovation, accountable care, and health system operations. Karen's expertise spans value-based care, clinical program growth, health equity, and technology integration across various payer models. She holds multiple professional certifications in health IT and clinical informatics, serves as an adjunct faculty member at Jefferson University, and has been on the Board of Directors for NAACOs. Her work in driving ROI, value-based transformation, and leveraging technology for system-wide growth has made her a key figure in reshaping the healthcare industry landscape globally.

Dr. Olga Kagan, Ph.D., RN, FHIMSS, FAAAAI: Principal OKHCC; Adjunct Associate Professor CUNY SPS; Adjunct Faculty Molloy University. A registered professional nurse with over 25 years in the industry, her experience spans various clinical and academic settings, including Mount Sinai Health System, Lenox Hill Hospital, Molloy University, CUNY School of Professional Studies, and within professional organizations, including the American Nurses Association, the American Academy of Allergy Asthma and Immunology, the Health Information Management System Society, the Eastern Nursing Research Society, and the Society of Nurse Scientists, Innovators, Entrepreneurs, and Leaders.

Tatyana Kanzaveli: Open Health Network. Tatyana Kanzaveli is the Founder and CEO of Open Health Network. With extensive experience in the healthcare and technology sectors, Tatyana has been a leading force in integrating AI and GenAI-driven solutions to enhance clinical trial processes and patient care. Prior to founding Open Health Network, she held senior executive positions at prominent tech companies and has been recognized globally for her contributions to healthcare innovation and digital transformation.

Dr. Eileen Kasda, DrPH.: SafeTower Baltimore, Md. Eileen is the Vice President of Patient Safety at SafeTower, a spinout from Johns Hopkins Medicine. Dr. Kasda is a recognized leader in the field of patient safety, dedicated to transforming safety practices and culture using innovative technology with more than 14 years of experience in patient safety. She specializes in applying AI to solve problems in patient safety and grievance reporting and analysis. Prior to joining SafeTower, Eileen led the development and management of a novel, AI-driven patient safety reporting solution at Johns Hopkins Medicine in Baltimore.

Dr. Avneesh Khare – BrainX AI, USA: Dr. Avneesh Khare, a former anesthesiologist and pain management specialist, is a thought leader, educator, advisor, and consultant at the intersection of AI and medicine. As a LinkedIn Top Voice, he has established "The Med AI Capsule" initiative and contributes to "BrainX AI", focusing on machine learning in healthcare for good. Based in India, Dr. Khare is a co-founder of the "Doctors AI" online community, advocating for AI education for medical professionals. His views have been recognized and featured internationally, including at the G20 Consultation, Times Square, and Forbes.

Inderpal Kohli: Inder is the VP of IT and CIO at Englewood Health and has 25+ years of leadership in healthcare technology. He oversees IT, biomedical engineering, and digital transformation for a health system with 150+ locations. Previously, he held key roles at the Hospital for Special Surgery and Columbia University Medical Center. Kohli holds a master's in technology management, speaks at industry events, and has taught healthcare informatics at Weill Cornell Medical College.

Durga Malleswari Koratani: Durga is an aspiring EPIC Analyst with a Master of Science in Healthcare Informatics from Sacred Heart University. She completed an internship at Optimus Healthcare, where she gained hands-on experience with EPIC systems. She is passionate about leveraging technology to improve healthcare outcomes.

Craig Kwiatkowski, PharmD: Craig is Chief Information Officer and Senior Vice President of Enterprise Information Services at Cedars-Sinai. He has over 25 years of experience in healthcare, having led numerous technology initiatives aimed at improving care delivery, outcomes, user experience, and operational efficiency. Prior to joining Cedars-Sinai in 2009, Kwiatkowski held various operational and clinical leadership roles at the University of Chicago Hospitals. He holds a Doctor of Pharmacy degree from the Chicago College of Pharmacy.

Jian Liu: Jian is a highly accomplished Senior Health IT Executive with over 20 years of experience in the healthcare sector. His expertise spans strategic and digital health planning, governance, digital transformation and integration, and IT operations management. Throughout his career, Jian has shown a deep commitment to driving digital health innovation to improve healthcare quality and safety. Currently serving as the Chief Digital Health Officer and CIO at the Sydney Children's Hospitals Network, he spearheads efforts to orchestrate and optimize digital transformation initiatives within the organization.

Rohit Mahajan: Rohit is an experienced entrepreneur, investor, and leader with a demonstrated history of working in the Digital Health and Healthcare Industry. He has worked with IBM and Wipro in the past. He is the Managing Partner and CEO at BigRio and Damo Consulting. He holds a Bachelor's degree in Electronics and Communications Engineering, is a Wharton School Fellow and a graduate of the Harvard Business School. He has recently completed the Global Healthcare Leaders Program from

Harvard Medical School. His first full-length book, Quantum Care: A Deep Dive into AI for Health Delivery and Research, has been published and has been trending #1 in several categories at Amazon.

Dr. Kamal Maheshwari MD: Kamal completed anesthesia training in India (2004) and the United States (2009). He did a fellowship in Regional Anaesthesia and Acute Pain Management at Cleveland Clinic (2010). He graduated from the MPH (2015) program at Johns Hopkins Bloomberg School of Public Health with a specialization in health policy and management. He also received a certificate in Quality Patient Safety and Outcomes Research from the Johns Hopkins Bloomberg School of Public Health. He (2016) founded the Center of Perioperative Intelligence at the Cleveland Clinic Foundation to focus on artificial intelligence applications in perioperative medicine. He has published more than 100 peer-reviewed publications focused on improving perioperative outcomes. He founded (2022) Roojh Health, a digital health company focused on empowering doctors and patients, especially in the developing world.

Gabriella Marcelja: International Medical Community (IMC): Gabriella Marcelja is a co-founder and the CEO of the International Medical Community (IMC). She is an entrepreneur, legal, IT, and strategy global advisor with over ten years of experience, active in four working languages. Topics of interest include criminal and international law, strategy, innovation, technology, conflict analysis, peace resolution, mediation, and foreign investments. She is also an Investor in impact projects, a startup supporter, a speaker at international and UN forums, and a university lecturer on topics such as law and technology, multilateral diplomacy, and sustainability.

Dr. Kathleen McGrow DNP, MS, RN, PMP, FHIMSS, FAAN: Dr. Kathleen McGrow, the Global Chief Nursing Information Officer at Microsoft, is a pioneering leader in the integration of innovative technologies within healthcare. With a doctor of nursing practice from the University of Maryland, Baltimore, Dr. McGrow combines her extensive clinical experience in trauma critical care with her expertise in information technology to drive digital transformation in healthcare. Her work focuses on addressing critical issues such as workforce crises, enhancing patient and consumer engagement, and leveraging cognitive computing to create a learning health system. Internationally recognized for her contributions to the intersection of clinical care and technology, Dr. McGrow has delivered numerous educational presentations, including at the prestigious International Congress of Nursing in Montreal, Canada. Her scholarly work, published in peer-reviewed journals, explores the transformative potential of artificial intelligence (AI) in healthcare, including her recent publication on foundation models and generative AI in nursing. In addition to her role at Microsoft, Dr. McGrow co-leads the HIMSS Nursing Innovation Advisory Committee and serves as an adjunct clinical instructor at the University of Alabama at Birmingham School of Nursing. Her leadership and insights continue to shape the future of healthcare, making her a vital voice in the ongoing evolution of clinical practice and technology integration.

Dr. Ashkan Memari, PhD, MEng, BEng, FHEA, is an academic and researcher at Central Queensland University in Australia, with international experience spanning the Middle East, South Asia, and Australia. Ashkan's research area revolves around sustainability, and one of his articles in the field of sustainable supplier selection ranks among the top ten most cited works globally in this field. Dr. Memari teaches a wide range of Project Management courses catering to both undergraduate and postgraduate students.

Malissa Miot is Senior Director of Sales and Delivery at Signature Performance. Signature Performance is a leading provider of healthcare administrative solutions and services. Malissa is passionate about helping hospitals and health systems adopt innovation and workflows that improve patient outcomes, increase productivity for the administrative and care teams and reduce costs. She has served as Co-chair of the CIO Council for the New England HIMSS (NEHIMSS) Chapter. Malissa is a past president of the NEHIMSS Chapter and has been a volunteer to the NEHIMSS Board since 2013.

Shreya Mishra: Experienced Researcher in Computational Biology (Genomics) with a demonstrated history of working in the higher education industry. Skilled in Graph Signal Processing, Network Analysis, and Algorithm Development in Genomics, Machine Learning, Data Science, and Python. Strong research professional with a Doctor of Philosophy and Ph.D. focused on Computational Biology from Indraprastha Institute of Information Technology, Delhi.

Kristin Myers: Northwell Health. Kristin Myers joined Northwell Health as the Chief Digital Officer in January 2024. She is a visionary leader with over 20 years in the healthcare industry with a focus on maturing, integrating, and harnessing the power of digital, data, and advanced technologies to enhance patient care and enrich community experiences. Prior to joining Northwell Health, Ms. Myers was the Chief Digital and Information Officer and Dean for Digital and Information Technology at Mount Sinai Health System.

Logan Nye: Logan Nye is a physician and computer scientist at Carnegie Mellon University. He is a founder of Galen Health, a medical technology platform using AI to solve complex health challenges, such as early detection and intervention of cancer.

Richard Ong, MBA, MSc, FACHE, CHCIO, CDH-E, CSPO: Over the past 15 years, Richard Ong has served in various CxO-IT roles and is currently Summa Health's Vice President of IT – Digital Product Development. He earned his MBA (Waynesburg University) and Master of Science (University of Oxford). He is a fellow of the American College of Healthcare Executives (FACHE), a Certified Healthcare CIO (CHCIO), a Certified Digital Health Executive (CDH-E), and a Certified Scrum Product Owner (CSPO).

Jennifer Owens, MS, has been working in healthcare and life sciences since 2007. Her responsibilities have included bench research, biospecimen collection, and genomics in her current role in IT with a focus on innovative projects. A longstanding interest in healthcare data led her to start her podcast, "Health Data Ethics", in 2023.

Anthony Papay: Anthony is an undergraduate student at Kent State University with a major in business management and analytics.

Brittany Partridge: Brittany Partridge is a recognized expert in healthcare technology, bringing extensive experience in integrating advanced AI solutions to enhance patient care in her role as virtual care technical manager at UCSD Health. She's honored to be a fellow of the American Medical Informatics Association, where she serves on the policy committee. Brittany has led numerous projects that bridge the gap between technology and healthcare delivery, making significant strides in improving clinical outcomes.

Matt Partridge: Matt Partridge, co-founder of the Trustworthy Technology and Innovation Consortium (TTIC), is a leading figure in the field of AI and healthcare. His work focuses on developing and implementing trustworthy AI systems that ensure safety, efficacy, and ethical standards. Matt's contributions to TTIC have been pivotal in setting industry standards for AI in healthcare, fostering innovation while maintaining rigorous compliance.

Anupriya Ramraj: Principal at PwC's Cloud Practice, Anu is a recognized expert in healthcare digitization and transformation. With a distinguished career spanning over 28 years, Anu has held pivotal global leadership roles at Unisys, DXC Technology, and Hewlett-Packard Enterprise. She has a proven track record of scaling cloud practices, engineering groundbreaking products, and driving digital innovation in healthcare leveraging cloud and AI. She is a regular contributor to Forbes Tech, and her contributions to the field have earned her prestigious accolades such as the Cloud Girls Rising Trailblazer Award and recognition as one of Consulting Reports's Top 25 Digital Transformation Leaders. Anupriya's strategic vision and technical expertise continue to propel innovative healthcare solutions on a global scale, making her a leading voice in the intersection of cloud technology and healthcare.

Wael Saasouh: Board-certified anesthesiologist with work experience at multiple major academic centers. Established clinical research record with a focus on perioperative medicine, medical innovation, noninvasive monitoring, medical technology, and medical informatics.

Vinaya Sree Samala: Vinaya is a recent graduate with a Master's in healthcare informatics from Sacred Heart University. Vinaya is a dentist from India by profession with over one year of experience and has also worked as a dental assistant in Canada for more than two years before moving to the United States for further studies. Passionate about integrating technology and healthcare, Vinaya aims to bridge the gap by using data for better and more valued healthcare outcomes through innovative solutions.

Dr. Anna E. Schoenbaum, DNP, MS, RN, NI-BC, FHIMSS: Dr. Anna Schoenbaum is Vice President of Application and Digital Health at Penn Medicine. With over 30 years of experience in healthcare, she began her career as a pediatric intensive care nurse. Dr. Schoenbaum leads complex transformation projects aimed at enhancing the health ecosystem, with a focus on advancing health and advocating for health equity. She also serves as the co-chair of the HIMSS Innovation Advisory Nursing Workgroup and participates in several advisory and informatics committees. Additionally, she is an adjunct faculty member at the University of Maryland School of Nursing. In recognition of her contributions to the Health IT field, Dr. Schoenbaum received the 2023 HIMSS and ANI Changemaker Nursing Informatics award was inducted into the American Academy of Nursing in early 2025.

Michael Schostak: Michael is a seasoned healthcare leader with a proven track record in delivering excellence and innovation within the dynamic realm of perioperative care. His career journey has been marked by a relentless commitment to enhancing patient care, streamlining healthcare logistics, and optimizing healthcare operations. He is committed to staying at the forefront of healthcare innovation, currently pursuing education in artificial intelligence in healthcare. This forward-thinking approach reflects my dedication to shaping the future of healthcare leadership.

Greg Skulmoski, PhD, MBA, BEd, CITP, FBCS: Greg is an award-winning project manager who teaches project and risk management at Bond University, Australia. With 15 years of healthcare project experience in the Middle East and Canada, his research is practitioner-oriented and aligned with best practices found in global standards. He wrote *Shields Up: Cybersecurity Project Management* (Business Expert Press, 2022) and *Cybersecurity Training: A Pathway to Readiness* (Business Expert Press, 2023). Dr. Skulmoski and Dr. Ashkan Memari wrote *Quantum Cybersecurity Program Management* (Business Expert Press, 2025).

Alan Smith: Lifepoint Health. Al is the Chief Information and Innovation Officer at Lifepoint Health. He has 35+ years working in IT across multiple industries, with the last 25+ years working exclusively in US healthcare companies. Prior to joining Lifepoint, he was the CIO at RCCH Healthcare and Capella Healthcare. He is also a Venture Partner with Caduceus Capital Partners and serves on multiple vendor customer advisory boards.

Kannan Srinivasan: A proven award-winning leader and strategist having 24 years of experience recognized for translating business imperatives into actionable deliverables using a range of influencing skills to obtain stakeholder buy-in at all levels. A very active member in building and supporting the cybersecurity community by giving keynote addresses, webinars, and conducting sessions for SMB organizations.

Kumar Subramaniam, DBA: SafeTower, Inc. Baltimore, USA. Kumar is the President and CEO of SafeTower, a spinout of Johns Hopkins Medicine. He has more than 24 years of experience working in the healthcare sector in various leadership roles in health systems and health plans. Prior to joining SafeTower, Inc., Kumar led the solutions and innovation business unit at Johns Hopkins Health Plans in Baltimore, MD.

Kimberly Szymczak, MSN, APRN-GCNS, SCRN: Kim Szymczak serves as Summa Health Stroke Program Coordinator and has worked with the stroke population for more than 15 years and with Summa for almost 35 years. She earned her BSN from the University of Akron and her MSN from Kent State University. She is certified as a Gerontological Clinical Nurse Specialist, Stroke Certified Registered Nurse, along with having a Fellowship as an Acute Neurovascular Advanced Practitioner.

Ginny Torno, Administrative Director of Innovation and Clinical Systems at Houston Methodist, has over 23 years of technical leadership experience, with over 12 of those years at Houston Methodist in progressive leadership roles. Her current role spans strategy and leadership for inpatient clinical systems involving nursing, virtual health, medical device integration, imaging, pharmacy, lab, operating rooms, emergency departments, cardiology, and research systems.

Ginny also plays an instrumental role in the Center for Innovation at Houston Methodist, focusing on smart hospital functionality and technologies that advance and improve the patient, nurse, and physician experience. One current initiative is a large-scale, multi-pronged initiative internally branded as "Care Redesign", which transforms patient care through technology and processes. Voices of patients and care teams play a significant role in this transformation, with the goal of eliminating computers from patient rooms by enabling patient interactions through voice-enabled technology.

Khalid Turk, MBA, PMP, PMI – ACP, CHCIO, CDH-E, ITIL: As a seasoned executive IT leader with over two decades of experience in the healthcare IT sector, Khalid has consistently driven digital transformation and strategic initiatives that enhance operational efficiency and patient care. His journey from hands-on technical roles to leading IT divisions showcases Khalid's ability to innovate and lead. He specializes in building and directing high-performing teams to implement cutting-edge technology solutions, with extensive experience in implementing Epic EHR systems across multiple organizations.

Addobea Twum: International Medical Community (IMC). Addobea Twum is a co-founder and the Legal Lead at IMC. She has years of experience in legal consulting, managing ISO compliance projects in the oil and shipping sector and conducting GRC and ESG training for public sector agencies in the utilities sector. She has professional experience in International Development. Conducting in-country security assessments, drafting subcontractor agreements for USAID solicitations and leading on GAC, GTZ/GIZ funded projects. She is a member of the Commonwealth Association of Legislative Counsel and the International Association of Legislation (IAL). She holds an LLB from Lancaster University, UK and an LLM from Université Paris Panthéon-Assas, France.

Shareni De La Rosa Xochitiotzi: International Medical Community (IMC): Shareni De la Rosa Xochitiotz is a Co-founder and the Innovation Lead of the International Medical Community (IMC). She is an Industrial Designer from Mexico, driven by a strong social consciousness and a commitment to enhancing the quality of life through design as a powerful tool to address social challenges and, as a result, create a positive impact on society. Her experience includes research and development of innovative products by employing user-centered practices, social design methodologies, and collaborative processes rooted in the study of people's needs.

Voices of Innovation in Healthcare Series

We published the original *Voices of Innovation: Fulfilling the Promise of Information Technology in Healthcare* in the Spring of 2019. Little did we know that less than a year later, COVID-19 would completely disrupt life as we knew it. Innovation and Digital Transformation became everyday vernacular and *Voices* went on to sell very well. Our publisher returned in late 2022 asking for a second Edition. The publisher made a good point in that there were so many new stories of innovation born from the pandemic that it would help the industry to update the book. We updated almost half of the content with COVID-19-inspired innovations. *Voices of Innovation: Fulfilling the Promise of Information Technology in Healthcare, 2nd Edition,* was published in July 2023.

With the success of the books, we heard requests from many other communities for *Voices* that were increasingly specific to their healthcare vertical or focused on a particular topic.

We came out of the gate with *Voices of Innovation - Payers*. Like their provider counterparts, payers also long to transform, and innovation is a catalyst to spark change of such magnitude. With Sachin Jain MD writing the Foreword, we published *Voices of Innovation - Payers* in July 2024. An immediate best-seller, it was the first book ever written addressing the leverage of technology in the payer community.

With all the buzz surrounding artificial intelligence, large language models, and robotic process automation, our readers began to ask for *Voices of Innovation – AI*. While there are many books already written on the topic with more to follow, *Voices of Innovation – AI* differentiates itself by focusing on repeatable processes, not strictly examples, which quickly lose impact given the rapid nature of AI innovation. While we applaud these books, *Voices of Innovation – AI* is meant to be a handbook to help practitioners today and tomorrow in their AI-related innovations.

The beauty of *Voices* is that the books remain a set of global best practices where peers openly share their playbooks for transformation around a common structure for innovation that is easily adaptable for any size organization. A leader can pick up a copy of *Voices* and instantly have access to a tried and tested framework for innovation with multiple "case studies" of how other payer organizations have succeeded, complete with results. This is the reason for the success of all the *Voices* books. Look for more *Voices* in the future.

Voices of Innovation—AI Prologue

Everyone talks about innovation, and we can all point to random examples of innovation inside of healthcare information technology, but few repeatable processes exist that make innovation more routine than happenstance. How do you create and sustain a culture of innovation? What are the best practices you can refine and embed as part of your organization's DNA? What are the potential outcomes for robust healthcare transformation when we get this innovation mystery solved? Through timely essays from leading experts, the first edition showcased the widely adopted healthcare innovation model from HIMSS and how providers could leverage it to increase their velocity of digital transformation. Regardless of its promise, innovation has been slow in healthcare.

Voices of Innovation – AI leverages the same framework and construct but zeroes in on artificial intelligence to include large language models, voice, and robotic process automation.

The hype of AI has certainly reached a fever pitch in 2024, and at this time we don't see the excitement slowing down. We believe AI holds more promise than previously hyped technological advances such as Cloud and Blockchain. Our reasoning is simple. AI has actually been around in some form for a generation, so the foundations are strong. As computing power becomes more ubiquitous and data accessible, use cases demonstrating value are now routine. Many experiments have now transitioned to mainstream utilization. AI is already embedded in numerous processes and technologies. Vendors have embraced AI as a prerequisite for long-term success and most products today are AI-enabled. AI is not only here to stay, but will continue to proliferate exponentially.

When I served as Chief Information Officer at Cleveland Clinic, we announced AI as the #2 most critical medical innovation of 2019. Even 5 years ago, AI was already front and center in the healthcare community. In my talk, I stressed AI as "augmented intelligence", not purely "artificial intelligence". You will find this subtle yet critical nuance in the innovations shared in each chapter. We highlight the steps in the innovation process where you can leverage AI as a partner in enabling transformation at scale.

Inside you will find over 30 real-world examples (and two AI-generated) where leaders share how they innovated with AI and the impacts on their organizations. We include examples from providers around the world that apply to small organizations as well as those hyper-complex. We demonstrate the impacts in multiple areas, including clinical outcomes, financial performance, and overall experience. No matter the size of your organization or the number of your staff, *Voices of Innovation – AI* will accelerate your capability to generate value from this amazing technology asset. In fact, those who fail to embrace AI will have difficulty in our complex industry, which is under constant disintermediation by new and emboldened entrants. Survival of the Digitialist.

As with all *Voices* titles, 100% of author royalties are donated to charities whose focus is to eliminate cancer. *Voices of Innovation – AI* proceeds will fund cancer research at the Mayo Clinic.

Innovation Framework

AI Statement

Essay authors in Chapters 3 and 8 leveraged ChatGPT3 to source additional documented examples of AI in healthcare to compliment the others used in the article. We leveraged AI the same way we would search for examples using traditional methods such as Google or a public library for basic research.

Chapter 1

Blend Ethics and Governance

Prioritize Patient Welfare, Respect Patient Autonomy, and Ensure Informed Consent

While the integration of artificial intelligence (AI) in healthcare holds tremendous promise, offering capabilities to enhance diagnostics, treatment, and operational efficiency, the increasing application of AI in healthcare also raises significant ethical and governance challenges. Ethical principles and robust governance structures are essential to ensure that AI technologies enhance patient care, maintain trust, promote fairness, and support professional integrity.

Prioritizing ethics and governance in AI applications will be crucial to achieving a future where technology enhances, rather than undermines, the quality and equity of patient care.

BLEND ETHICS AND GOVERNANCE | THE DEBATE ON THE GOVERNANCE AND ETHICS OF ARTIFICIAL INTELLIGENCE | *BY ANTHONY PAPAY, FRANK PAPAY, AND PIYUSH MATHUR*

> The development of full artificial intelligence could spell the end of the human race.
>
> **—Stephen Hawking**
> *(Cellan-Jones, 2014)*

DOI: 10.4324/9781032715155-1

AI has rapidly advanced in recent years, raising critical ethical concerns and the need for effective governance (Hawking et al., 2014). The above quote by renowned physicist Stephen Hawking encapsulates the chilling implications of AI governance (Naib, 2021). It highlights the potential risk to humanity associated with the uncontrolled advancement of AI technology. Hawking's quote serves as a fearful reminder of the need for responsible and ethical governance to ensure the safe development and deployment of AI systems worldwide.

> Artificial Intelligence is the future, not only for Russia but for all humankind. It comes with colossal opportunities, but also threats that are difficult to predict. Whoever becomes the leader in this sphere will become the ruler of the world.
>
> **—Vladimir Putin**
> *(Polyakova, 2018)*

In contrast, this quote by Vladimir Putin can be seen as arguing against the governance of AI. It highlights the belief that AI holds immense potential and that the competition to lead in this field is a global race for power. By emphasizing the opportunities and uncertainties associated with AI, Putin implies that strict governance could hinder a country's ability to become a dominant force in the AI landscape. In addition, inhibiting any progression of AI may produce an imbalance of power in the world, potentially subjugating those who do not have such intelligence. This perspective suggests that pursuing unrestricted AI development and deployment is necessary to secure a position of balanced influence and power in the future. However, it is important to note that this quote does not represent a comprehensive argument against governance, as ethical considerations and potential risks associated with AI are not addressed in Putin's statement.

Currently, there has not been enough effort to initiate AI governance and how to control its potential for society while limiting its societal harm (Mäntymäki, 2022). Dafoe (2018, p. 121) states,

> The emerging field of 'AI governance'…explores how humanity can best navigate the transition to advanced AI systems. We expect that such governance will prove difficult given the strategic importance of the technology, its diverse applications, and the uncertainty associated with its developmental trajectory.

To help bridge this knowledge gap in the development of AI control, this essay examines the debate concerning the ethics and governance of AI, exploring the urgent challenges and arguments posed by its uncontrolled development and the amazing potential versus destructive deployment (Koniakou, 2022). This contemporary topic is relevant and involves controversial issues on which people hold varying strong opinions, which leads to the persuasive argument of whether there should be an urgent debate on the importance of effective governance in the field of AI (Leslie et al., 2023). What is the current governance and ethical framework necessary to address AI's potential risks and implications, ensuring its responsible and beneficial integration into society? Who is responsible and accountable for developing and using AI systems that produce harm?

While proponents argue for accountability to ensure ethical behavior, others highlight traceability's technical limitations and human oversight's importance (Koulu, 2020). Striking a balance between human rights and responsibility compared to the constraint of AI is vital for harnessing its potential while preventing potential harm (Jelinek, 2021). Who will design and police such AI constraints? Is self-regulation by industry and AI developers trustworthy, or should governments be involved? There also remains a question as to if ethical principles stated by developers of AI will influence the development of safe and beneficial AI rather than just a public display of "smoke and mirrors" to bypass public scrutiny (Seger, 2022).

AI systems operate autonomously, which in most cases makes unsupervised decisions with immediate to far-reaching consequences. Holding them accountable aligns with human ethical principles. Accountability ensures that appropriate measures are taken when an AI system causes harm, such as correcting the situation, preventing future damage, and compensating affected individuals. Accountability will incentivize AI's responsible use and promote trust between AI systems, AI developers, and society.

The difficulty in identifying the accountable person(s) in AI systems is because of its complexity. The complexity of algorithms involved in AI systems represents a "black box" of unknowns, unexplainable algorithms, and software coding processes (Adadi and Berrada, 2018). This "black box" effect makes it challenging to trace the decision-making processes of AI systems. The traceability of coders and developers of AI systems that can be developed through an open-source coding mechanism creates a more significant complex problem in identifying who are the responsible creators of such systems. This lack of understanding and traceability of AI systems raises concerns about potential unjust or inaccurate accountability (Mora-Cantallops et al., 2022). AI algorithms should be designed to be transparent and explainable.

This enables AI users to comprehend how the algorithms arrived at their conclusions and facilitates the detection of potential biases. Explainable AI empowers individuals to challenge and hold AI systems accountable for unfair or biased outcomes.

Simply put, AI systems are the creations of humans, and therefore, the AI human creators should bear a significant portion of the responsibility for their actions, whether intentional or not. Rather than focusing solely on holding AI systems accountable after misuse or harm, external and internal human oversight throughout the AI development, deployment, and operations should be established early in the process. Responsible designers should be named as accountable authors. Understandable design practices, ongoing testing, and transparent design decision-making throughout AI development can reduce potential risks and ensure that AI systems align with societal values (Barredo Arrieta et al., 2020).

A more selective approach may be necessary rather than absolute accountability for all involved in the misuse and harm of AI systems. Should AI systems be judged on their decisions and actions within the scope of their intended use and capabilities? The level of automated decisions made by AI systems should be closely monitored, and the potential for immediate human intervention at any given time should always be considered (Antoniadi et al., 2021). This approach acknowledges the sensitive interaction between AI and human involvement, striking a balance between the benefits and limitations of AI systems. The constant role of human oversight throughout open AI creation and transparent implementation is essential. The accountability of individuals related to the outcome and consequences of AI systems will ensure that humans retain control over all aspects of AI, ensuring that AI is always aligned with human values.

Additionally, AI governance should prioritize protecting personal privacy and data. Part of the AI protective measures should include informed consent, transparency in data collection, usage, and storage practices, as well as safeguards and regulations to prevent unauthorized access and breaches. Respecting privacy rights and ensuring the safe handling of personal data should be a fundamental universal consideration in AI governance (Mazurek and Małagocka, 2019).

AI developers should also prioritize safety and security from the outset. This includes rigorous testing, verification, and validation processes to identify and mitigate potential risks and vulnerabilities (Schwartz et al., 2019). Implementing best practices, such as secure coding standards, ensures that AI systems are resilient against attacks and maintain data integrity and functionalities. Developers should establish clear guidelines and standards regarding the use of AI technology, particularly in sensitive areas such as healthcare, finance, and law.

AI developers and organizations should be responsible for continually monitoring AI systems after deployment to identify and address emerging threats (Raji, 2020). Regular updates should be released to monitor and solve security risks and ensure that AI systems stay up-to-date with evolving standards and best practices. A timely response to identifying such vulnerabilities is essential to maintaining the safety and security of AI systems. AI developers should actively collaborate and share knowledge within the AI community to collectively enhance the safety and security of AI systems. Sharing best practices, research findings, and threat intelligence helps foster a culture of responsibility and accountability. Transparency helps external oversight, including regulatory bodies and auditors, assess AI systems' safety and security measures.

AI systems must be developed and governed to uphold fairness and non-discrimination. Monitoring and auditing data inputs, model training, and evaluation processes are necessary to prevent the perpetuation of discriminatory AI practices (Nazer et al., 2023). AI biases can perpetuate unfairness and unequal treatment, leading to far-reaching societal consequences. Addressing biases in AI algorithms begins with the data used for training. AI developers must prioritize diverse and representative data sources. This involves incorporating data from various demographic groups, cultures, and backgrounds into training datasets. By including a wide range of unbiased data, biases can be minimized, leading to fairer decision-making outcomes. Developers should also use internal testing techniques to identify and mitigate biases in AI algorithms before use. Once biases are identified, developers can implement corrective measures such as adding broad representative data, algorithm retraining, or modifying the decision-making process to mitigate biases and promote fairness. Explainable AI empowers individuals to challenge and hold AI systems accountable for unfair or biased outcomes. AI bias evaluations should include real-world use cases and simulated scenarios to identify biases impacting decision-making (Hickok, 2020). Prioritizing fairness enables us to harness the potential of AI technology while safeguarding against the perpetuation of biases, thereby advancing a more equitable society.

Collaboration between governments, industry organizations, and research institutions is also necessary to develop and enforce standards and regulations that promote fairness and equal treatment. Care must be taken not to produce "proxy discrimination" hidden behind the use of AI systems and misguided development (Prince and Schwarcz, 2020). Preventive guidelines should outline the ethical responsibilities of AI developers and organizations in preventing discriminatory proxy practices, emphasizing the importance of addressing biases and ensuring fairness early in decision-making processes.

Privacy regulations should mandate de-identification techniques to protect individual privacy, such as in healthcare personal data storage (Murdoch, 2021). Personally identifiable information should be carefully removed or encrypted to ensure data cannot be traced back to individuals. Guidelines should require security measures to protect data throughout its lifecycle. Transparent reporting mechanisms should be in place to inform individuals about how their data is being used and provide avenues for redress in case of any data mishandling. Guidelines should also explicitly prohibit using sensitive data for discriminatory or unethical purposes. AI systems in healthcare should adhere to principles of fairness, ensuring that decisions and outcomes are not influenced by factors such as race, gender, or socioeconomic status.

The rapid advancement of AI has also raised concerns about the potential ethical implications of job displacement (Agrawal et al., 2023). As AI-driven automation replaces specific job roles, individuals and communities may face significant challenges. What are the strategies for businesses and governments to mitigate the negative social and economic consequences for affected individuals and communities? Losing employment can lead to financial instability, income inequality, and reduced social mobility. Furthermore, individuals and communities may need a greater sense of purpose and identity, expanding existing social issues. Therefore, ethical considerations should include evaluating potential economic disparities, job displacement, and systemic biases. By addressing these social impacts, AI governance can ensure that AI serves the greater good and contributes positively to society on several levels.

Businesses and governments should bear some responsibility for investing in lifelong learning and reskilling programs to empower individuals facing job displacement by AI. By providing access to affordable and relevant education and training, affected individuals can acquire new skills that align with emerging job opportunities, including working closely with AI systems such as robotics (Vrontis et al., 2023). Governments can incentivize businesses to participate in such programs and foster a culture of continuous learning and adaptability. Governments can also provide comprehensive support to individuals transitioning into new employment. This includes career counseling, job placement assistance, and financial aid during the transitional period. Support networks, mentoring programs, and access to job retraining resources can ease the burden on affected individuals and facilitate a smoother transition.

In light of the potential long-term challenges associated with AI-driven job displacement, governments should explore implementing a solution, such as a universal basic income or similar safety net programs. These controversial safety net programs ensure a minimum income level for all individuals, irrespective of employment status. Such programs can help mitigate the negative consequences of job displacement, provide financial stability, and promote social and economic well-being (Furman and Seamans, 2019).

AI is a global phenomenon, with its development and deployment spanning national borders. To ensure AI's responsible and ethical use, it is crucial to establish international collaborations and agreements to develop standardized ethical guidelines and governance frameworks, Luc Steels has contributed significantly to AI ethics, notably co-launching the Barcelona Declaration for the Proper Development and Usage of Artificial Intelligence in Europe in 2018 (Steels and Lopez de Mantaras, 2018). International collaborations are necessary to address these challenges collectively and foster consistent standards. International collaborations enable diverse stakeholders to pool resources, knowledge, and expertise (West and Allen, 2018). Governments, industry leaders, academic institutions, and civil society organizations can collaborate to develop universal ethical guidelines and governance frameworks that reflect various cultural perspectives and experiences. Shared responsibility fosters a sense of collective ownership, leading to more comprehensive and practical solutions.

International standardized ethical guidelines help create a level playing field for AI development and deployment worldwide (Jobin et al., 2019). An international agreement among ethical standards avoids the risk of jurisdictional discrepancies and prevents unethical practices from being carried out in regions with weaker regulations. When AI technologies adhere to global standards, users, consumers, and stakeholders can trust their reliability, fairness, and accountability more. Organizations such as the United Nations, the European Union, and global industries have already made strides in developing ethical guidelines for AI (Hogenhout, 2021). By leveraging these initiatives, global collaborations can accelerate the development of standardized ethical frameworks and avoid duplicative efforts. International collaborations offer opportunities to share best practices and lessons learned.

Countries can refine their ethical guidelines and governance frameworks by learning from each other's successes and challenges. By recognizing shared responsibility, harmonizing ethical standards, building trust, leveraging existing initiatives, establishing multilateral agreements, sharing best practices, providing capacity building, and ensuring continuous review, the international community can work together to promote AI's responsible and ethical use across borders.

Healthcare is just starting to realize the benefits and caveats of AI. Medical AI ethics in healthcare is a critical field that addresses the moral implications and societal impacts of deploying AI technologies in medical settings. As AI systems become increasingly integrated into healthcare for diagnostics, treatment planning, and patient care, it is essential to ensure these technologies are used responsibly. Ethical considerations include ensuring patient privacy and data security, as AI systems often rely on vast amounts of personal health data. Additionally, there is a need to address bias in AI algorithms, which can arise from unrepresentative training data and lead to disparities in healthcare outcomes. Transparency and accountability are also paramount, as healthcare professionals and patients must understand how AI systems reach their decisions. Furthermore, the integration of AI should enhance, rather than replace, the human touch in medical care, preserving the empathy and compassion that are central to healthcare. Developing robust ethical frameworks and regulatory standards will be crucial to harnessing the benefits of AI while mitigating potential risks and ensuring equitable and just healthcare for all.

Key concerns of AI medical use include data privacy and security, as AI systems often require access to vast amounts of personal health data, making it crucial to ensure this data remains secure and private to prevent unauthorized access to sensitive information. Bias and discrimination are also significant issues, as AI algorithms can inherit biases from their training data, potentially leading to disparities in treatment and care for certain groups if the data is not representative of the entire population. Additionally, the accuracy and reliability of AI systems are paramount, as inaccurate or incomplete data can lead to erroneous diagnoses or treatment recommendations, potentially harming patients. The lack of transparency in many AI algorithms, especially those using deep learning, makes it difficult for healthcare providers to trust and validate AI-generated recommendations. Over-reliance on AI technology poses a risk as well, potentially causing healthcare providers to neglect their clinical judgment and expertise, which could lead to a decline in the quality of patient care if the AI system fails or makes a mistake.

Ethical concerns, such as informed consent, autonomy, and the potential for dehumanization of patient care, must be addressed to ensure AI systems are used in ways that respect patients' rights and dignity. The evolving regulatory and legal environment for AI in healthcare necessitates robust frameworks to ensure the safety, efficacy, and ethical use of AI technologies, addressing issues such as liability in case of AI errors. Moreover, the high cost of implementing AI technologies can widen the gap between well-funded and under-resourced healthcare facilities, posing a challenge to ensuring equitable access to AI advancements. Addressing these dangers requires a multifaceted approach, including rigorous testing and validation of AI systems, continuous monitoring for bias, robust data security measures, transparent algorithm development, and the establishment of comprehensive regulatory and ethical guidelines.

As we continue to develop AI systems and utilize one of humankind's greatest and perhaps last inventions, we must continue to be vigilant watchmen in addition to demanding the urgent ethical imperatives of controlling AI for the good of all. Fallible humans create AI systems that operate independently, making decisions and implementing actions that have the most profound effects on individuals and society across the globe. To date, AI systems have no emotions or remorse and continue to learn and act based on their programmable intellect. Therefore, the danger of AI systems emanates from the incentives of AI developers (creators) either through unknowing naiveness or malintent. Unfortunately, being naïve is not an accountable crime, and malintent is usually hidden from oversight. Because of these hidden unknowns, we must continue to scrutinize each AI system as if there is potential future harm to the world society. Nick Bostrom, a futurist and philosophy professor at Oxford University, recently reflected on the need for heightened awareness and scrutiny of the development of AI systems (Times News, 2023):

> We are moving towards transformative AI capabilities that will potentially shape the future of our species and our life on this planet. AI can carry existential risks but can also help solve many problems. It would be wrong to meet it with indifference or complacency.

BLEND ETHICS AND GOVERNANCE | TRANSFORMATIVE IMPACT OF AI IN HEALTHCARE: ETHICAL CONSIDERATIONS AND FUTURE DIRECTIONS | *BY OLGA KAGAN, KATHLEEN MCGROW, AND ANNA E. SCHOENBAUM*

"What all of us have to do is to make sure we are using AI in a way that is for the benefit of humanity, not to the detriment of humanity."

—Tim Cook
(MIT Technology Review, 2017)

Introduction

AI serves as a pivotal element in healthcare, bestowing upon systems a semblance of human intellectual processes. AI is typically understood as machine capabilities that mimic cognitive abilities associated with human intelligence (Lawry, 2022). It aids clinicians by analyzing extensive healthcare data to discern patterns, forecast outcomes, and aid in the formulation of diagnoses and therapeutic approaches.

Healthcare is being transformed by AI through the enhancement of clinical judgments, operational efficiency, and patient care quality. AI can assist in understanding health results and streamline care provision, utilizing advances in machine learning (ML), natural language processing (NLP), and computer vision (Bekbolatova, et al., 2024). Utilized across the spectrum in diagnostics, medical imaging, surgery assistance, and patient management, AI assists clinicians, tailors individual treatment plans, and improves overall public health.

AI plays a pivotal role in improving patient outcomes. ML algorithms analyze vast datasets to predict disease progression, identify high-risk patients, and recommend personalized treatment plans (Kitsios et al., 2023). For instance, ML models can predict readmissions or adverse events, allowing proactive interventions. NLP extracts valuable insights from unstructured clinical notes, enabling a better understanding of patient histories, symptoms, and treatment responses.

Additionally, AI-powered computer vision aids in early disease detection, such as identifying tumors or anomalies in radiology scans (Kitsios et al., 2023). AI algorithms accurately interpret medical images (X-rays, MRIs, etc.), reducing radiologists' workload and minimizing diagnostic errors (Kitsios et al., 2023). AI facilitates early detection, flagging subtle abnormalities that might be missed by human eyes, leading to timely interventions. Moreover, AI identifies genetic markers and predicts treatment responses, enabling personalized therapies.

AI provides valuable assistance in surgical settings. Robot-assisted surgery, driven by AI, enhances precision and minimizes invasiveness during complex procedures. Intraoperative decision support leverages real-time data analysis, providing insights to optimize surgical outcomes.

AI-powered virtual health assistants benefit patient-centric care. These chatbots offer 24/7 support, answering patient queries, scheduling appointments, and providing health information (Bekbolatova et al., 2024). Personalized treatment plans, based on individual patient profiles, consider comorbidities, preferences, and socioeconomic factors. Additionally, remote monitoring using wearable devices and AI algorithms tracks patient vitals, alerting care teams to deviations and preventing complications. Lastly, AI contributes to population health management (Bekbolatova et al., 2024). Predictive analytics models forecast disease outbreaks, identify at-risk populations, and allocate resources efficiently. Social determinants of health are considered, addressing disparities and improving overall community health.

Ethical Principles

Ethical principles are crucial in ensuring the responsible and equitable use of AI in healthcare. Healthcare organizations must take ownership of AI systems' outcomes. Clear lines of accountability ensure that decisions made by AI models are traceable and justifiable (Murphy, et al., 2021). When AI affects patient care, it is crucial to have accountability systems in place to ensure transparency, fairness, and responsibility. AI algorithms should explain their decisions transparently (Ross et al., 2024b). Clinicians and healthcare leaders need to understand how AI arrives at specific recommendations. Explainability builds trust and facilitates informed decision-making. When clinicians comprehend the rationale behind AI-generated insights, they can confidently incorporate them into patient care.

AI systems should be designed to serve diverse patient populations. Ensuring inclusivity means addressing biases and disparities, especially in underrepresented groups. By considering various demographic factors, AI can assist in ensuring equitable care and avoid exacerbating existing health disparities (Murphy, et al., 2021). Efforts should be made to minimize bias in AI algorithms (Alowais, et al., 2023). Rigorous testing and ongoing monitoring are necessary to prevent unintended discrimination. Bias-free AI ensures that recommendations are based on clinical evidence rather than perpetuating existing biases.

Openness about AI's capabilities, limitations, and data sources is essential. Transparent communication fosters trust among patients, clinicians, and stakeholders. When healthcare leaders are transparent about AI's role, patients can make informed decisions, and clinicians can collaborate effectively (Murphy et al., 2021). AI should align with ethical guidelines and legal frameworks. Responsible use involves considering patient privacy, safety, and the impact on healthcare workflows. By adhering to responsible practices, healthcare organizations can maximize the benefits of AI while minimizing risks. Ethical AI adoption is critical for advancing healthcare while safeguarding patient well-being and trust. AI is a powerful tool that is transforming healthcare delivery. However, successful implementation requires robust data governance, clinician collaboration, and ongoing evaluation. Integrating AI in healthcare requires addressing ethical, legal, and social considerations and ensuring AI is used responsibly (Bekbolatova et al., 2024).

Ethical Implication in Clinical Practice, Education, and Research

Ethical application of AI is particularly important in the healthcare sector, including in practice, education, and research. AI-driven and enabled technology must be thoroughly vetted and examined not only for its benefits but also for unintended consequences. Relationships between patients and clinicians are rooted in trust. Can trust be developed with AI, our newer partner, in this equation? Emerging AI technologies can be intimidating to healthcare professionals, as some can feel unprepared or have a fear of the unknown and are at times resistant to change due to a lack of understanding or familiarity with them. Post the COVID-19 pandemic, clinicians across disciplines, including nurses and physicians, remain overburdened by technology (e.g., EHR documentation burden) and experience burnout (e.g., clinician burnout). Similarly, healthcare academics and researchers are faced with AI-driven technologies that can offer many opportunities yet bring out challenges that can be difficult to decipher. These professionals and leaders need to have a roadmap and resources to guide the adoption and integration of AI-driven technologies in their respective areas in the most ethical and thoughtful manner. This requires close collaboration and continual dialogue between industry professionals, clinicians, government entities, researchers, and academics. Some of this work has been underway by The Coalition for Health AI (CHAI) with a framework called the Assurance Standards Guide, which outlines industry-agreed standards for AI deployment in healthcare; the Translational Evaluation of Healthcare AI (TEHAI) framework that accounts for AI capability, utility, and adoption (Reddy et al., 2021); and the HIMSS Nursing Innovation Advisory Workgroup for the HIMSS Healthcare Innovation and AI Toolkit (2024), just to name a few.

AI in Clinical Practice Example

Healthcare leaders responsible for the deployment of AI in their organizations must become familiar with or employ and/or form teams of professionals like nurse informatics specialists, data scientists, and engineers to provide guidance with the selection, customization, and implementation of AI-driven solutions. AI tools offer direct advantages not only for clinicians but also for healthcare leaders, by employing AI-powered business intelligence tools. These tools can help enhance productivity, optimize or create KPIs, and inform strategic staffing decisions, budgets, and organizational performance, including resource allocation for patient engagement, and employee experiences.

In 2024, as part of the HIMSS Healthcare Innovation and AI Toolkit, Ross, Freeman, McGrow, and Kagan developed the *5 Rights of AI in Healthcare* as a resource for clinicians and healthcare leaders to critically appraise AI-driven technologies. The "5 Rights of AI" concept draws inspiration from the "Five Rights of Medication", which originated in early 20th-century nursing practices. These rights guided nurses in administering medication safely and accurately to enhance patient safety and improve quality. The adaptation of these principles for AI considers recommendations from the World Health Organization (WHO) and the White House AI Bill of Rights (2023). This practical framework is aimed at applying and managing AI by clinicians in healthcare settings and assists in planning, using, and integrating AI technologies, ensuring optimal application and achieving safe, compassionate, and effective outcomes (HIMSS 2024). More specifically, the *5 Rights of AI in Healthcare* addresses the right objective with a focus on the problem and population, the right approach that encompasses workflows and technologies, the right competency, including intelligence and clinical acumen, the right data with reasonable logic, and the right safeguards that include checks and balances, with additional details outlined in Figure 1.1.

5 Rights of AI in Healthcare

Artificial Intelligence in healthcare must apply a systematic and standardized approach to ensure its application is optimal, safe, effective, and compassionate.

Right Objective

Problem & Population

A clear understanding of the problem to solve informs the design of appropriate workflows, key metrics, outcomes, and aids in validation to evaluate responses for biases.

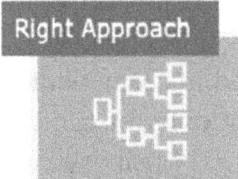

Right Approach

Workflow & Technology

The right solution and perspective are key success factors. It is essential to have a testing phase, to fine-tune and optimize the logic and performance.

Right Competency

Clinical & Intelligent

A well-trained project team can effectively recognize and mitigate biases in both data and algorithms. Knowledgeable clinical leaders are crucial for informed decision-making and successful integration for meaningful healthcare application.

Right Data

Reasonable Logic

Validating the accuracy of the data source, dataset, and algorithms is critical. This ensures that the AI system operates with reliable and trustworthy information.

Right Safeguards

Checks and Balances

Ensuring compliance with regulatory requirements is key to guaranteeing transparency, data integrity, privacy, and security. Clinicians help ensure responsible & ethical use of this technology.

Figure 1.1   5 Rights of AI in Healthcare. Courtesy of https://gkc.himss.org/resources/five-rights-ai-healthcare

Responsible use of AI requires dialogue, stakeholder engagement, and continual evaluation to ensure its successful implementation and adoption.

AI in Education Example

Learning occurs on a continual basis within and outside of academic institutions, including in clinical settings. Education within health professions has seen a surge of AI-driven tools, including AI-powered interactive learning platforms that adapt to employees' learning pace, preferences, and styles with personalized content that enhances engagement and knowledge retention. Additionally, AI-assisted assessment tools help identify education gaps and potential skill deficiencies by analyzing student data, tailoring educational interventions, and improving overall competency. Despite many opportunities, the proliferation of AI-driven tools in education also raises many ethical concerns that include but are not limited to pedagogical impact, job displacement, bias and fairness, privacy, transparency, autonomy and dependence, ethical literacy, accountability, equity, and short-term and long-term effects.

For example, from the pedagogical perspective, AI can change teaching dynamics, compelling educators to adapt their methods to complement AI tools and, in turn, ensure job security instead of job displacement. Additionally, AI algorithms may inherit biases from their training data, and educators must work with developers to ensure fairness by auditing and refining AI models. Moreover, protecting student privacy is crucial, as AI tools collect vast amounts of student data. This leads to further questions about who has access to this data, how it is used, and whether students' consent is obtained. Educators need transparency to trust and interpret AI-generated recommendations. As students rely on AI tools, there is also a significant concern about diminishing students' autonomy while balancing independent learning and critical thinking. Educators and students need to understand AI's ethical implications, which must be integrated into education at undergraduate and graduate levels. In cases of AI failure, one must know who is accountable and what the process is for reporting and documenting errors and/or AI hallucinations. Moreover, academic leaders must ensure equitable access to AI tools for all learners and educators regardless of their socioeconomic status or language preferences, including investments into AI-enabled accessibility tools to accommodate learners with disabilities.

Lastly, one needs to assess both short-term and long-term effects of AI on teaching and learning to keep a competitive edge, as many students will be transitioning into practice in a high-tech healthcare environment for which they must be prepared during their academic journey. For example, the American Association of Colleges of Nursing (AACN, 2021) emphasizes the impact of informatics and technology on patient outcomes, clinical thinking, and healthcare processes, which are now core competencies for nursing students at undergraduate and graduate levels. Academic programs are encouraged to fully integrate basic informatics competencies into nursing curricula, leveraging advanced technology to enhance instruction (Ross et al., 2024a). Multimedia tools, synchronous and asynchronous programs (webinars and podcasts), conferences, and involvement within professional organizations serve as complementary educational opportunities on AI in healthcare.

AI in Research Example

Healthcare delivery is rooted in evidence that is generated by scientists across disciplines and care settings, ranging from bench research to public health studies where researchers have been increasingly employing AI-driven tools for the recruitment of subjects for clinical trials to literature review and data analysis of large datasets and reporting, just to name a few. It is important to note that all data entered by scientists, clinicians, and other professionals in healthcare can become part of the ML algorithms that generate models and make predictions to help generate new knowledge (e.g., evidence-based practice), to inform the care of the patient (e.g., precision health), and to facilitate compliance (e.g., information blocking or quality improvement) and reporting standards (e.g., disease surveillance).

It is imperative that all involved treat data responsibly, ensuring its timeliness, accuracy, completeness, consistency, and truthfulness. This ensures that data is useful, transparent, and robust as ethical challenges in research continue to center around safety and transparency, algorithmic bias and fairness, and patient data privacy. For example, while most data are reported as an aggregate number and may not be traceable, unique identifiers like DNA or fingerprints may. Responsible and ethical use of AI in research is highly desirable as we strive toward faster discovery of curative and preventative treatments, minimally invasive procedures, and novel technologies (e.g., robotics, prosthetics, and nano-technologies).

Future of AI in Healthcare

The future of AI in healthcare is unfolding rapidly, presenting transformative opportunities across clinical practice, academia, and research. Healthcare organizations must begin thinking strategically about how to effectively use AI. It is not about if but when and how to integrate it into clinicians' workflows, academic settings, and research endeavors. Understanding AI systems and their applications is crucial, alongside vigilance about ethical considerations and the potential for beneficial use.

Ethical considerations and the potential use of AI are critical factors for healthcare leaders tasked with developing comprehensive plans and support models for AI integration. Leveraging frameworks like the CHAI Assurance Standards Guide and the AI Maturity Roadmap offers guidance. The CHAI framework sets forth industry-agreed standards for AI deployment in healthcare, emphasizing AI capability, utility, and adoption (CHAI, 2024). Meanwhile, the AI Maturity Roadmap delineates critical focus areas for health systems, including culture, governance, business implementation, value, maintenance and operations, and information architecture, thereby guiding AI strategy and organizational alignment (Durlach et al., 2024). Additionally, the HIMSS Healthcare Innovation and AI Toolkit (HIMSS, 2024) complements these frameworks by providing additional support to healthcare leaders. Together, these resources furnish essential guidance to align technology with clinical objectives, optimize resource allocation, refine implementation strategies, and navigate regulatory and ethical landscapes effectively.

Recommendations for the future of AI in healthcare:

1. **Applying AI**: The principles proposed by Mollick (2024) can be applied in healthcare as we navigate how to integrate AI effectively.
   - **Invite AI to the table**: Consider AI solutions as possible tools in guiding decision-making processes to leverage insights and enhance clinical outcomes.
   - **Be the human in the loop**: Ensure that human oversight is maintained in AI systems to guide and validate AI-driven decisions.
   - **Treat AI like a person (but tell it what kind of person it is)**: Clearly define AI's role and capabilities, ensuring that its functions align with clinical and ethical standards.
   - **Assume that this is the worst AI we will ever use**: Maintain a critical perspective on AI's current and future capabilities; rapid advancement is ongoing, and this is just the beginning.

2. **Strategic Planning for AI Integration**: Strategic planning for AI integration should include establishing governance and working groups, assessing AI solutions, and developing a clear roadmap for implementation. Change management should set clear aims, foster constructive conversations, and ensure widespread agreement and commitment to AI implementation. Investment in education and training is crucial to prepare the healthcare workforce for AI adoption. Collaboration with AI experts, data scientists, application leaders, and ethicists is essential to navigate the complex landscape of AI in healthcare.

3. **Resource Allocation and Infrastructure**: The deployment of AI systems requires significant resources to support infrastructure, data management, and continuous improvement. Investments in high-performance computing, secure data storage solutions, and scalable AI platforms are necessary to facilitate robust AI integration. Interdisciplinary teams, including IT professionals, data scientists, clinicians, and ethicists, are crucial to ensuring the effective implementation and maintenance of AI systems.

4. **Ethical Considerations and Transparency**: Ethical considerations must remain at the forefront of AI deployment. Ensuring transparency, fairness, and accountability in AI systems is essential to building trust among patients and clinicians. Ongoing monitoring and evaluation of AI systems will help identify and mitigate any unintended consequences, ensuring that AI remains a tool for enhancing patient care and outcomes.

5. **Collaboration and Continuous Learning**: Fostering a culture of collaboration and continuous learning is critical for the successful integration of AI. Healthcare organizations should promote partnerships with academic institutions, technology companies, and regulatory bodies to stay at the forefront of AI advancements. Providing continuous education and training opportunities for healthcare professionals will ensure they are equipped to work alongside AI technologies effectively.

Conclusion

The exploration of the transformative impact of AI in healthcare and the ethical considerations necessitates a comprehensive approach, as it is evident that AI holds immense potential to revolutionize clinical practice, education, and research. From enhancing diagnostic accuracy and personalized treatment plans to improving operational efficiencies and population health management, AI's applications are broad and impactful. However, the responsible integration of AI requires careful navigation of ethical principles, transparency in decision-making, and continuous evaluation of its outcomes.

AI resources like those provided by the CHAI Assurance Standards Guide, the AI Maturity Roadmap, and the HIMSS Healthcare Innovation and AI Toolkit offer invaluable guidance in ensuring AI deployment aligns with patient-centric care, fairness, and accountability. These frameworks emphasize the importance of explainability in AI algorithms, mitigation of biases, and safeguarding patient privacy—critical elements in building trust among stakeholders.

Looking forward, strategic planning and robust governance structures will be essential for maximizing AI's benefits while minimizing risks. Education and training programs must equip healthcare professionals with the necessary skills to effectively collaborate with AI technologies and uphold ethical standards. Partnership across disciplines, continuous learning, and adaptation to evolving technological landscapes will be key in harnessing AI's full potential in healthcare.

As we move into the future, understanding AI in healthcare requires proactive engagement, ethical leadership, and a commitment to leveraging technology for the betterment of patient care and outcomes. By adhering to these principles and frameworks, healthcare organizations can navigate the complexities of AI integration responsibly, ensuring a future where AI enhances, rather than replaces, the human touch in healthcare delivery. AI's journey in healthcare is not merely about innovation but about fostering a future where technology and humanity collaborate harmoniously to achieve optimal health outcomes for all.

BLEND ETHICS AND GOVERNANCE | ARTIFICIAL INTELLIGENCE—ARE WE REACHING A TURNING POINT OR A PRECIPICE? | *BY PAUL BRIAN CONTINO*

The greatest opportunity offered by AI is not reducing errors or workloads, or even curing cancer: it is the opportunity to restore the precious and time-honored connection and trust.

Eric Topol (2019)

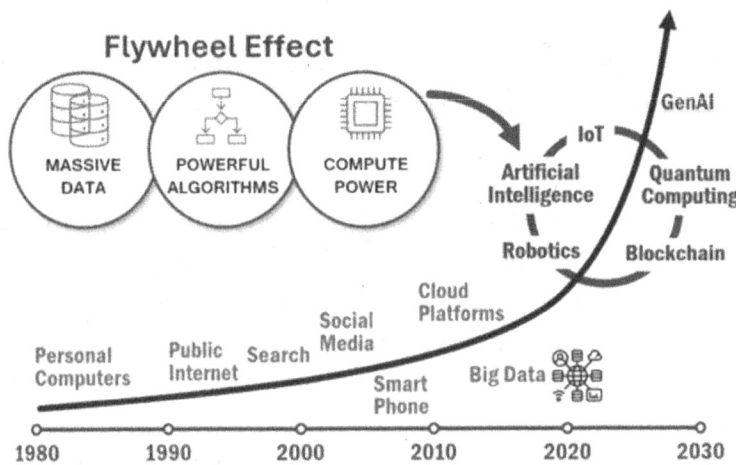

Figure 1.2 The Flywheel Effect of Big Data, Algorithms and Computational Power.

AI looks to be one of the most transformative technologies of our time.

We have explored the myriad of use cases and examples of how ML, AI, and generative AI are impacting healthcare and the practice of medicine.

This is an exciting time as we are seeing the confluence of several fields and disciplines coming together to create a "flywheel" effect that I expect will accelerate the pace of innovation we have previously seen.

The flywheel effect I am referring to is the impact of big data, algorithms, and computational power (Figure 1.2) that provides a self-reinforcing cycle. This synergistic relationship is where each element contributes to and amplifies the capabilities of the others.

But first, let us review the technological advancements that have shaped the current landscape of AI:

- **Personal Computers (PCs)**: The proliferation of personal computers democratized access to computing power. PCs allowed individuals to experiment with programming, learn about algorithms, and develop software. As more people gained computer literacy, the foundation for AI research and development expanded.
- **Public Internet**: The advent of the Internet revolutionized information sharing. Researchers worldwide could collaborate, access vast knowledge repositories, and share code. Online forums, mailing lists, and open-source communities facilitated AI discussions and accelerated progress.
- **Search Engines** like Google made information retrieval efficient. Researchers could quickly find relevant papers, datasets, and code snippets. Search engines also fueled the growth of NLP by enabling large-scale text analysis.

- **Social Media** platforms collect massive amounts of user-generated content. ML algorithms analyze this data to personalize recommendations, detect trends, and understand user behavior. Social media data fuels sentiment analysis, recommendation systems, and content generation.
- **Smartphones** brought computing to our pockets. Their sensors (such as cameras, accelerometers, and GPS) generate diverse data streams. AI algorithms process this data for applications like image recognition, location-based services, and health monitoring.
- **Cloud Platforms** and cloud computing provide scalable infrastructure for AI workloads. Researchers and developers can access powerful GPUs, TPUs, and storage without investing in expensive hardware. Cloud platforms enable training large neural networks, deploying models, and handling big data.
- **Big Data** is the lifeblood of AI. The exponential growth in data volume, velocity, and variety fuels ML models. AI algorithms learn from diverse datasets, improving accuracy in tasks like image classification, speech recognition, and recommendation.

The Flywheel Effect of Big Data, Algorithms, and Computational Power

Big Data

Remember the big data craze a decade ago, with every company on the Internet trying to aggregate, analyze, and, in many cases, monetize the datasets they had. Everyone from Google to Amazon to Facebook was hiring the best talent in the field of data science and looking for ways to leverage these massive datasets. Big data refers to the vast and complex datasets that organizations collect from a wide variety of sources. This includes both structured and unstructured data, such as social media interactions, sensor data, online activities, and search and transaction records, for example. The more data an organization has, the better it can understand patterns, trends, and correlations.

So as it turns out, big data was not a passing fad but an important on-ramp to the advancement of ML algorithms and the field of AI. Big data provides the raw material necessary for creating robust and accurate AI models. The effectiveness of large language models (LLMs) hinges on the quality of the data they are trained on. These sophisticated systems thrive on clean, high-quality data, relying on patterns and nuances in the training data.

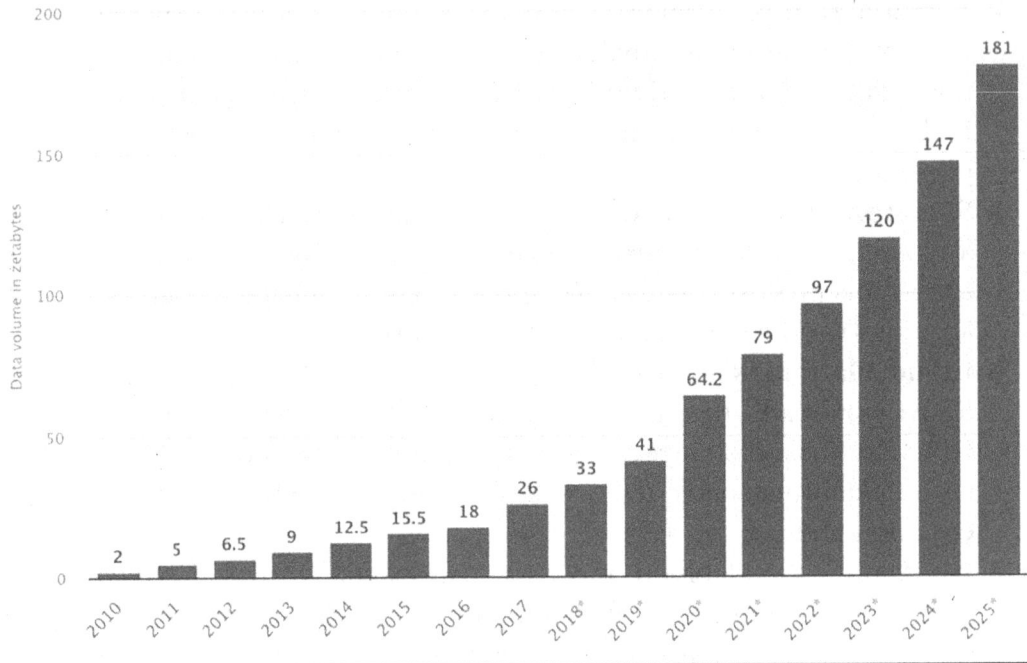

Figure 1.3   Digital Data Created Per Year.

To put the magnitude of big data into context, in the past two years alone, a staggering 90% of the world's data has been generated. This exponential growth underscores the rapid pace at which information is being produced, highlighting the dynamic nature of our digital landscape. Factors such as the widespread use of the Internet, the surge in social media interactions, and the proliferation of connected devices (IoT) have collectively contributed to this unprecedented data generation. The ability to harness and make sense of this immense volume of information presents both challenges and opportunities, influencing how we approach data management, analysis, and the development of technologies like AI and ML.

IDC predicts that the total amount of digital data created per year will reach 180 zettabytes by 2025 (Fortune Business Insights, n.d.) In 2022, the global big data analytics market size was valued at $271.83 billion and is projected to grow from $307.52 billion in 2023 to $745.15 billion by 2030 (IDC, 2017) (Figure 1.3).

Algorithms

Algorithms are sets of instructions or rules that guide the computer in performing specific tasks or making decisions. In the context of big data, advanced algorithms, especially ML algorithms, can extract meaningful insights, patterns, and predictions from these vast datasets.

As algorithms process and analyze big data, they can discover complex relationships and patterns that would be impossible to detect using traditional methods. This, in turn, helps organizations make more informed decisions, reduce risk, and uncover new opportunities. Moreover, big data contributes to the training and refinement of ML models. The more the data available for training, the better the models can understand the underlying patterns and nuances within the data. The importance of big data for ML and AI lies in its capacity to fuel the learning process, improve model accuracy, and enable real-time decision-making, ultimately enhancing the overall capabilities of these advanced technologies. Algorithms are the core components of ML systems and are designed to improve their performance over time as they are exposed to more data.

Computational Power

Computational power facilitated by advancements in hardware and cloud computing plays a pivotal role in advancing the capabilities of AI. Improved computational power enables the training of more sophisticated ML models, allowing organizations to tackle more complex problems and process larger datasets in less time.

Graphics processing unit (GPU)-accelerated computing has become instrumental to the field of AI due to its parallel processing capabilities, which make it well-suited for handling the complex computations involved in AI workloads. We are now seeing an exponential growth in computing power that is no longer following Moore's law of doubling every 2 years (Figure 1.4).

Quantum computers, while still in the early stages of development, hold intriguing promise for AI. Researchers are exploring how the unique properties of quantum systems could enhance various aspects of AI where quantum computing can provide advantages over classical computing.

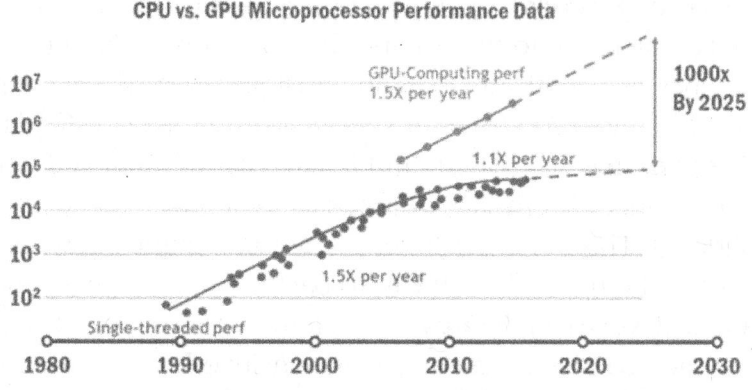

Figure 1.4   CPU vs GPU Microprocessor Performance Data.

AI Unchartered Waters: Risks and Ethical Challenges

Inordinate Power

Concerns have been raised that the development of AI is concentrated in the hands of too few companies, potentially granting them excessive control over this rapidly evolving technology. The rise of AI, fueled by models like OpenAI's ChatGPT, has sparked what some call an "AI arms race" among tech giants like Microsoft and Google. These companies are investing significant resources to develop and deploy large-scale AI models trained on massive amounts of data. The tech giants' control over data not only gives them a competitive edge but also raises questions about the equitable distribution of AI's benefits and highlights the potential for monopolistic practices. Companies like Google, Meta, Microsoft, and Apple unilaterally control access, aggregation, and distribution of data, impacting AI development. (Cyberscoop, n.d.)

AI in healthcare and medicine offers immense potential, but it also comes with several risks and ethical challenges that need to be carefully considered.

- **Patient Harm Due to AI Errors**: AI systems, while powerful, can still make mistakes. Errors in diagnosis, treatment recommendations, or patient monitoring could lead to harm. Ensuring robust testing and validation of AI algorithms is crucial to minimizing such risks.
- **Misuse of Medical AI Tools**: If AI tools are not used appropriately, they may yield incorrect results or mislead healthcare providers. Proper training and guidelines are essential to prevent misuse.
- **Bias in AI and Health Inequities**: AI algorithms can inadvertently perpetuate biases from the data they are trained on. These biases may amplify existing health disparities, affecting patient outcomes. Ensuring fairness and equity in AI systems is a critical challenge.
- **Lack of Transparency**: Some AI models operate as "black boxes," making it challenging to understand their decision-making process. Transparency is essential for building trust and ensuring accountability. Understanding how AI arrives at specific outputs is vital (Explainable AI).
- **Data Provenance**: The origin and lineage of AI-generated content (data provenance) is crucial. We need to trust that the content is reliable and validated. This is especially important in healthcare, where critical decisions are being made that can impact the lives of our patients.
- **Privacy and Security Issues**: AI systems rely on patient data, which raises privacy concerns. Safeguarding sensitive health information and preventing unauthorized access are paramount.

■ **Gaps in Accountability**: As AI becomes more integrated into health-care, defining clear lines of responsibility becomes crucial. Who is accountable for AI decisions? How do we address errors or adverse outcomes? These questions need thoughtful consideration.

Balancing the benefits of AI with these risks is essential for creating an ethical and effective healthcare system that leverages technology for the well-being of patients and providers alike.

To ensure that the promise of AI is realized while safeguarding against its potential perils, we must have responsible use of this powerful technology. We need to embrace the challenge of making AI a force for good, enhancing our lives, and empowering humanity.

We stand at a crossroads—will AI lead us to a brighter future or a precarious edge?

Time will tell, but it will take human intelligence and wisdom. I'm hopeful.

Bibliography

AACN Essentials. 2021. www.aacnnursing.org/Portals/0/PDFs/Publications/Essentials-2021.pdf

Adadi, A., & Berrada, M. (2018). Peeking inside the black-box: A survey on explainable artificial intelligence (XAI). *IEEE Access*, vol. 6, pp. 52138–52160. https://doi.org/10.1109/ACCESS.2018.2870052

Adadi, Amina, & Mohammed Berrada. "Peeking Inside the Black-Box: A Survey on Explainable Artificial Intelligence (XAI)." *IEEE Access*, vol. 6, 2018, pp. 52138–52160, ieeexplore.ieee.org/document/8466590, https://doi.org/10.1109/access.2018.2870052

Agrawal, Y. et al. "AI-Driven Job Displacement and Economic Impacts: Ethics and Strategies for Implementation". 2023. Retrieved from https://www.researchgate.net/publication/380676017_AI-Driven_Job_Displacement_and_Economic_Impacts_Ethics_and_Strategies_for_Implementation

Alakbarov, Naib. "Artificial Intelligence and the End of Capitalist System." *The Impact of Artificial Intelligence on Governance, Economics and Finance*, vol. I, 1 Jan. 2021, pp. 165–178, https://doi.org/10.1007/978-981-33-6811-8_9. Accessed 21 June 2023.

Alowais, S.A., Alghamdi, S.S., Alsuhebany, N., Alqahtani, T., Alshaya, A.I., Almohareb, S.N., Aldairem, A., Alrashed, M., bin Saleh, K., Badreldin, H.A., al Yami, M.S., al Harbi, S., & Albekairy, A.M. "Revolutionizing Healthcare: The Role of Artificial Intelligence in Clinical Practice." *BMC Medical Education*, vol. 23, no. 1, 2023, p. 689. https://doi.org/10.1186/s12909-023-04698-z

Antoniadi, Anna Markella, et al. "Current Challenges and Future Opportunities for XAI in Machine Learning-Based Clinical Decision Support Systems: A Systematic Review." *Applied Sciences*, vol. 11, no. 11, 31 May 2021, p. 5088, https://doi.org/10.3390/app11115088

Barredo Arrieta, A., Díaz-Rodríguez, N., Del Ser, J., Bennetot, A., Tabik, S., Barbado, A., Garcia, S., Gil-Lopez, S., Molina, D., Benjamins, R., Chatila, R., & Herrera, F. (2020). Explainable Artificial Intelligence (XAI): Concepts, taxonomies, opportunities and challenges toward responsible AI. *Information Fusion*, vol. 58, pp. 82–115. https://doi.org/10.1016/j.inffus.2019.12.012

Barredo Arrieta, Alejandro, et al. "Explainable Artificial Intelligence (XAI): Concepts, Taxonomies, Opportunities and Challenges toward Responsible AI." *Information Fusion*, vol. 58, no. 1, June 2020, pp. 82–115, arxiv.org/pdf/1910.10045.pdf, https://doi.org/10.1016/j.inffus.2019.12.012

Bekbolatova, M., Mayer, J., Ong, C.W., & Toma, M. "Transformative Potential of AI in Healthcare: Definitions, Applications, and Navigating the Ethical Landscape and Public Perspectives." *Healthcare*, vol. 12, no. 2, 2024, p. 125. https://doi.org/10.3390/healthcare12020125

Berretta, S., Tausch, A., Ontrup, G., Gilles, B., Peifer, C., & Kluge, A. "Defining Human-AI Teaming the Human-Centered Way: A Scoping Review and Network Analysis." *Frontiers in Artificial Intelligence*, vol. 6, 2023, p. 1250725. doi:10.3389/frai.2023.1250725

Cellan-Jones, Rory. "Stephen Hawking Warns Artificial Intelligence Could End Mankind." *BBC News*, 2 Dec. 2014, www.bbc.com/news/technology-30290540

Coalition for Health AI (CHAI). "Assurance Standards Guide Coalition for Health AI (CHAI)." CHAI-Assurance-Standards-Guide, 2024. https://chai.org/wp-content/uploads/2024/06/CHAI-Assurance-Standards-Guide-6-26-2024.pdf

CyberScoop (n.d.), Safeguarding data is our best hope to control AI, https://cyberscoop.com/safeguarding-data-is-our-best-hope-to-control-ai/

Dafoe, A. (2018). The governance of artificial intelligence: A framework for policymakers. *In Journal of AI and Society*, vol. 33, no. 1, pp. 121–139.

Dafoe, Allan, & Journal of International Affairs. "Global Politics And The Governance Of Artificial Intelligence." *Journal of International Affairs*, vol. 72, no. 1, 2018, pp. 121–126, www.jstor.org/stable/26588347

Durlach, P., Fournier, R., Gottlich, J., Markwell, T., McManus, J., Merrill, A., & Rhew, D. "The AI Maturity Roadmap: A Framework for Effective and Sustainable AI in Health Care." *New England Journal of Medicine Artificial Intelligence*, 2024. https://ai.nejm.org/doi/full/10.1056/AI-S2400177

Fortune Business Insights, Big Data Analytics Market (n.d.), https://www.fortunebusinessinsights.com/big-data-analytics-market-106179

Furman, Jason, & Robert Seamans. "AI and the Economy." *Innovation Policy and the Economy*, vol. 19, no. 1, Jan. 2019, pp. 161–191, https://doi.org/10.1086/699936

Greiman, V.A. "Human Rights and Artificial Intelligence: A Universal Challenge." *Journal of Information Warfare*, vol. 20, no. 1, 2021, pp. 50–62, www.jstor.org/stable/27036518

Hawking, S., et al. (2014, May 1) https://www.independent.co.uk/news/science/stephen-hawking-transcendence-looks-at-the-implications-of-artificial-intelligence-but-are-we-taking-ai-seriously-enough-9313474.html

Hickok, Merve. "Lessons Learned from AI Ethics Principles for Future Actions." *AI and Ethics*, vol. 1, no. 1, 6 Oct. 2020, pp. 41–47, https://doi.org/10.1007/s43681-020-00008-1

HIMSS. "HIMSS Nursing Innovation Advisory Workgroup's Healthcare Innovation & AI Toolkit: 5 Rights of AI in Healthcare." The Five Rights of AI in Healthcare, 2024. https://www.himss.org/resources/five-rights-ai-healthcare

Hogenhout, L. (2021). A framework for ethical AI at the United Nations. arXiv preprint arXiv:2104.12547. Retrieved from https://arxiv.org/abs/2104.12547

Hogenhout, Lambert. "A Framework for Ethical AI at the United Nations." *ArXiv:2104.12547 [cs.CY]*, 9 Apr. 2021, arxiv.org/abs/2104.12547. https://doi.org/10.48550/arXiv.2104.12547

IDC (2017). Data Age 2025: The Evolution of Data to Life-Critical. Seagate. Retrieved from https://www.seagate.com/files/www-content/our-story/trends/files/Seagate-WP-DataAge2025-March-2017.pdf

Jelinek, T. "The Ethics and Governance of Artificial Intelligence". 2021. Retrieved from https://www.researchgate.net/publication/349821936_The_ethics_and_governance_of_artificial_intelligence

Jobin, A., Ienca, M., & Vayena, E. (2019). Artificial Intelligence: The global landscape of ethics guidelines. *Nature Machine Intelligence*, vol. 1, no. 9, pp. 389–399. https://doi.org/10.1038/s42256-019-0088-2

Jobin, Anna, et al. "The Global Landscape of AI Ethics Guidelines." *Nature Machine Intelligence*, vol. 1, no. 9, Sept. 2019, pp. 389–399, www.nature.com/articles/s42256-019-0088-2, https://doi.org/10.1038/s42256-019-0088-2

Kitsios, F., Kamariotou, M., Syngelakis, A.I., & Talias, M.A. "Recent Advances of Artificial Intelligence in Healthcare: A Systematic Literature Review." *Applied Sciences*, vol. 13, no. 13, 2023, p. 7479, https://doi.org/10.3390/app13137479

Koniakou, V. "From the 'Rush to Ethics' to the 'Race for Governance' in Artificial Intelligence". *Information Systems Frontiers*, vol. 24, no. 3, 2022, pp. 577–593.

Koulu, R. (2020). Automating Fairness? Artificial Intelligence in the EU Justice System and the Future of Human Oversight. In M. Belov (Ed.), *Courts and Automation: The New Face of Justice* (pp. 111–135). Springer.

Koulu, Riikka. "Proceduralizing Control and Discretion: Human Oversight in Artificial Intelligence Policy." *Maastricht Journal of European and Comparative Law*, vol. 27, no. 6, Dec. 2020, pp. 720–735, https://doi.org/10.1177/1023263x20978649

Lawry, T. *Hacking Healthcare* (1st ed.). Productivity Press, 2022. https://doi.org/10.4324/9781003286103

Leslie, D., Rincón, C., Briggs, M., Perini, A., Jayadeva, S., Borda, A., Bennett, S.J., Burr, C., Aitken, M., Katell, M., Fischer, C., Wong, J., & Kherroubi Garcia, I. *AI Ethics and Governance in Practice: An Introduction*. The Alan Turing Institute, 2023.

Mäntymäki, Matti, et al. "Defining Organizational AI Governance." *AI and Ethics*, vol. 2, no. 4, 24 Feb. 2022, pp. 603–609, https://doi.org/10.1007/s43681-022-00143-x

Mazurek, G., & Małagocka, K. (2019). Perception of privacy and data protection in the context of the development of artificial intelligence. *Journal of Management Analytics*, vol. 6, no. 4, pp. 344–364. https://doi.org/10.1080/23270012.2019.1671243

Mazurek, Grzegorz, & Karolina Małagocka. "Perception of Privacy and Data Protection in the Context of the Development of Artificial Intelligence." *Journal of Management Analytics*, vol. 6, no. 4, 2 Oct. 2019, pp. 344–364, https://doi.org/10.1080/23270012.2019.1671243

Mora-Cantallops, Marçal, et al. "Traceability for Trustworthy AI: A Review of Models and Tools." *Big Data and Cognitive Computing*, vol. 5, no. 2, 4 May 2021, p. 20, https://doi.org/10.3390/bdcc5020020

Mora-Cantallops, M., Sierra, C., & Martínez-Torres, M. R. (2022). Traceability for trustworthy AI: A review of models and tools. *Computers*, vol. 11, no. 2, p. 20.

Murdoch, B. "Privacy and Artificial Intelligence: Challenges for Protecting Health Information in a New Era". *BMC Medical Ethics*, vol. 22, no. 1, 2021, p. 122. https://doi.org/10.1186/s12910-021-00687-3

Murphy, K., di Ruggiero, E., Upshur, R., Willison, D.J., Malhotra, N., Cai, J.C., Malhotra, N., Lui, V., & Gibson, J. "Artificial Intelligence for Good Health: A Scoping Review of the Ethics Literature." *BMC Medical Ethics*, vol. 22, no. 1, 2021, p. 4, https://doi.org/10.1186/s12910-021-00577-8

Mollick, E. *Co-intelligence: Living and working with AI*. Penguin Random House, 2024.

Nazer, Lama, et al. "Bias in Artificial Intelligence Algorithms and Recommendations for Mitigation." *PLOS Digital* Health, vol. 2, no. 6, 22 June 2023, p. e0000278, https://doi.org/10.1371/journal.pdig.0000278, Accessed 1 July 2023.

Neeley, Tsedal. "8 Questions about Using AI Responsibly, Answered." *Harvard Business Review*, 9 May 2023, http://hbr.org/2023/05/8-questions-about-using-ai-responsibly-answered

NVIDIA: Growth Beyond Moore's Law. Seeking Alpha. https://seekingalpha.com/article/4502479-nvidia-growth-beyond-moores-law

Polyakova, A. "Weapons of the Weak: Russia and AI-Driven Asymmetric Warfare. Brookings." 2021. www.brookings.edu/articles/weapons-of-the-weak-russia-and-ai-driven-asymmetric-warfare/. Accessed 14 July 2023.

Prince, Anya E.R., & Schwarcz, Daniel. "Proxy Discrimination in the Age of Artificial Intelligence and Big Data." *Iowa Law Review*, vol. 105, 2019, p. 1257, http://heinonline.org/HOL/LandingPage?handle=hein.journals/ilr105&div=35&id=&page=

Prince, A. E. R., & Schwarcz, D. (2020). Proxy discrimination in the age of artificial intelligence and big data. *Iowa Law Review*, vol. 105, no. 3, pp. 1257–1318.

Raji, I. D., Buolamwini, J., & Gebru, T. (2020). Actionable auditing: Investigating the impact of publicly naming biased performance results of commercial AI products. In Proceedings of the 2020 Conference on Fairness, Accountability, and Transparency (pp. 429–439). ACM. https://doi.org/10.1145/3351095.3372830

Raji, Inioluwa Deborah, et al. "Closing the AI Accountability Gap." *Proceedings of the 2020 Conference on Fairness, Accountability, and Transparency*, 22 Jan. 2020, https://doi.org/10.1145/3351095.3372873

Reddy, S., Rogers, W., & Makinen, V.P., et al. "Evaluation Framework to Guide Implementation of AI Systems into Healthcare Settings." *BMJ Health & Care Informatics*, vol. 28, no. 1, 2021, p. e100444, doi:10.1136/bmjhci-2021-100444

Ross, A., Freeman, R., McGrow, K., & Kagan, O. "Implications of Artificial Intelligence for Nurse Managers." *Nursing Management (Springhouse)*, vol. 55, no. 7, July 2024a, pp. 14–23, DOI: 10.1097/nmg.0000000000000143

Ross, A., McGrow, K., Zhi, D., & Rasmy, L. "Foundation Models, Generative AI, and Large Language Models." *CIN: Computers, Informatics, Nursing*, vol. 42, no. 5, May 2024b pp. 377–387. https://doi.org/10.1097/CIN.0000000000001149

Santoni de Sio, F., & Mecacci, G. (2021). Four responsibility gaps with artificial intelligence: Why they matter and how to address them. *Philosophy & Technology*, vol. 34, pp. 1057–1084. https://doi.org/10.1007/s13347-021-00450-x

Schwartz-Narbonne, D. (2019). *Daniel Schwartz-Narbonne shares how automated reasoning, a branch of AI tech, can help prove the security of boot code.* AWS Security Blog.

Schwartz, Reva, et al. *Towards a Standard for Identifying and Managing Bias in Artificial Intelligence*, vol. 3. US Department of Commerce, National Institute of Standards and Technology, 15 Mar. 2022, https://doi.org/10.6028/nist.sp.1270

Seger, E. "In Defence of Principlism in AI Ethics and Governance". *Philosophy & Technology*, vol. 35, no. 2, 2022, p. 45. https://doi.org/10.1007/s13347-022-00538-y

Statista, Worldwide Data Created (n.d.), https://www.statista.com/statistics/871513/worldwide-data-created

Steels, Luc, & Lopez de Mantaras, Ramon. "The Barcelona Declaration for the Proper Development and Usage of Artificial Intelligence in Europe." *AI Communications*, vol. 31, no. 6, 21 Dec. 2018, pp. 485–494, https://doi.org/10.3233/aic-180607. Accessed 21 Sept. 2019.

Topol, E. (2019). *Deep medicine: How artificial intelligence can make healthcare human again*. Basic Books.

Times News. "Is AI Existentially Dangerous or Not?" *Time News*, 30 June 2023, https://time.news/is-ai-existentially-dangerous-or-not/?p2=%5EEQ%5Eaug22%5E&prod=HP&cmpgn=aug22&locale=en_us&annot=false&sameTabLaunch=false&o=APN12175&installSource=direct&geo=us&browser=chrome&darkMode=false&ueid=1b85e424-f983-4fb6-b415-1ee71a9025b0&doi=2022-09-05. Accessed 1 July 2023.

United Nations. "Towards an Ethics of Artificial Intelligence | United Nations." *www.un.org*, Dec. 2018, www.un.org/en/chronicle/article/towards-ethics-artificial-intelligence

Vrontis, D. "Artificial Intelligence and the Future of Work: A Critical Analysis of Potentials and Challenges". *Technological Forecasting and Social Change*, vol. 180, 2023, p. 121689. https://doi.org/10.1016/j.techfore.2022.121689

West, D., & Allen, J. (2018). *How artificial intelligence is transforming the world*. Brookings Institution.

West, Darrell M., & Allen, John R. "How Artificial Intelligence Is Transforming the World. Brookings". 24 Apr. 2018, www.brookings.edu/research/how-artificial-intelligence-is-transforming-the-world/

World Health Organization. "WHO Calls for Safe and Ethical AI for Health." 2023. www.who.int/news/item/16-05-2023-who-calls-for-safe-and-ethical-ai-for-health

White House Office of Science and Technology Policy. "Blueprint for an AI Bill of Rights Making Automated Systems Work for the American People." 2022. www.whitehouse.gov/wp-content/uploads/2022/10/Blueprint-for-an-AI-Bill-of-Rights.pdf

Chapter 2

Blend Cultures

Include the organization's larger community and ensure that institutional leaders are engaged and supportive of the proposed innovative strategies.

One of the first things you need to do to improve the odds of innovation success is to ensure support and engagement from key organizational leaders. Innovation is hard to do in a vacuum. Often it takes a team, some of whom are directly involved and others who provide resources and political cover. As you embark on your innovation, take inventory of key decision-makers, influencers, and culture. Identify both the individuals who will help you and those who might hurt you. The more organizational community and leadership engagement you develop, the higher the likelihood of overcoming the obstacles that will be on your path to innovation.

BLEND CULTURES | ENGAGING THE ENTERPRISE ON AI | *BY SARAH HATCHETT*

The integration of artificial intelligence (AI) into healthcare organizations has brought about a revolutionary shift, presenting both challenges and unprecedented opportunities. Chief information officers (CIOs) must develop strategies to both engage and educate all levels of the organization to prepare the enterprise for the multifaceted impact of AI. AI has transcended its role as a mere tool and has become an integral part of healthcare teams, with implications reaching far beyond the realms of traditional

 DOI: 10.4324/9781032715155-2

collaboration and decision-making. This shift opens up new possibilities for teamwork and efficiency in healthcare delivery.

The opportunities for transformation are vast. In the operational sector, futurists predict general productivity gains of 20–30% for knowledge workers. On the clinical front, fundamental changes in health delivery models are anticipated that streamline workflows and enable care providers to work at the top of the license. Whether clinical or operational, the support of these technologies necessitates the evolution of technical teams, who must acquire new skills and adapt to innovative ways of working. There are heightened expectations for optimized performance and enhanced patient care through the strategic utilization of AI capabilities.

CIOs play a crucial role in this transformative journey, starting with the need to inform Executive Leadership about the indispensable nature of AI in the development and execution of business, clinical, and research strategies. Making a compelling case for the integration of AI into organizational goals is key. Here are some key strategies to consider in informing and educating the executive team on AI:

- **Strategic Alignment**:
  - Emphasize how AI aligns with the overall strategic vision and mission of the organization.
  - Illustrate how AI can enhance the organization's competitive position and contribute to long-term sustainability.
- **Case Studies and Success Stories**:
  - Share relevant case studies and success stories from other organizations that have successfully implemented AI in healthcare.
  - Highlight measurable improvements, financial gains, and positive impacts on patient outcomes achieved by similar implementations.
- **Cost–Benefit Analysis**:
  - Present a detailed cost–benefit analysis that outlines the investment required for AI implementation against the anticipated returns.
  - Clearly define the short-term and long-term financial implications, showcasing the potential return on investment.
- **Risk Mitigation Strategies**:
  - Address concerns related to risks, including data security, privacy, and potential resistance from employees.
  - Present comprehensive risk mitigation strategies to assure executive leadership that these challenges are being proactively addressed.

- **Continuous Communication**:
  - Foster an open dialogue to address any concerns or questions that may arise during the decision-making process.

CIOs must also form partnerships with clinical and operational leadership to establish a shared vision, recognizing that AI initiatives cannot be developed in isolation but require collaboration across departments.

- **Align to Organizational Value Paradigms**:
  - Conduct a thorough business impact assessment to demonstrate how AI aligns with organizational goals and can drive positive outcomes.
  - Clearly articulate the potential benefits, such as increased efficiency, cost savings, improved patient care, and competitive advantages.
- **Collaboration Opportunities**:
  - Identify collaboration opportunities with other departments, institutions, or industry partners that can strengthen the organization's AI initiatives.
  - Emphasize the potential for creating synergies and fostering innovation through strategic partnerships.
- **Educational Workshops and Seminars**:
  - Conduct educational workshops and seminars to provide a comprehensive understanding of AI concepts, technologies, and their relevance to the healthcare industry.
  - Invite external experts or thought leaders to share insights and perspectives on the transformative power of AI.
- **Pilot Programs and Demonstrations**:
  - Implement small-scale pilot programs to demonstrate the tangible benefits of AI in a controlled environment.
  - Showcase prototypes or simulations to give executive leadership hands-on experience with AI technologies and their potential applications.
- **Regulatory Compliance**:
  - Demonstrate a deep understanding of relevant regulations and compliance standards in the healthcare sector.
  - Outline how AI implementations will adhere to these standards, ensuring legal and ethical practices.

Educating and activating the workforce is equally vital, with grassroots innovation being fostered through education and evangelization. Engaging employees in the transformation process is crucial for successful implementation. Additionally, effective change management, addressing both technical and organizational challenges, is essential to overcome operational issues that may surface during implementation.

- ▪ **User-Centric Design Workshops**:
  - – Host user-centric design workshops that involve front-line staff in the creation and refinement of AI tools.
  - – Encourage employees to share their insights on workflow challenges and opportunities where AI can make a positive impact.
  - – Encourage employees to contribute ideas and suggestions during the development process, including the accessibility and usability of solutions as they are integrated into workflows.
- ▪ **Interactive Training Sessions**:
  - – Offer interactive training sessions on AI concepts and applications tailored to the specific roles of front-line staff.
  - – Provide hands-on experience with AI tools in a simulated environment to build familiarity and confidence.
- ▪ **Feedback Mechanisms**:
  - – Establish open channels for continuous feedback to gather insights from front-line workers regarding their experiences with AI applications.
  - – Actively address concerns and suggestions to demonstrate a commitment to improvement.
- ▪ **Champion Programs**:
  - – Identify and empower AI champions among front-line staff who can act as advocates for AI adoption.
  - – Provide these champions with additional training and resources to support their peers in embracing AI technologies.
- ▪ **Incentive Programs**:
  - – Implement incentive programs or recognition schemes to reward front-line staff for their contributions to AI innovation.
  - – Highlight success stories and acknowledge individuals or teams that have successfully integrated AI into their workflows.
  - – Introduce gamification elements to make the learning process and AI engagement more enjoyable.
- ▪ **Skill Development Programs**:
  - – Offer skill development programs to empower front-line staff with the necessary knowledge and capabilities to work alongside AI technologies.
  - – Provide training on how to interpret and utilize insights generated by AI systems.

■ **Community Building**:
  – Establish a community or forum where front-line staff can share their experiences, insights, and best practices related to AI adoption.
  – Facilitate peer-to-peer learning and collaboration.

Communication is important at all three levels: executive, leadership, and front-line teams. Establish continuous communication channels with each stakeholder group, providing regular updates on AI developments, progress, and milestones.

Maintaining ethical standards in AI implementation requires effective enterprise governance, establishing frameworks for ethical AI deployment, and ensuring compliance with regulations and guidelines. Moreover, subject matter expertise should be actively involved in validation and testing processes to balance technological advancements with domain-specific knowledge.

The accountability for innovation and ethical considerations must be broadened, making it an integral part of the scope and focus of AI initiatives. Educating stakeholders about the ethical dimensions of AI deployment ensures a responsible and transparent integration into healthcare practices.

The future holds a world of possibilities for AI in healthcare. Envisioning algorithmic medicine, diagnostic interpretations, precision medicine, intelligent wearables, predictive analytics, virtual health assistants, and remote patient monitoring, the potential applications of AI are vast.

The Cleveland Clinic has taken initial steps by defining use cases and piloting AI programs, with a five-year outlook for sustained implementation. Thoughtful consideration is being given to building an "AI foundation," contemplating the people, tools, and processes needed to deploy AI at scale across the enterprise. Fundamental alignment with care priorities, including patient care, caregiver support, organizational well-being, and community health, is a guiding principle in the Cleveland Clinic's approach to AI implementation.

The impact of AI on the healthcare workforce is transformative, offering unprecedented opportunities for efficiency and innovation. CIOs play a pivotal role in ensuring a smooth transition, promoting ethical practices, and embracing future trends. As organizations like the Cleveland Clinic pioneer AI initiatives, the healthcare landscape stands at the forefront of a technological revolution, promising enhanced patient care, streamlined operations, and improved overall well-being.

BLEND CULTURES | SYNERGISTIC BLEND OF AI EXPERTS AND HEALTHCARE EXPERTS FOR THE DEVELOPMENT OF AI IN HEALTHCARE | *BY RAGHAV AWASTHI, SHREYA MISHRA, AND PIYUSH MATHUR*

BrainX AI Research, BrainX, LLC

The COVID-19 pandemic presented a significant opportunity to use AI to save lives (Syrowatka et al. 2021; Tzachor et al. 2020; Ashique et al. 2024), leading to the development of various AI solutions ranging from AI-powered chatbots and diagnostic tools to AI-guided resource allocation (Syrowatka et al. 2021; Ashique et al. 2024; Tzachor et al. 2020; Chang et al. 2021). However, we have observed limited real-world application of these AI models (Wynants et al. 2020; Roberts et al. 2021; Syrowatka et al. 2021), which can be attributed to factors such as data quality and lack of collaboration with AI experts and healthcare experts ("When AI Systems Systemically Fail," n.d.; Vela et al. 2022; Santa Clara University, n.d.).

Developing AI solutions entails a comprehensive process: from ideation to data collection to model training, deployment, and continuous monitoring. Throughout this process, healthcare experts play a crucial role in assessing data quality, ensuring the integrity of data, evaluating models, providing feedback, and addressing ethical considerations.

At BrainX, we cultivate a culture that integrates AI expertise with deep domain knowledge from healthcare experts. Below are some key points that are important we follow while building a strong team of AI experts and healthcare experts:

- ■ **Understanding the Multidisciplinary Nature of AI**: AI has multiple components like machine learning, deep learning, natural language processing, computer vision, and reinforcement learning, each requiring expertise in computer science, mathematics, statistics, and information science. Healthcare data, including EHRs, genomic data, and clinical trials, adds complexity (Gunatilleke 2022; Wright 2023). It is unrealistic to expect one AI professional to possess all skills. So it is important to build the AI team based on the nature of the AI project.

- **AI experts are Sometimes Not Software Developers**: Deploying AI models requires building interactive and secure platforms, which demands a different skill set. Therefore, having an expert with platform development skills enhances the team's strength.
- **The Importance of Cross-Disciplinary Knowledge in Healthcare and AI**: Domain experts in healthcare should have a basic understanding of data and AI, while AI experts should be familiar with healthcare terminology. Although healthcare and AI are distinct fields, it is crucial for experts in both areas to have some cross-disciplinary knowledge.

Establishing a structured working environment and effective communication channels is crucial for maintaining a strong team where all members feel comfortable and aligned with the project progress. We advocate for regular group meetings and 1–1 sessions to ensure clear communication within the team. Team leads are encouraged to understand each individual's expertise and work habits to assign project tasks effectively. Furthermore, we have a culture that respects and encourages open communication between team leads and all team members. Additionally, we create an environment where team members support each other in improving the quality and reproducibility of work. This includes activities such as code reviews and providing explanations of code details to healthcare experts.

To ensure timely project delivery, we divide the project into distinct parts and assign tasks based on individual expertise. We begin with a clear project vision established through an extensive literature review and deep discussions among team members. Healthcare experts contribute insights on the project's objectives, clinical significance, and potential data sources, while AI experts focus on data handling, AI model selection, and evaluation strategies. Healthcare experts play a crucial role in providing feedback on data quality and conducting qualitative evaluations of models. For instance, in one of our projects (Mishra et al. 2021), healthcare experts manually assessed the text output of question-answering-based AI models that queried clinical notes with questions like "Does this patient have a stroke?" This evaluation helped us identify patterns where models excelled and where improvements were needed. This collaborative approach helped our solutions reach the deployment level.

Similarly, we collaborated with AI experts and healthcare professionals to write an award-winning essay for a Kaggle competition titled "Ethical AI Is All We Need!!" ("Ethical AI Is All We Need!!" 2023). In this essay, a team of healthcare experts and AI experts together performed data-driven experiments to evaluate various aspects of AI ethics, such as diversity and fairness, transparency, privacy and data governance, societal and environmental well-being, and accountability.

After successfully completing projects, it's crucial to make them accessible to the public, either through publication or as software tools. In both scenarios, we continue to collaborate closely to document our research findings or develop software. We encourage all team members to contribute to paper writing, whether by drafting subsections of the paper or offering suggestions for software design during development. This inclusive approach cultivates a sense of ownership and ensures that our work reflects diverse perspectives and expertise.

Other than diversity in expertise, we believe in demographic diversity such as gender, age, race, and ethnicity within the team. This diversity enriches our environment, nurtures creativity, and promotes understanding of new cultures and perspectives. Also, fun is very important, so we prioritize creating a supportive and enjoyable atmosphere where team members can bond, relax, and recharge together. This helps build strong relationships and enhances overall team morale and productivity.

Overall, at BrainX AI Research, this synergistic blend of expertise and diversity drives data-centric, model-centric, and human-centric AI with innovation, while also ensuring ethical, patient-centered AI solutions that advance healthcare delivery and enhance patient outcomes.

BLEND CULTURES | BUILDING AND DILIGENCING AI ORGANIZATIONS' DEVELOPMENT PLANS REQUIRES BLENDING CULTURES | *BY BRITTANY PARTRIDGE, MATT PARTRIDGE, KIERAN DONALDSON, ARTHUR DOUVILLE, AND SHERRI DOUVILLE*

While there are mixed perspectives on generative AI being ready for primetime in medicine, it's predicted to drive dramatic productivity and financial impacts due to generative AI, large language models, and LLMs that no executive can ignore. At the same time, most organizations don't have a highly functioning AI product owner in place with the authority to build the capabilities it really takes to drive value from AI in a healthcare enterprise-wide context. It's therefore every leader's responsibility to drive a new level of organization-wide literacy and competence with respect to AI and GenAI. This essay is brought to you by a trusted coauthor team with a repeated best-selling track record specific to introducing new technology paradigms and frameworks in healthcare. As an industry, we must focus on integrating the essential new technical and AI team members that we need to partner with GenAI talent, including GenAI talent themselves. Every leadership team must define and pursue their own development plan as a team and individuals, including leaders, because no AI talent in isolation can help you derive value from AI in an enterprise context.

Blending Cultures

For a long time, the culture of medicine has been based on a salaried workforce. This doesn't work for top tech talent. Healthcare can more easily integrate AI engineers from a vendor perspective when there is an opportunity to build equity and value.

Engineering talent is accustomed to equity ownership and well-compensated opportunities in the tech sector. Healthcare technology companies that are successful in creating these kinds of potential for wealth generation and career opportunities for engineers will be successful in integrating them into healthcare.

Further, since being successful in healthcare technology requires understanding and aligning with physician and clinical work, experienced engineering leaders have a chance to pioneer and define a winning future career path that may not be currently obvious. We think this would entail:

1. Building a high-quality publication record.
2. Focusing on cross-disciplinary communication and public speaking.
3. Honing leadership skills by advancing engineering organizations like IEEE or AI organizations like the American Board of AI in Medicine, ABAIMED.

Though hiring an engineer who understands and can build AI models and applications is a worthwhile goal, there's an organizational roadmap that needs to be in place to drive value for all stakeholders.

This includes:

■ Productizing engineering.
■ Addressing data quality.
■ Planning for the right infrastructure.

- Having data science and data engineering skills that underpin sound model development.
- Testing and validation.

The Promise of AI and Large Language Models in Healthcare

In many contexts, professionals who integrate AI into their work will be able to amplify their capabilities and elevate their roles. All computer work can be enhanced with AI. Leveraging contemporary LLMs is like accessing a skilled team that is always ready and eager to help. Such human-AI collaboration can increase job satisfaction and reduce the risk of burnout, particularly when routine tasks are delegated to AI. The resultant boost in productivity can ideally then lead to the ability to produce higher-quality work to benefit healthcare professionals, their respective organizations, and the patients they serve.

Potential applications in healthcare include assistance in differential diagnosis, language translation in telemedicine sessions, composing nuanced emails, and authoring patient education.

Vision for the Future

It's crucial for AI in healthcare to achieve an error rate substantially lower than humans and ensure that any mistakes have minimal consequences. As we transition to more natural language-based APIs, there will be heightened security risks. Potential threats, like data breaches by LLM providers, underscore the importance of robust protective measures.

Looking further ahead, we can anticipate AI systems that possess the collective knowledge of many professionals, enhanced by superior analytical capabilities, eventually leading to advanced robotic applications.

Shifting Organizational Culture

Organizations are now recognizing the need to place AI at the center of their operational strategies. In the foreseeable future, overlooking the use of advanced tools like LLMs, especially when the situation calls for it, will be viewed negatively. Eventually, it would be like choosing a typewriter over a computer in today's context. This evolving landscape necessitates that staff are equipped with updated training, introducing them to innovative workflows and effective AI interactions. The goal is to nurture an environment where professionals can confidently collaborate with and delegate tasks to AI and master the nuances of effective AI communication, from prompt engineering and beyond.

Organization-wide AI literacy is required to drive value out of AI. To facilitate that, a core team will need to be on a development plan to enable being true partners for our engineering and AI talent that consists of the following.

What to Look for in Diligence for AI Vendors

As AI applications are being integrated into more aspects of healthcare, baseline knowledge of AI applications and their underlying code becomes necessary. Technical staff will ultimately be the ones implementing these applications, so it is useful for them to understand how they are created. Having a basic understanding of a coding language paired with an understanding of how AI applications are built can go a long way in further maximizing the impact of such applications when they are implemented in your organization. While an organization's AI and engineering talent already exceeds this knowledge level, this baseline understanding can equip your other technical staff so they can become better partners with that talent. In many instances, it will enable them to ask better questions and make sure that the applications that are being implemented actually provide additional value to the organization.

Implementing a development plan for all staff that will be interacting with AI applications is in the best interest of the organization to get the most out of AI. Because the introduction of powerful large language models in the enterprise is in the early stages, the gap between novice and expert remains relatively small, specifically in terms of delivering value to patients, clinicians, and organizations through LLMs. To capitalize on this, it's a good idea to implement a development plan for all staff that will be interacting with AI application developers and implementers so that your staff can speak about AI fluently and ask educated questions about potentially implemented AI. While there is no one-size-fits-all development plan, the following steps can ensure a baseline understanding of the AI space for your technical and technical operations IT staff.

First, a basic level of coding understanding is necessary to comprehend the vocabulary surrounding the technical aspects of the AI conversation. This can be paired with a basic education of how language models are created to equip your technical team with the basic skills to have high-level conversations around the AI space.

Once this basic level is achieved, the next steps depend on how your organization looks to use AI both in the present and in the future. For many, this will be a sufficient level of AI knowledge. For those looking for further development, a good next step is to gain an understanding of how to build AI applications and specifically how to build the AI program your organization will be using. This will further increase vocabulary and improve the conversations that can be had around creating, implementing, and maximizing the effectiveness of the applications. This will also improve the level of brainstorming you are able to have at an internal level around AI.

Lastly, it is important to take a step back when implementing AI, that is, to use AI as a solution to a problem you are currently or potentially looking to solve, not implementing AI and looking for a problem that it may fix. This will ensure that your organization isn't wasting time and resources implementing the newest technology that doesn't address your organization's shortcomings or pain points.

Once your technical team begins on their AI development plan, they can be leveraged to bring along some of your organization's non-technical staff who will be interacting with AI applications on a lower level. This is a dual purpose. First, it reinforces the things learned through the development plan by the technical staff, and second, it begins to give the non-technical staff a better level of understanding, so they are able to maximize the effectiveness of the applications and provide better feedback for the improvement of the applications. In general, those who interface with AI technical teams should have a skills development plan that will drive literacy, some experience, and understanding of programming, algorithms, machine learning, deep learning, neural networks, and large language models. Leadership overseeing AI and technology needs further additional skills around AI-specific governance, compliance, medical ethics, and cybersecurity to make it operational (not just aspirational) and to enable acceptance by clinicians in all types of settings.

Great Practices Which Should Be on Your Radar That also Apply to AI

As a general manager, one author of this section recommends leveraging GenAI for non-confidential or non-PHI content development and marketing and knowledge management. The road to making it operational > aspirational is about managing the risks, including cybersecurity, and that can be tackled from a total team perspective, frameworks.

There is also the requirement to manage the deployment project for impact including change management (Partridge, 2021).

Further, to handle data and applications safely, organizations must have a robust third party management strategy, which can be well-informed by all the relevant frameworks and regulations outlined in Chapter 10 of Advanced Health Technology, "Managing Third-Party Risk: Framework Details for Risk Management in Medical Technology" (Parker et al., 2023).

Making It Real

Some great impacts we've seen include work being done now at UCSD Health.

A recent article out of UC San Diego Health walked through the challenges of AI through the lens of Sepsis prediction models being criticized for inaccuracy.

> Errors in sepsis prediction are often highlighted both in anecdotal and health system-wide failures that can be traced to poor implementation approaches, rudimentary ML algorithms, application of algorithms outside their intended use, or without proper maintenance.
>
> *(Wardi et al., 2023)*

There is always risk when implementing technology and AI in healthcare, so consistent exploration of error reduction must be part of the technical operating model. To reduce this error and improve AI models in healthcare, the authors proposed and expanded upon the following steps:

Focus on the Data

1. **Data Enrichment**: The process of taking first-party data from internal sources and combining it with disparate data from other internal systems or external data. Not limiting data sources to the EHR but focusing instead on additional data sets that will broaden the model, such as multimodal data from bedside monitors, IV pumps, mechanical ventilators, and imaging studies.
2. **Actively Involve AI in Data Generation**: Most current AI protocols don't actively seek and collect data; they rely on already collected data. When an AI model determines predictive certainty is low, it could be

used to order further diagnostics or request additional nursing assessments to obtain additional data. While this approach could improve
accuracy, it is important to tool accurately to minimize costs (to both
patients and systems) and workflow disruptions.

Decrease the Implementation Gap

Even the most promising AI systems in medicine need to be implemented clinically, evaluated with adequate safety nets in place, and
iteratively improved over time to be successful. Yet, implementation of these models into clinical practice is too often an afterthought compared with the investment of model development.

(Wardi, et al, 2023)

1. **Workflow testing in the form of real-time case reviews**: Meant to
   get feedback from the clinical staff about how the AI works in practice,
   including timing and appropriateness of alerts. These iterative improvements and slight model changes are crucial but often overlooked steps
   during implementations.
2. **Silent trials**: A type of study where the AI model is tested on real
   patients in the production environment but is only accessible by key
   stakeholders and is not involved in clinical care. Beyond just improving
   a model's predictive ability, it allows the technical teams to study UX and
   UI as well as develop content to educate end-users on the new model.
3. **Using A/B testing**: Tests where users are randomly given design A or
   design B are very common outside of healthcare but are slower on
   clinical implementation. This could greatly enhance the UX of AI
   models and decrease the snooze/ignore rates.

All of these implementation strategies and tests should be part of the
operating model of a learning health system as part of their local quality
improvement efforts. In a presentation titled *Bridging AI's Proof-Of-Concept
to Production Gap*, Andrew Ng reiterated this challenge.

There Is a huge gap between what works in a research lab vs.
what will run in production. This is true not just for healthcare.
One thing we should work on both from the research and on the
practical engineering side is better tools and processes to make
sure our model is generalized to different datasets.

(Ng. 2020)

Rigorous Testing

1. **Focus on prospective studies rather than retrospective**: At the time of this writing, the vast majority of sepsis ML studies are retrospective, meaning they look at data from the past, which have flaws that limit generalizability. For example:
   a. A model trained on an administrative definition of sepsis might perform poorly at hospitals that rely on Center for Medicare and Medicaid Definition.
   b. A model that has a high AUCroc score might still generate many false alarms, resulting in workflow disruption and unnecessary anxiety for patients and physicians.

Constantly Learning and Adapting

2. **Focus on new approaches that can lead to increased generalizability**: Evolution and availability of nation-wide data sets as well as novel approaches like transfer learning and conformal prediction should be studied and leveraged in learning healthcare systems.
3. **"I Don't Know"**: Program and Empower AI models to say they don't know when they detect unfamiliar patients/situations arising from erroneous data, missingness, distributional shift, and data drifts.

The technical and administrative teams in healthcare systems are acutely aware that clinicians are being bombarded by an increasing number of tasks. Many products are foisted onto physicians in what feels like an intrusion into their workflows.

If these models are implemented poorly, they will lead to mistrust, frustration, and potentially inadvertent harm. In most use cases, the default workflow should require physician oversight. It is therefore our role to ensure that we are consistently learning, training, and testing so that we can implement the best, most trustworthy options with input and co-design from the clinicians that will use it. "Finally, we need to recognize the limit of AI: it may alert us to a patient with sepsis, but—unlike chess—it does not yet know the next move."

Next Steps

Beyond the proof-of-concept to production gaps with implementation, another key "make or break" area is data quality. It will therefore be critical for executive and IT teams to define and pursue a data quality and governance strategy in parallel with an AI workforce upskilling plan to deliver real results in saving and improving patient lives, reducing the cost of care, and improving the clinician's work and patient experience.

BLEND CULTURES | ENHANCING PATIENT ENGAGEMENT AND BOOSTING PROVIDER PRODUCTIVITY THROUGH AI | *BY KHALID TURK*

Introduction

The healthcare landscape is undergoing a rapid transformation fueled by technological advancements. AI has emerged as a powerful force, offering unprecedented opportunities to revolutionize patient care. At Santa Clara Valley Healthcare, we recognized the immense potential of AI to enhance patient engagement and increase provider productivity.

For good reason, healthcare represents a fifth of the US economy and is ripe for AI, especially augmented intelligence. Because healthcare involves life-and-death decisions, AI is unlikely to completely replace human judgment anytime soon. Rather, having a medical professional in the middle to validate AI recommendations should lead to better health outcomes and lower costs.

This article delves into our journey of integrating AI with our electronic medical record (EMR), highlighting the key strategies and challenges encountered while aligning with the HIMSS Innovation Pathways framework.

Identifying the Need for AI Integration

Our journey began with a comprehensive analysis of our current operations. We were determined to identify pain points hindering both patient engagement and provider efficiency. Our analysis revealed several areas ripe for improvement:

- **Patient Communication Challenges**: Patients often experience delays in receiving responses to their queries, leading to frustration and a sense of disconnect with their healthcare providers.
- **Administrative Burden**: Providers were burdened by tedious administrative tasks, significantly impacting the time they could dedicate to direct patient care.

- **Data Overload**: The vast amount of patient data often impeded timely access to crucial information, hindering clinical decision-making.
- **Language Barriers**: Communication gaps due to language differences posed a significant challenge in delivering optimal care to non-English-speaking patients.

Based on these findings, we established clear goals for our AI integration:

- **Revolutionize Patient Engagement**: Foster personalized and timely communication between patients and providers, leading to a more positive and effective healthcare experience.
- **Streamline Provider Workflows**: Automate routine administrative tasks, allowing providers to dedicate more time to patient interaction and clinical care.
- **Enhance Clinical Decision-Making**: Leverage AI to analyze vast amounts of patient data, providing clinicians with readily accessible and insightful summaries for informed decision-making.
- **Break Down Language Barriers**: Implement AI-powered translation tools to bridge the communication gap between providers and non-English-speaking patients.

Fostering a Collaborative Culture

Successfully introducing AI into our complex healthcare system demanded the active participation and support of key stakeholders, including:

- **Healthcare Providers**: Clinicians needed to understand the potential benefits of AI and feel comfortable integrating it into their daily workflows.
- **Administrative Staff**: Staff responsible for administrative tasks needed to be trained on new AI-powered tools to ensure a smooth transition.
- **Leadership**: Leaders needed to be on board with the initiative, providing resources and promoting a culture of innovation.

To achieve this collaborative environment, we adopted a multi-pronged approach:

- **Open Communication and Transparency**: We conducted workshops and meetings to discuss the potential benefits and limitations of AI.

This fostered an open dialogue where concerns could be addressed, building trust in the initiative.

■ **Education and Training**: We developed comprehensive training programs to ensure all staff members were comfortable using the new AI tools. This included hands-on training sessions and readily available user guides.

■ **Executive Sponsorship**: Secured the endorsement of our Chief Executive Officer (CEO) and Chief Medical Officer (CMO). Their active involvement sent a strong message of support and encouraged broader participation from all levels of the organization.

Engaging Key Stakeholders

Introducing AI into a complex healthcare system necessitated the buy-in and support of key stakeholders, including healthcare providers, administrative staff, and leadership. To achieve this, we organized a series of workshops and meetings to discuss the potential benefits of AI and address any concerns. This collaborative approach was essential to ensuring that everyone was on board and had a clear understanding of the initiative. We emphasized transparency, communication, and inclusivity throughout this process.

One of the critical strategies was the partnership between the Chief Healthcare Information Officer (myself) and the Chief Medical Information Officer (CMIO). Together, we took the proposal to the Generative AI Review Committee, which comprised the County CIO, CTO, Chief Compliance Officer, CISO, and Counsel. This comprehensive review process was designed to inform organizational leaders at every level, generate buy-in, and alleviate any concerns. Given the risk-averse nature of healthcare leadership, it was crucial to address concerns regarding AI bias, data privacy, and security before implementation.

Developing a Strategic Roadmap

With stakeholder support secured, we embarked on developing a detailed strategic roadmap outlining the steps for successful AI integration. This roadmap encompassed several key elements:

■ **Technology Assessment**: We meticulously evaluated various AI technologies available, considering factors such as functionality, scalability, and compatibility with our existing infrastructure.

- **Phased Implementation**: We opted for a phased implementation approach, starting with pilot programs to test the effectiveness of AI solutions in controlled settings before wider-scale deployment.
- **Change Management Strategy**: Recognizing the potential challenges associated with organizational change, we devised a comprehensive change management strategy. This strategy focused on fostering a culture of innovation, addressing potential resistance, and providing ongoing support to staff throughout the AI integration process.
- **Metrics and Evaluation**: We established a framework for measuring performance and evaluating the impact of AI on patient engagement, provider productivity, and overall operational efficiency.

Implementing AI Solutions

Based on our strategic roadmap, we introduced several AI solutions designed to enhance patient engagement and increase provider productivity. These included:

- **Patient/Provider Communication**: AI-powered tools were integrated into the Epic EMR system to streamline communication between patients and providers. This included the use of AI to draft responses to patient messages in the in-basket, significantly reducing the time providers spent on this task. Providers could review, edit, and personalize AI-generated responses, ensuring accuracy and empathy while maintaining efficiency.
- **Summarization of Care**: Generative AI capabilities were employed to create comprehensive summaries of patient care. These summaries provided clinicians with an overview of a patient's medical history, recent visits, and relevant clinical information, enhancing the clinician's ability to make informed decisions quickly. The AI system cited sources for the summarized information, allowing clinicians to verify details as needed.
- **Translation**: To overcome language barriers, AI-driven translation tools were implemented to assist with translating patient communications, including in-basket messages and discharge instructions. This capability ensured that non-English-speaking patients received timely and accurate information, improving their overall healthcare experience.

Overcoming Challenges through Change Management

Our journey was not without challenges. Initial resistance from some staff members, concerns about data privacy, and the complexity of integrating AI with existing systems required careful management. We addressed these issues through several strategies rooted in effective change management:

- **Reactive and Proactive Change**: We recognized the need to address both reactive changes to close performance gaps and proactive changes to seize opportunities. Reactive changes, such as automating routine tasks, were easier to implement and provided immediate relief. Proactive changes, like integrating AI-driven patient engagement tools, required more effort but promised significant long-term benefits.
- **Identifying Innovators and Early Adopters**: We identified key individuals who were enthusiastic about AI and could act as innovators. These innovators helped secure the commitment and support of early adopters. Early adopters, in turn, influenced others, creating a critical mass of support that facilitated broader acceptance of AI solutions.
- **Phased Approach to Organizational Change**: Our change management process unfolded in three phases. The mobilization phase involved unfreezing the organization and preparing it for change. The movement phase was where substantive changes were made, including the implementation of AI tools. Finally, the sustain phase, or "refreeze," focused on embedding these changes into the fabric of the organization to ensure they became part of the standard operating procedures.
- **Transparent Communication**: We kept all stakeholders informed about the progress and benefits of the AI integration, ensuring a clear understanding of the initiative.
- **Data Security Measures**: We implemented stringent data protection protocols to ensure that patient information remained secure and confidential.
- **Technical Support**: We provided ongoing technical support to staff to help them navigate any issues with the new AI tools, ensuring a smooth transition and continuous improvement.

Measuring Success

We established a framework for measuring performance and evaluating the impact of AI on patient engagement, provider productivity, and overall operational efficiency.

- **Patient Engagement Metrics**: We tracked metrics such as patient satisfaction scores, response times to inquiries, and appointment adherence rates to assess the impact of AI on patient communication and overall healthcare experience.
- **Provider Productivity Metrics**: We monitored metrics like the time physicians spend on administrative tasks, the number of patient appointments completed, and documentation turnaround times to evaluate the impact of AI on provider workflow efficiency.
- **Operational Efficiency Metrics**: We tracked metrics such as appointment scheduling times, error rates in administrative tasks, and overall resource utilization to assess how AI streamlined workflows and improved operational efficiency.

This data-driven approach allowed us to continuously monitor the effectiveness of our AI integration and make adjustments as needed. By analyzing the results, we could identify areas for further improvement and refine our AI solutions to achieve optimal outcomes.

Conclusion

The integration of AI into Santa Clara Valley Healthcare has proven to be a transformative endeavor, significantly enhancing patient engagement and boosting provider productivity. By following a meticulously planned strategic roadmap, engaging key stakeholders, and continuously monitoring performance, we successfully harnessed the power of AI to transform our healthcare delivery. Our experience underscores the importance of a thoughtful and inclusive approach to innovation, ensuring that technology serves to enhance, rather than disrupt, the healthcare experience.

By prioritizing patient engagement and provider productivity through the thoughtful integration of AI, Santa Clara Valley Healthcare has set a new standard for excellence in healthcare delivery, demonstrating that with the right strategies and support, AI can be a powerful tool for positive change.

BLEND CULTURES | AI ENABLEMENT THROUGH GOVERNANCE AND CULTURE | *BY KRISTIN MYERS*

Introduction

AI is revolutionary, not only reshaping the way we live, work, and collaborate but also transforming every industry, including healthcare. As AI continues its evolution and maturity, health systems and other organizations across the country continue making substantial investments in this space, dedicating considerable resources, time, and financial capital to this transformative technology. Using our own institution—the Mount Sinai Health System and its Icahn School of Medicine—AI is not just an imperative but also a competitive differentiator, aligning seamlessly with our organizational mission to "provide compassionate patient care with seamless coordination and to advance medicine through unrivaled education, research, and outreach in the many diverse communities we serve." By harnessing AI's power and potential in innovative ways, we are transforming how we operate and deliver healthcare with the clear aim of enhancing patient experience, elevating the quality of care, and driving better healthcare outcomes.

The use and development of AI continues to expand within our organization across many domains, including clinical, operational, research, education, digital, and more. It has become increasingly apparent that a comprehensive strategy and plan are needed to steer our AI investments and initiatives to meet our needs. The strategy will need to offer key objectives, increased visibility into AI initiatives, measurable outcomes and value, and collaboration and input across the health system and school. Achieving these objectives hinges on the support from our leadership team and the participation and collaboration of the broader organizational community across the different domains. The two foundational pillars for addressing these needs are governance and culture. Governance serves as the cornerstone, establishing clear guidelines, highlighting roles and responsibilities, and establishing decision-making processes. Through governance, we foster accountability, transparency, and alignment with our leadership and organizational mission and objectives. Culture is equally indispensable, acting as the driving force behind our core values and shaping the behaviors of our employees. A strong culture propels innovation, enhances employee engagement, and contributes substantially to the success of our organization. Another way to conceptualize the relationship between governance and culture is to view governance as a top-down approach and culture as a bottom-up approach. Governance and culture work together to engage the right individuals and teams within our health system and school, creating awareness, building consensus, and garnering support for the enablement of AI. This synergy will help increase the pace, value, and impact of AI on our organization and ultimately our patients and community.

AI Governance

While some may perceive governance as a hindrance, an unnecessary roadblock to the advancement of AI and innovation, the reality is quite the opposite. Governance is an enabler of innovation, a foundational requirement for the success of AI. Governance does not have to be heavy-handed and bureaucratic to be effective. It should be nimble yet comprehensive and focused on the areas that matter most to the organization. The establishment of effective AI governance hinges on several critical steps. It first necessitates securing leadership alignment, ensuring that key stakeholders are aligned on the same page regarding AI's importance and potential. Subsequently, it involves defining the precise objectives underpinning the need for AI governance. From there, a governance structure will need to be defined with its associated committees and specific responsibilities. These committees and associated processes collectively form the governance framework, a robust structure that maintains a constant pulse on leadership and stakeholders, keeping them informed and involved in critical decision-making processes.

■ **Leadership Alignment**: The initial step always involves the identification of critical leadership—such as the Board of Directors, C-level executives, and department heads—who possess not only authority but also wield influence and exhibit a strategic, innovative mindset. Engaging in meaningful discussions with these key leaders is essential, as it allows us to convey the strategic significance of AI, emphasizing its alignment with the organization's core missions and overarching goals. Simultaneously, we also need to communicate the multifaceted landscape of AI, which includes both its substantial benefits and inherent risks, which drives the need for a robust AI governance framework with strong leadership sponsorship and support. At Mount Sinai, AI is a strategic priority supported by the highest levels of the organization. These leaders not only endorse the AI initiatives but also drive our AI governance. It is a combination of education, communication, and a clear value proposition that will drive leadership buy-in, alignment, and advocacy for AI.

■ **AI Governance Objectives**: With leadership alignment on AI's strategic importance, our focus then should be articulating the objectives and outcomes we aim to attain through AI governance. While organizations may embark on the path of establishing AI governance for a multitude of reasons, the ultimate aim should be to enable effective decision-making and oversight of AI. AI has been an integral part of our organization long before the unveiling of ChatGPT, which led to the surge in AI's popularity and excitement. Our organization has always been innovation-driven, with AI already leveraged in many different clinical departments, research, education, and operational areas. Our need for governance stemmed from the rapid increase in the exploration, utilization, and development of AI across the health system and school. Though the AI initiatives are decentralized across many different teams and functions, we recognized the need for central governance of AI as an enterprise capability. It is important to achieve consensus on the governance objectives among all members of the governance committee. Key objectives within our AI governance framework include the promotion of ethical and responsible AI practices, robust risk management and compliance, accountability/visibility into AI, tangible value realization, and the cultivation of a culture that empowers AI innovation.

■ **AI Governance Structure**: AI governance structures can vary significantly based on an organization's specific requirements and the maturity level of AI within the organization. These structures may also evolve over time, just as they did at Mount Sinai. In early 2021, we initiated a single AI committee (the AI Ethics Committee) aimed at addressing AI bias and ethical concerns while mitigating associated risks. More recently, we have further expanded our governance structure to provide enterprise oversight over all AI. We established an AI Executive Committee, which plays a pivotal role in providing strategic direction and approving the overall AI investment strategy in alignment with our organizational objectives. To ensure a thorough and domain-specific approach, we have also instituted AI committees dedicated to education, research, and clinical and operations. We also renamed our original AI Ethics Committee to be AI Risks, Ethics, and Policy Committee to identify and mitigate risks, address AI bias and ethics issues, and develop policies to monitor the utilization of both internally developed AI solutions and third-party AI tools and integrations. These four committees feature leadership representation across the entire health system and school. They all maintain a direct reporting line to the AI Executive Committee, ensuring alignment, oversight, and an efficient mechanism for escalations. This multi-tiered approach empowers our organization and community to drive transformative AI advancements while maintaining a focus on the unique requirements and objectives of each domain.

■ **AI Governance Responsibilities**: AI Governance committees may have varying charters and objectives depending on their unique purpose, function, and specific needs. Nonetheless, all committees should incorporate certain elements from a program management perspective. First, a consistent intake process must be established, complete with clearly defined prioritization criteria. This intake process plays a pivotal role in guiding leadership toward areas where their investments and efforts are most needed. Effective project management is another essential responsibility which entails oversight of project timelines, budget allocation, resource allocation, risk assessment, and dependency management. Perhaps the most challenging and frequently overlooked aspect of innovation pertains to value realization. This is a key driver and input that influences the future AI investment strategy. It is subject to review not only by individual project stakeholders but also holistically by AI leadership, finance, AI governance, and other key decision-makers.

Governance is a multi-disciplinary approach, drawing on the expertise and participation of leadership and stakeholders across multiple domains, including strategy, technology, legal, risk, ethics, clinical, operations, research, and more. It serves as a mechanism to bring like-minded and innovative thought leaders from across an organization together to collaborate, promote, and accelerate AI.

Innovation-Driven Culture

Cultivating the right culture is a key element for ensuring the sustained success of AI initiatives. Within Mount Sinai, we place an emphasis on fostering a culture that champions innovation, encourages seamless collaboration, and embraces cutting-edge technologies. In this innovation-driven environment, we actively promote continuous learning, nurture creative thinking, and advocate for data-driven decision-making processes. Our overarching goal is to instigate a transformative shift in employees' mindsets and behaviors, encouraging them to readily embrace new approaches to thinking and working—a foundational requirement for the effective integration of AI technology. This cultural transformation is critical for the success of AI, as we recognize that leadership alignment and governance, while critical for proper AI execution, are insufficient in guaranteeing widespread adoption and acceptance. Establishing this culture necessitates a focus on several key areas, including a leadership vision, comprehensive training and education, adept organizational change management, robust collaboration mechanisms, policy development, and a commitment to fostering diversity and inclusion throughout the AI journey.

- **Leadership Vision**: The AI vision needs to be established and agreed upon at the highest levels in the organization and championed by the AI Executive Committee. The AI vision also needs to be aligned with the overarching enterprise strategy and objectives and will serve as the north star for all AI initiatives.
- **Training and Education**: As AI becomes an integral part of our environment, it becomes paramount to equip and empower our employees with comprehensive training and upskilling opportunities. This education should encompass understanding AI's fundamentals, its varied applications, the value it delivers, inherent risks, and its broader impact on both the community and individuals. Fear of new and advanced technology is a common challenge to widespread adoption, making it imperative to nurture data literacy and AI education throughout the organization. This proactive approach of increasing education and providing training programs not only diminishes apprehension but also kindles excitement, anticipation, and heightened utilization of AI within our organization.
- **Organizational Change Management**: The introduction of new AI technology rollouts or initiatives necessitates a comprehensive change management strategy to ensure that the impacted community is fully prepared. This approach encompasses effective communication, user testing, targeted training programs, dedicated technology support, the establishment of continuous feedback mechanisms, and more. It's important to recognize that the level of engagement from key stakeholders directly correlates with the success and rate of adoption of these initiatives.

- **Collaboration**: AI is not confined to the realm of "IT" but rather stands as a "cross-functional" technology. No single group has sole responsibility for AI, making it imperative to engage multiple teams, including technology, data science, cybersecurity, infrastructure, clinical, operational, legal, risk/compliance, intellectual property, marketing, and various other functional areas. The orchestration of cross-functional teams is pivotal in designing and executing successful AI initiatives.
- **Policy Development**: Policies and guidelines play an essential role in ensuring the responsible and consistent utilization of AI technology, providing a standardized means of communication and enforcement for the broader community. Ethical guidelines governing the use, development, and deployment of AI technology are necessary to uphold responsible and ethical AI practices. Alignment with regulations and ongoing monitoring of changes is crucial, in addition to continuous communication with the community to keep them informed and compliant.
- **Diversity and Inclusion**: At Mount Sinai, diversity, equity, and inclusion are a top priority and embedded in all our behaviors and work efforts. The significance of diversity within our teams and diversity of thought becomes even more pronounced in the context of cutting-edge technologies like AI, serving as the foundation for fostering an innovative culture. While developing and utilizing AI tools and services, it is imperative that we carefully consider accessibility and equity, ensuring they are integral components of our approach.

As we drive an innovative culture to impact AI, it is important to acknowledge that AI itself will also influence our culture. The key factor lies in ensuring organizational readiness for the coming changes and transformation. Our overarching objective revolves around empowering employees to proactively contribute new ideas, actively participate in innovation, embrace the digital landscape, and readily adopt AI-driven solutions and capabilities.

Conclusion

AI is not just another technology; it stands as a transformative capability that will reshape our workforce and transform our approach to work. To successfully steer and drive the AI journey within an organization, we require not only the engagement and support from the highest levels of leadership but also the collective support from the entire community. The establishment of a robust governance framework, concurrently with the cultivation of an innovative culture, serves as a dual force that engages all levels of the organization and ensures alignment in AI communications and initiatives. It starts with the formulation of a leadership-driven AI vision, bolstered by a comprehensive governance structure and supported by a strong innovative culture. This fusion enables organizations to swiftly and creatively innovate, enhance AI decision-making, and deliver cutting-edge AI solutions. Ultimately, this synergy allows us to fully maximize the potential of AI, driving business growth and optimized operations while simultaneously making healthcare advancements to positively impact our patients and community.

Acknowledgment

The coauthor team would like to acknowledge our book series COO, Keith Duemling, Senior Director of Cybersecurity Technology Protection at the Cleveland Clinic and Chair-Elect, Association for Executives in Healthcare Information Security (AEHIS), Book Series COO.

Bibliography

Ashique, Sumel, Neeraj Mishra, Sourav Mohanto, Ashish Garg, Farzad Taghizadeh-Hesary, B. H. Jaswanth Gowda, and Dinesh Kumar Chellappan. 2024. "Application of Artificial Intelligence (AI) to Control COVID-19 Pandemic: Current Status and Future Prospects." *Heliyon* 10 (4). https://doi.org/10.1016/j.heliyon.2024.e25754

Chang, Zhoulin, Zhiqing Zhan, Zifan Zhao, Zhixuan You, Yang Liu, Zhihong Yan, Yong Fu, Wenhua Liang, and Lei Zhao. 2021. "Application of Artificial Intelligence in COVID-19 Medical Area: A Systematic Review." *Journal of Thoracic Disease* 13 (12): 7034.

Gunatilleke, Janak. 2022. *Artificial Intelligence in Healthcare: Unlocking Its Potential*, https://www.alumni.cam.ac.uk/benefits/book-shelf/artificial-intelligence-in-healthcare-unlocking-its-potential

Kaggle, "Ethical AI Is All We Need!!" 2023. July 16, 2023. https://kaggle.com/code/shreyamishra610/ethical-ai-is-all-we-need

Mishra, Shreya, Raghav Awasthi, Frank Papay, Kamal Maheshawari, Jacek B. Cywinski, Ashish Khanna, and Piyush Mathur. 2021. "DiagnosisQA: A Semi-Automated Pipeline for Developing Clinician Validated Diagnosis Specific QA Datasets." *medRxiv*. https://doi.org/10.1101/2021.11.10.21266184

Ng, A. 2020. "Bridging AI's Proof-of-Concept to Production Gap." *Stanford HAI*, September.

Partridge, Brittany. 2021. "Driving Value from Technical Innovation: Dramatic Change Management Skills and Leadership at All Levels Is Required." In

Douville, S. (Ed.), *Mobile Medicine: Overcoming People, Culture, and Governance* (1st ed.). Productivity Press. https://doi.org/10.4324/9781003220473

Parker, Mitch et al. 2023. "Managing Third-Party Risk: Framework Details for Risk Management in Medical Technology." In Douville, S. (Ed.), *Advanced Health Technology: Managing Risk While Tackling Barriers to Rapid Acceleration* (1st ed.). Productivity Press. https://doi.org/10.4324/9781003348603

Roberts, Michael, Derek Driggs, Matthew Thorpe, Julian Gilbey, Michael Yeung, Stephan Ursprung, Angelica I. Aviles-Rivero, et al. 2021. "Common Pitfalls and Recommendations for Using Machine Learning to Detect and Prognosticate for COVID-19 Using Chest Radiographs and CT Scans." *Nature Machine Intelligence* 3 (3): 199–217.

Santa Clara University. n.d. "Human-AI Collaboration in Health Care." Accessed July 4, 2024. https://www.scu.edu/ethics/healthcare-ethics-blog/human-ai-collaboration-in-health-care/

Stanford HAI. "When AI Systems Systemically Fail." n.d. Accessed July 4, 2024. https://hai.stanford.edu/news/when-ai-systems-systemically-fail

Syrowatka, Ania, Masha Kuznetsova, Ava Alsubai, Adam L. Beckman, Paul A. Bain, Kelly Jean Thomas Craig, Jianying Hu, Gretchen Purcell Jackson, Kyu Rhee, and David W. Bates. 2021. "Leveraging Artificial Intelligence for Pandemic Preparedness and Response: A Scoping Review to Identify Key Use Cases." *Npj Digital Medicine* 4 (1): 1–14.

Tzachor, Asaf, Jess Whittlestone, Lalitha Sundaram, and Seán Ó. Héigeartaigh. 2020. "Artificial Intelligence in a Crisis Needs Ethics with Urgency." *Nature Machine Intelligence* 2 (7): 365–366.

Vela, Daniel, Andrew Sharp, Richard Zhang, Trang Nguyen, An Hoang, and Oleg S. Pianykh. 2022. "Temporal Quality Degradation in AI Models." *Scientific Reports* 12 (1): 1–12.

Wardi, Gabriel MD, MPH1,2; Robert Owens MD2; Christopher Josef MD3; Atul Malhotra MD2; Christopher Longhurst MD4; Shamim Nemati PhD5. 2023. "Bringing the Promise of Artificial Intelligence to Critical Care: What the Experience with Sepsis Analytics Can Teach Us." *Critical Care Medicine* 51(8): 985–991, August. https://doi.org/10.1097/CCM.0000000000005894

Wright, Avery. 2023. *AI in Healthcare: How Artificial Intelligence Is Transforming Medicine*. Independently Published, https://www.amazon.com/AI-Healthcare-Artificial-Intelligence-Transforming-ebook/dp/B0BTBZDVBY

Wynants, Laure, Ben Van Calster, Gary S. Collins, Richard D. Riley, Georg Heinze, Ewoud Schuit, Elena Albu, et al. 2020. "Prediction Models for Diagnosis and Prognosis of Covid-19: Systematic Review and Critical Appraisal." *BMJ* 369 (April). https://doi.org/10.1136/bmj.m1328

Chapter 3

Use People with IT

Do not create an over-reliance on people or on technology; use both resources in concert.

Often we rely too heavily on technology as we embark on innovation. Sometimes innovation starts at the other extreme with people but little incorporation of automation or tools. The best innovations tend to be the result of a strong balance at the intersection of people and technology. Always take an inventory of people and technology to ensure balance. It is the ability to take the best of people and technology, and then meld them together that ignites innovation.

USE PEOPLE WITH IT | (R) EVOLUTION OF THE LUNG NODULE PROGRAM | *BY BRIAN BAUMAN*

There has truly been a (R)evolution in the diagnosis and treatment of lung cancer over the past decade, driven by rapid technological and scientific advances. Health care providers can now paint a picture of hope for a disease once perceived to be universally fatal. In 1970, Dr. Paul Carbone published a statement in The Annals of Internal Medicine: "At present lung cancer is recognized late. Opportunities to improve survival are through earlier detection, accurate localization, and curative therapy." Not until recently did we begin to see these improvements in care delivery materialize.

Merriam-Webster (2021) defines *revolution* as a fundamental change in the way of thinking about or visualizing something: a change in paradigm.

DOI: 10.4324/9781032715155-3

It defines *evolution* as a process of constant change from a lower or simple state to a higher or more complex state. Building the lung nodule program at Summa Health required a paradigm change, a revolution of sorts, against the traditional identification of potential malignancy and the referral process, which led to missed diagnoses, gross delays in treatment, and unnecessary anxiety for our patients. Furthermore, the growth and success of the lung nodule program have been a process of constant change by utilizing technological advances to deliver timely, precise, and personalized high-quality care.

Lung cancer remains the #1 cause of cancer-related death, exceeding that of breast, prostate, colon, and pancreatic cancers combined. While breast, prostate, and colon cancer have similar incidences, lung cancer is more often diagnosed at a late stage, thus contributing to its high mortality. In 2011, the National Lung Cancer Screening Trial demonstrated a 20% reduction in lung cancer mortality by using low-dose CT scans to detect lung cancer in at-risk individuals. This ultimately led to the approval of lung cancer screening by the Centers for Medicare and Medicaid Services, and today, to a shift toward lower-stage diagnosis and reduced mortality. Unfortunately, a minute fraction—4.5% of at-risk patients nationally per the American Lung Association—undergo lung cancer screening. Opportunities exist to utilize the electronic medical record.(EMR) to identify and notify at-risk patients and providers of screening eligibility.

Despite the acceptance and increased utilization of lung cancer screening, the majority of lung cancers are still identified incidentally on CT imaging completed for other reasons. In fact, rapid technological improvements in CT scans, including lower costs, faster scanning, higher resolution, and reduced radiation doses, have resulted in the utilization of CTs not only for lung cancer screening but also for the widespread use to diagnose a number of other conditions, most commonly in the Emergency Department (ED). At Summa and across the globe, it was recognized that to identify lung cancer early, programs would need to address both lung cancer screening and the management of incidental lung nodules (how lung cancer starts) in a highly organized manner. The idea of the lung nodule program was born.

Prior to the institution of lung nodule programs, high-risk, potentially cancerous lung nodules were left unrecognized only to have patients present later with advanced-stage malignancy and retrospectively identify that a small malignant nodule was present years earlier. A study in 2011 demonstrated that 21% of CT scans performed in the ED had a pulmonary nodule, but only 25% of the time were these nodules reported to the patient. A process was needed not only to ensure that these nodules were detected and reported to patients but also to facilitate a rapid and coordinated evaluation.

Before the initiation of the lung nodule program, the identification of lung nodules was sporadic, and the timeliness of action concerning nodules was highly variable. Once identified, patients with nodules may have been sent directly to oncology or thoracic surgery, often for ultimately benign diagnoses. The timeliness of these referrals varied from days to months, and these patients often believed that they had untreated cancer during these periods, creating unnecessary anxiety. Additionally, patients were often sent directly for dangerous, or unnecessary biopsy procedures with little to no follow-up for results. The importance of lung cancer staging for appropriate treatment was frequently an afterthought. This fragmented and variable care directly supported the need for a coordinated program; however, implementing the program required a cultural change. Time would teach that making this change required recognition of a clear benefit for patients and providers alike. It also required patience and champions with an unrelenting belief in the ultimate goodness of their work.

Lung nodule management and the subsequent treatment of lung cancer require a team. It involves multiple providers, from radiology to oncology, and truly becomes an orchestra, working in unison toward a single purpose. Pulmonary medicine was uniquely suited to promote lung cancer screening for at-risk individuals, identify concerning nodules on CT imaging, perform diagnostic procedures in the evaluation of lung nodules, treat non-malignant lung conditions, and orchestrate coordinated referrals for those identified with lung cancer to the first, best-treating provider based on the cancer stage. Pulmonary became the quarterback of the team.

Opportunities, including the advent of lung cancer screening and advances in bronchoscopic techniques, along with outstanding mentors, uniquely positioned me to develop the lung nodule program at Summa. Fortunately, I was surrounded by an outstanding team, which allowed us to succeed. Summa has long recognized the importance of people taking care of people. Prior to the birth of the lung nodule program, our breast and colon cancer programs utilized patient navigators to coordinate care. These navigators served as a direct resource for patients, empathetically walking with them through the trying process of cancer care. They coordinated testing, identified and addressed psychosocial barriers to care, and accompanied them to the myriad of appointments required to undergo cancer treatment. In essence, these navigators are a personal guide for patients as they proceed through the journey of cancer care.

In 2014, shortly after our lung cancer screening program humbly began (only 96 screening CTs were performed in 2013), Sandy Kohut, a registered respiratory therapist with a personal interest in lung cancer, was asked by her director to begin participating in the care of lung nodule patients being evaluated for lung cancer. She participated in our multidisciplinary tumor conference to understand and elucidate for patients the nuances of nodule evaluation and lung cancer treatment. She was mentored by the lung cancer navigator, Sally Olszewski, and they began to work as a team as patients transitioned from the diagnostic phase to the cancer treatment phase. The transition was seamless, and patients saw their evaluation and treatment as a truly coordinated, team effort.

By 2017, Summa performed nearly 800 screening CTs, and Sandy took on the lung nodule navigator role full-time. To clarify, when correctly implemented, lung cancer screening results in exponential program growth for several reasons. First of all, once a patient begins screening, these are continued at least annually until age 80 as patient health permits. Additionally, ongoing efforts to educate patients and referring providers result in increased utilization of lung cancer screening. Sandy, while incredibly organized, quickly realized that tracking patients enrolled in lung cancer screening became a job in and of itself. Patients required reminders to have repeat scans at varying intervals, and when abnormalities were identified, these patients required care coordination for numerous additional tests and appointments. Her Excel spreadsheet and Post-It notes simply could not keep up. Automated tracking tools, reminders, and reporting operated through the EMR became an option to get Sandy back to her initial purpose of direct patient care.

Furthermore, while lung cancer screening continued to grow, Laura Musarra, an exceptional member of our radiology department, implemented a natural language recognition software program by Nuance to identify incidental nodules found in our ED. This program identified concerning findings and routed these findings to our nodule navigator, who then was able to coordinate evaluation in our now highly functioning lung nodule clinic. With the optimization of this tool, Laura demonstrated a progressive growth of lung nodule detection and, more importantly, coordinated follow-up for patients at high-risk for loss to follow-up. Today we identify hundreds of incidental lung nodule patients who may have otherwise been lost to follow-up on a monthly basis from our ED alone, and in 2023 our incidental lung nodule program detected and treated over 200 patients identified with cancer. The combination of people and technology has made this possible.

As the lung nodule program grew, we added an additional navigator. Today, our navigators actively follow approximately 5000 patients through the screening and incidental lung nodule programs combined and manage a list of over 18,000 patients currently or previously participating in lung screening. Since the implementation and optimization of the Nuance search for ED patients in 2017, incidental nodule detection remained largely flat, correlating with ED CT volumes. We now have recognized an opportunity to expand this search to include CTs performed in the outpatient and inpatient settings as well. Given that our lung nodule navigators are responsible for managing high-risk Nuance search patients and that there is an expectation of greatly increased incidental nodule volume with the expanded search, we are now in the process of hiring an additional navigator. Additionally, technology options to off-load data management duties will allow our navigators to continue their best work, direct patient care. The key is that we are matching technology with clinical needs and clinical staff with the increased volumes related to technology implementation.

Lung nodule identification is complicated. Most lung nodules do not represent lung cancer. For example, only about 3% of nodules identified on screening CTs are malignant, but about 1/3 of screening CTs identify some abnormality. Radiologists are given the difficult task to note merely the presence of a lung nodule, particularly when CTs are performed for reasons other than looking specifically for nodules, let alone to characterize nodules as changing or potentially malignant. Technology, and specifically AI, has specific solutions for this daunting task and can now not only identify nodules but characterize them to better predict malignancy risk. There are programs which seamlessly integrate into radiology work flows and reporting systems, ensuring that nodules are appropriately identified and risk-stratified. When combined with a highly functioning process of care such as the lung nodule program, technologies such as this provide massive benefits to improve outcomes, limit missed diagnoses, and drive volumes for health systems.

Technology improvements such as natural language recognition software and AI not only improve nodule detection but also allow for the identification and treatment of cancer. Bronchoscopy, a minimally invasive technique to perform lung biopsies through a small camera, has dramatically changed with the development of GPS-like software programs that allow the operator to accurately localize and sample very small nodules in virtually any part of the lung. This technique, termed navigational bronchoscopy, has allowed for earlier diagnosis of lung cancer, placement of markers for targeted radiation treatments, and localization for minimally invasive surgical resection of tumors. It also provides a means to obtain cancer tissue for specialized molecular testing to identify genetic mutations, which may be targets for highly personalized cancer treatments. These bronchoscopic navigation programs utilize AI to continuously improve software algorithms and improve accuracy. Today, the accuracy of these techniques approaches 90% and allows providers to confidently determine appropriate treatments.

Today, our lung nodule and lung cancer team includes a variety of providers, which include physicians, nurses, navigators, financial assistants, and research coordinators. No longer are patients randomly directed to various providers. Technology allows high-risk nodules to be rapidly identified by radiology and subsequently routed to our lung nodule navigators, who facilitate evaluation by a dedicated team of pulmonary providers skilled in advanced bronchoscopy techniques. These providers in turn actively participate in the follow-up of these patients, directing their treatment to the appropriate surgical and oncologic specialists. Patient satisfaction has dramatically improved. Timeliness of care and anxiety associated with delays have been greatly reduced. Cancer specialists now see a higher volume of lung cancer patients who have been thoroughly evaluated and preemptively selected to be more appropriate for cancer treatment. Technology has become a vital tool, but our navigators are the glue that holds the entire web of care together. Everyone benefits, most importantly our patients.

Today, we seek to continuously improve on our already highly effective program. We utilize EMR data and a team of data analysts to help identify gaps and delays in care. The data allows us to identify pain points, such as a lack of scanners or an insufficient number of providers, and implement solutions. As our program grew, our navigators went from serving as empathetic and knowledgeable healthcare providers to constantly managing a large database. Technology solutions utilizing EMR data relieve this burden and allow us to continuously recognize patients in need of clinical services. Engaged and inquisitive team members identified the clinical needs and actively sought out technological solutions to improve outcomes and patient and provider satisfaction. The results are impressive. Our program continues to grow exponentially and receive national accolades.

The lung nodule program is a shining example of how technology, including AI, has taken a once haphazard process of care to an accurate, highly personalized, seamless one. Patients with high-risk findings who once went unnoticed are now rapidly guided through evaluation and treatment. Technology allows us to identify and encourage high-risk patients to undergo screening. Today, we screen nearly 4000 patients annually. In 2023, over 100 of these screening patients were diagnosed with lung cancer, and most importantly, the vast majority, at an early, curable stage. Technology assists our navigators to keep track of these patients and to coordinate subsequent testing and follow-up. Additionally, AI tools allow our radiologists and navigators to identify high-risk nodules and facilitate evaluation, ensuring that asymptomatic lung cancer does not go unrecognized. Advances in bronchoscopy, radiation, surgical, and oncologic treatments allow for highly targeted and personalized care. The program would not have started without healthcare providers focused on outstanding patient care, but it would not have continued to thrive without technologies to improve quality, reduce logistical burdens, and improve diagnostic accuracy. By pairing people and IT, lives are saved, providers are satisfied, and patients express genuine gratitude for truly (R)evolutionary care.

USE PEOPLE WITH IT | THE ROLE OF THE BUSINESS RELATIONSHIP MANAGER | *BY JENNIFER OWENS*

Too often, healthcare professionals and healthcare IT divisions find themselves in conflict despite having nearly identical goals of improving patient care, reducing the burden on providers, and providing care to patients at lower costs. This is particularly evident in attempts to use artificial intelligence (AI) to provide better patient care and reduce the burden on caregivers—but why? What makes AI different?

The cultural narrative around AI has created a terrifying dichotomy in which AI simultaneously will replace medical professionals by providing better care than humans, but also harm innumerable patients by providing worse care than humans and creating artificial barriers to care. Neither, of course, is strictly true, but these fears loom large in many discussions about AI implementation in healthcare. Additionally, the AI regulatory environment significantly lags the technology, leaving hospital systems to create governance criteria for themselves. The technology's capabilities and clinical needs are not always well-matched, and the hype and cultural conversation around AI's capabilities are often overblown. In this article, we will discuss some common challenges to implementing AI in healthcare and illustrate how the role of the Business Relationship Manager, or BRM, can smooth this path to implementation through a hypothetical project idea and evaluation process.

But first, what is the role of the Business Relationship Manager? Philosophically, the business relationship manager role is any role that leverages positive relationships to increase value in the organization. This role, often filled by a certified BRM, maintains relationships with key leaders on both the clinical and IT sides. One of the BRM's main functionalities is to connect IT-related project ideas (and those that have them) with processes for evaluation and implementation resources. A good BRM will be a trusted advisor/strategic partner to their clinical leadership and a respected voice for the clinical "customer" within IT. The BRM role brings special expertise to these conversations since they are familiar with both the clinical workflows and the technical requirements of the IT division. They can speak fluidly with both providers and technical teams and help navigate implementation processes. A good BRM will advocate for responsible innovation, hold teams accountable to adhere to processes, and ensure that the value proposed by new technology is realized.

The BRM role really shines in a situation where a clinician is bringing a technology solution for a clinical or operational problem. Let us follow a hypothetical example and say that a clinician has just returned from a conference where several vendors presented technical solutions for digital documentation support. The clinician is frustrated with the time spent responding to inbox messages from patients and feels that these vendors may be able to help. Here, the BRM role gives a voice to a frustrated "consumer" of healthcare IT services and products and creates a formal space for idea discussion. The first action on the part of the BRM is to sit down with the clinician and create a document containing the entire problem and proposed solution.

> **Problem:** Inbox messaging takes up too much time for the clinician.
> **Solution:** Implement one of the solutions from MDNoteFlow/ChartEase/MSGSync which will take 30 minutes and solve 100% of our problems.

In this not-exactly complete document, we can see one of the challenges of AI implementation in healthcare. The stated problem is overly broad—how are we defining "too much time?" What is the right amount of time? What kind of messaging is in scope? The solution is vague. Several vendors are offering very similar products, with unrealistic expectations about implementation effort and value offered.

Without a BRM involved, this idea might get rejected by IT out of hand as unrealistic. The BRM's job now is to flesh out both the description of the problem and the proposed solution with information that will help the IT division evaluate and prioritize the project. Expanding and interpreting an initial idea into a standardized framework is a large part of the BRM's role in the strategic partnership between IT and clinical divisions. This might take the form of additional requirements documentation, more description about the problem, estimates about the size of the lift to actually implement the solution, and proposed financial impact. After this editing passes by the BRM, which often involves follow-up meetings with the requestor and with impacted parties in the IT division, our request might look like this:

Problem: Inbox messaging takes up too much time for the clinician. Over the past five years, time spent responding to inbox messages from both patients and other providers has increased by 13%. Most of that increased time is spent outside of official work hours, resulting in increased "pajama time" which causes provider burnout and inefficient work. Many of the messages require similar responses, which a chatbot or other AI tool could draft for the provider to read, edit, and send. This would reduce provider time spent responding to messages.
Solution: Several vendor solutions exist in this space, as well as a native AI message draft tool within the electronic health record (EHR). Each of these should be evaluated for their ability to ingest message content and suggest appropriate responses. We should also consider the difficulty of implementing each of these solutions within our IT ecosystem and evaluate whether using the product as designed will reduce provider time spent responding to messages. We will need to estimate the effort for training providers on how to use this technology, as well as the effort for the reporting teams to develop dashboards to track success metrics. This request will require evaluation by our AI Governance Board.

The BRM has brought their clinical workflow knowledge to bear on the problem described, understanding that inbox messaging flows from providers as well as the patient and clearly documenting the increase in pajama time as an issue for providers. The BRM has also used their technical knowledge to remove the vendor's promise that implementation would take 30 minutes and substituted instead several reality-based criteria for evaluation. Finally, the

BRM has identified an additional governance group that will need to weigh in as this project is evaluated. With the assistance of the BRM, this healthcare AI project has avoided early common complications of poorly scoped problems, poorly defined value, and early rejection by IT groups.

When the BRM communicates their efforts back to the requesting provider, the conversation shifts quickly to frustration with the process. "Why do we have to have all this extra information? I already gave you the solution," says the provider. The BRM explains the intake and evaluation process and illustrates the value of a thorough evaluation prior to implementation. Luckily, the BRM has contacts at another institution that has just paused its pilot of an AI message bot due to its inaccurate message suggestions. This anecdote helps underline the importance of the evaluation process to the provider. They are not happy about it, but they understand a bit. Although frustrations with the process are not unique to AI projects, the novelty of AI can complicate routine evaluations, as we will see in the next few steps of our hypothetical project evaluation.

Now that the project has a more detailed scope and proposed solution, the next step is to bring the proposed project to IT for evaluation. In this example, IT has regular evaluation meetings where all IT teams can ask questions, detail the work their team would need to perform to complete the project, give estimates of the time it would take, and approve moving the project forward. Getting this project on the schedule is no problem, and when this project comes up on the agenda, several of the teams have follow-up questions and comments.

Cybersecurity:

Can we detail how the vendors will be accessing the information in the provider's messages?

What additional information from the patient record will need to be accessed to generate a message back to the patient?

How is the vendor storing information? For how long? Is the vendor training their language model on our data?

What is the plan if the vendor experiences an outage?

Integrations and Interfaces:

Are there documented APIs for integration?

How is identity managed?

Is the integration approach compatible with HL7, FHIR, or other existing communication protocols?

What triggers the passage of information between the EHR and the vendor?

How is additional information pulled?How often is information passed between the EHR and the vendor?

What is the lag time between requesting a message draft and the provision of the message draft?

IT Leadership:

What size (how many providers, how many messages, and how many weeks) is the proposed pilot, and are the vendors capable of scaling to enterprise volume?

What kind of training are the vendors providing? What is the ongoing support model?

What are the costs of implementation?

Can we document the efficacy and equity of the tool? Does it deliver similar results for all patients/providers with all content? If not, can we limit the tool to the content that it does deliver well?

How will we know if we are achieving our desired value? How will we measure reduced provider pajama time? What if patients or providers hate the messages and they require extended messaging?

Does using AI to respond to messages affect the patients' perspective of our medical expertise? How will we know if the message content is reliable? Does this place us at additional legal risk?

Should we pilot AI in such a patient-facing space? Would a better strategy be to find an AI use case that is more "internal" such as billing or risk scoring?

What legal agreements do we need to proceed with a pilot?

Some of these questions are routine for any technology implementation within a healthcare IT environment. However, some of these questions highlight ethical and philosophical concerns unique to AI. Questions about unintended consequences of large language models— "what if patients hate the messages and we actually spend MORE time messaging" can be recast as metrics for evaluating pilots. Questions about strategy, such as "should we pilot AI in such a patient-facing space or in a more internal area," are worthy of further discussion outside the format of the project evaluation process.

The IT division agrees to defer a decision about whether to proceed with a pilot until the BRM brings back some additional information. The BRM will not be able to generate all this information on its own. Gathering this information requires assistance from technical teams, the clinician, the vendor, and an assist from a business analyst or project manager with standardizing documentation. This takes time, and during this information-gathering process, the BRM is keeping the requesting clinician informed about progress as well as providing regular updates to the IT division.

When the requesting clinician reaches out to the BRM to voice impatience with the process, the BRM knows that part of the delay is that the AI Governance Board is still being spun up and is not yet formally meeting. The regulatory environment for healthcare AI is still forming, leaving hospitals to create their own governance structures and criteria. Our hypothetical hospital is doing well—they have seen the need for a governance board and identified a few people to be on it, but the governance process is not yet formalized, another common problem in healthcare AI.

The BRM brings the clinician directly to the proposed members of the AI Governance Board to advocate directly for their project. The clinician and BRM co-present a few slides clearly describing the problem and the proposed solution. The clinician's emotional description of the time spent responding to messages, paired with the BRM's neatly written documentation of the proposed pilots to evaluate an AI tool to help providers avoid burn out, resonates well with the Board. They decide to approve the project and ask that the clinician come back to present interim results from the pilots once the Board formally meets. The BRM is asked to provide a list of evaluation criteria for the pilots so that any similar cases that come before the board can be measured by standard metrics. In this case, the BRM has used their relationship skills to avoid a long delay while a governance board is formalized and helped create standard evaluation criteria.

After this discussion and the additional information provided by the BRM, the IT division approves moving forward with the pilots. Contracts are drafted, success metrics set, and the pilots begin. The BRM and requesting clinician stay involved throughout the process, ensuring that standard metrics are used for each pilot and that the clinician's desired result—less time spent composing messages—remains the goal. When the pilots end, the BRM brings the requestor and IT division back together to jointly give opinions on which pilots should continue, terminate, or expand. Finally, reporting metrics are handed off to the appropriate support team, and the BRM continues to confirm that the implemented solution is performing as expected.

Without a trusted partner to bridge gaps in IT processes and advocate for incoming ideas, projects and innovations can stall, especially innovations involving novel new technology such as AI. AI can overpromise results and is often seen as a universal solution for problems in healthcare IT. Those problems must be carefully defined if real value is to come from implementing a new technology. A new AI solution for healthcare should undergo scoping and requirements documentation so that it can be evaluated and prioritized by both IT and the clinical area.

The BRM role brings essential knowledge and relationships to this documentation, evaluation, and prioritization process. A good BRM will possess strong clinical workflow knowledge, including strong enough relationships to facilitate shadowing clinical workflows by IT team members and to generate powerful narratives to advocate for innovation. They will also have basic technical knowledge, including relationships with other institutions that have implemented similar technology. A BRM role will bring ability to bridge communication gaps and hold both sides accountable to the evaluation processes, including governance evaluation, success metrics, follow-ups, and post-go-live evaluations. With a good BRM, the road to innovative, safe AI in healthcare is much smoother.

USE PEOPLE WITH IT | THE DENTAL DETECTIVES, AI'S EVOLVING COLLABORATIVE ROLE IN EARLY CARIES DETECTION | *BY VINAYA SREE SAMALA*

Background

Dental caries significantly impact individuals and societies, affecting sleep, diet, social interaction, and self-esteem. The global cost of treating oral diseases exceeds 540 billion dollars annually (Khanagar et al., 2022). Early detection remains a challenge despite efforts. The limitations of traditional approaches, such as visual clinical inspections and radiographic examination, result in undetected lesions, delayed therapies, and inconsistent diagnoses, which depend on individual dentists' skills and experiences. It continues to be a serious concern in healthcare, despite advances in treatment at the expense of patient care.

To address the constraints, there is an increasing interest in using AI to increase the accuracy and efficiency of dental caries identification. It has the potential to transform dental care by offering automated, objective, and precise techniques for diagnosing caries lesions, resulting in improved patient outcomes and reduced healthcare expenditures. AI's method appears promising, as the models can reliably, impartially, and automatically evaluate dental X-rays to diagnose caries. A comprehensive evaluation of their accuracy and reliability is necessary, as is considering the balance between providers and use of this promising technology.

Qualitative Systematic Review of the Literature

A study was conducted to search and analyze current literature that addresses the research question of how AI improves dentist accuracy in early caries detection on radiographs. The study analyzed peer-reviewed English articles from 2019 to 2024, focusing on AI for caries diagnosis in permanent teeth. Literature was obtained from CINAHL, MEDLINE, and PubMed databases. The search terms included the keywords and Boolean Operators of AI, dental caries or caries, AND detect or diagnosis. Research unrelated to caries detection, with incomplete data, or in non-English languages was excluded. After an extensive systematic review of the results, 25 out of 30 studies were selected. These studies were further organized into four major themes: Assessing AI Model Precision for Detection, Exploration of Various AI Models, Image Processing Methods Analysis, and Cost–Benefit Analysis of AI Integration.

Assessing AI Model Precision for Detection

This research examined the effectiveness of AI models in detecting dental caries lesions by analyzing several key studies. Khanagar et al. (2022) and Mertens et al. (2021) reported high accuracy rates of 80% to 98% for various AI models, demonstrating their potential to enhance diagnostic precision. Musri et al. (2021) focused on deep learning approaches, particularly convolutional neural networks (CNNs), which achieved accuracy rates between 73% and 98%, indicating their superiority over conventional methods. Albano et al. (2024) confirmed that deep learning-based AI models often outperform traditional methods in both sensitivity and accuracy. Finally, Pérez De Frutos et al. (2024) compared the performance of advanced AI models to that of expert dentists, finding that the YOLOv5 model achieved significantly better results in analyzing X-rays, overcoming challenges like overlapping teeth and limited information from single views.

The integration of AI models for detecting dental caries lesions presents a significant leap forward in dental care. Research highlights the substantial benefits of AI, particularly its ability to enhance diagnostic precision. Studies report high accuracy rates, allowing for earlier and more accurate detection of cavities. This early intervention is critical, as it prevents cavities from progressing and ultimately improves patient outcomes. Deep learning approaches, like CNNs, offer a distinct advantage. These models can analyze large datasets of dental X-rays quickly and accurately, providing consistent and reliable results. This consistency empowers dentists with a crucial tool: the ability to make informed decisions based on reliable data, ultimately leading to more effective patient care. AI models go beyond simply enhancing accuracy. They address limitations inherent in traditional methods. For instance, overlapping teeth in X-rays can pose a challenge for traditional analysis. AI models like YOLOv5 overcome these limitations by providing more accurate and comprehensive diagnostic information. This information empowers dentists with a clearer picture of a patient's dental health, allowing for a more targeted and effective treatment plan. Dentists can then use this information to make informed decisions and develop tailored treatment plans for individual patients, ultimately improving patient care. The integration of AI in dental practice represents a paradigm shift in how dental diagnostics are conducted. AI offers a powerful combination of precision, efficiency, and ultimately, a greater benefit for patients.

Exploration of Various AI Models

Researchers in dentistry are focusing on AI models like CNNs and deep learning architectures. These models excel at analyzing complex dental X-rays, traditionally done by dentists, to identify potential cavities with high accuracy. Studies by Bayraktar & Ayan (2021) and Schwendicke (2019) showcase this effectiveness, highlighting the potential for earlier diagnoses and improved patient outcomes. Further research by Pérez De Frutos et al. (2024) examines various deep learning structures, comparing their performance to human experts. This research sheds light on the potential for AI as an assistive tool in clinical practice, providing dentists with valuable second opinions and confirmation of diagnoses.

The benefits of integrating AI extend far beyond just improved accuracy. AI plays a crucial role in streamlining workflows and increasing efficiency. These models can analyze complex X-rays rapidly, enabling faster diagnoses and quicker treatment decisions. Additionally, AI can alleviate dentist workload by handling routine tasks like X-ray analysis. This allows dentists to focus their expertise on more complex cases and dedicate more time to individual patients. The integration offers a multitude of advantages for dentistry.

Image Processing Methods Analysis

Delving deeper into the specifics of image processing methods, a study by Zanini et al. (2024) provides a broad overview, highlighting various computer-based approaches. It emphasizes supervised learning with machine learning algorithms, particularly the effectiveness of feature extraction techniques like semantic segmentation, object detection, and image classification. Deep learning architectures like U-Net and Faster R-CNN are noted for their proficiency in segmentation and detection. The study even suggests that some methods outperform human evaluations, especially for early lesions. The study by Anil et al. (2023) focused specifically on the application of AI, particularly machine learning and deep learning algorithms, emphasizing the role of CNNs in analyzing images and detecting caries. Support vector machines (SVMs) and random forests are also mentioned as potential tools. The study by Pérez De Frutos et al. (2024) builds on this by comparing different deep learning architectures for caries detection, noting that all the AI models performed as well as or better than the dentists, with the best model significantly exceeding human performance.

The advantages of these image processing methods are considerable. AI and deep learning techniques like U-Net and Faster R-CNN provide superior accuracy in detecting early lesions, which is vital for timely intervention and effective treatment. These methods can analyze images more precisely than human evaluators, reducing the likelihood of diagnostic errors. Additionally, the use of supervised learning and feature extraction techniques enhances the model's ability to identify and classify caries, streamlining the diagnostic process.

Cost–Benefit Analysis of AI Integration

Researchers are conducting cost–benefit analyses to assess the economic implications of using AI in various dental procedures. These analyses evaluate both the costs of implementing AI and the potential benefits it brings. One study by Schwendicke et al. (2022) focused on the value of using larger datasets to train AI models for cavity detection. Their findings suggest that even a moderate improvement in AI's ability to detect cavities can lead to significant cost savings, especially when treating high-risk patients. This study emphasizes the importance of considering factors like the stage of a cavity and a patient's overall risk profile when evaluating the cost-effectiveness of AI. Another study by Schwendicke et al. (2021) took a different approach, evaluating the long-term cost-effectiveness of an AI-based diagnostic tool for cavity detection. This research suggests that AI's higher accuracy in detecting cavities can lead to cost savings over time, despite potentially higher initial costs associated with implementing the technology.

The advantages of integrating AI into dental practices go beyond just improved diagnostic precision and streamlining workflows. Economically, AI offers significant cost savings through earlier detection and intervention. By catching issues early, the need for more complex and expensive procedures down the line is reduced. This is particularly impactful for high-risk patients, where early detection can prevent costly complications. Additionally, AI's consistent and accurate diagnoses minimize the risk of misdiagnosis and its associated costs. In the long run, the initial investment in AI technology is balanced by the savings from providing more efficient and effective patient care, making it a cost-effective solution for modern dental practices.

Strong Potential for AI to Improve Caries Detection through Early Intervention

Recent research highlights the significant potential of AI in improving caries detection. CNNs have emerged as a particularly successful AI technique. These algorithms demonstrate remarkable accuracy in analyzing dental X-rays, identifying the location and morphology of caries lesions with superior performance compared to traditional methods. This advancement signifies a major leap forward in caries detection, offering dentists a reliable tool for more precise diagnoses.

A crucial insight from this research underscores the importance of large datasets and consistent methodologies. AI models trained on extensive datasets exhibit improved diagnostic performance, leading to cost-effectiveness. This is particularly advantageous for high-risk patients, as it minimizes undetected lesions and translates to significant cost savings on treatment. The research emphasizes the need for further validation to ensure the responsible integration of AI into dental practice. By leveraging the power of AI, dentistry can move toward a future of more precise and optimized patient care. While the potential is undeniable, further research is essential to address current limitations, refine AI technologies, and facilitate their seamless integration into real-world clinical settings.

Future Use of AI and a Balanced Collaborative Role with Dentists

The significant potential of AI in dentistry is strongly supported by data, especially in enhancing radiograph-based early caries identification. This research highlights the main benefits of AI in dentistry, including improved diagnostic accuracy, cost-effectiveness, and enhanced image processing methods. AI continuously outperforms visual inspection and conventional radiography, providing more precise and useful diagnostic tools for locating dental caries lesions. Techniques like deep learning algorithms and feature extraction further increase diagnostic accuracy.

Standardized approaches are essential for consistency in future research. Optimizing AI-driven dental diagnostics requires larger datasets and robust ground truth annotations. Cost-benefit analyses indicate significant savings, especially in high-risk populations, with even modest increases in AI sensitivity. This means that the initial investment in AI technology is offset by the savings from more efficient and effective patient care.

Ultimately, AI acts as a second set of eyes for dentists, offering an automated, unbiased, and accurate tool for early detection and intervention of caries lesions. AI models provide dentists with a clearer picture of a patient's dental health, enabling them to detect and diagnose caries lesions earlier and more accurately. This collaborative role enhances the diagnostic process, allowing dentists to focus on more complex cases and improve patient outcomes. By integrating AI into dental practice, the global incidence of dental caries can be reduced, paving the way for a future where dental care is more precise, efficient, and patient-centric.

USE PEOPLE WITH IT | DRIVING THE VALUE JOURNEY | BY KAREN MARIE JOSWICK

Overview

The WHO constitution (1948) states, "Health is a state of complete physical, mental, and social well-being and not merely the absence of disease or infirmity." The speed of transformation in healthcare, particularly in the shift to value-based care (VBC), has had several impacts on healthcare organizations, providers, and patients. VBC represents a significant departure from the traditional fee-for-service model by focusing on delivering high-quality health-care that emphasizes outcomes, efficiency, and cost-effectiveness. By keeping people at the center of the value journey, organizations can realize success and maximize health IT investments that support the attainment of health, not the illness. As you develop your data-driven value journey, ensuring a balance between patients, providers, and technology innovation will be essential for the adoption of new payment and care models.

A Patient Engagement Mindset

The road ahead must involve experimentation with new care models and technologies. Healthcare organizations should remain open to innovation and be willing to pilot new approaches to care delivery, including alternative payment models, remote monitoring devices, and telemedicine solutions. The US Bureau of Labor Statistics (2020) projected a 34% growth in employment of home health and personal care aides from 2019 to 2029. According to Grand View Research (2021), the global remote patient monitoring market was valued at $4.3 billion in 2020 and is expected to grow at a CAGR of 17.9% from 2021 to 2028. These statistics illustrate the market movements and how forward-thinking organizations must plan for the workforce, site of care, and patient engagement strategies.

- **Patient-Centered Care as a Priority**: Patient-centered care places the patient at the core of healthcare decision-making and delivery. It recognizes that patients are unique individuals with distinct needs, preferences, and goals. By prioritizing the patient's well-being, healthcare organizations aim to improve patient satisfaction, treatment adherence, and overall health outcomes. This approach benefits patients and leads to cost savings and better population health management.
- **Engaging Patients through Education**: Healthcare organizations are increasingly focusing on patient education. Educated patients are better equipped to make informed decisions about their health and adhere to treatment plans. Providing easy access to accurate and comprehensible health information empowers patients to actively participate in their care. This engagement can lead to better health outcomes and lower health-care costs by preventing complications and unnecessary treatments.

Some examples to consider would be shifting the primary care and specialty relationship paradigm to improve access. This could be done by utilizing technology to facilitate virtual consultations that allow for timely, focused access. The promotion of remote monitoring of patients' health conditions outside of the acute care space is critical for sustainability in a value-based model. Leverage wearable devices, such as fitness trackers and smartwatches, to empower patients to actively engage in monitoring their health. These devices can collect real-time data, which can be shared with healthcare professionals to make more informed decisions. Finally, a refinement of the tools and workflows that improve the exchange of medical data between patients and healthcare providers is a growing area that needs more emphasis. Clinical workflow must be shaped to support care across the continuum, reflecting a change in the fee-for-service mindset driven by transactional care, not population health. This approach ensures that patients receive timely care and guidance, even from the comfort of their homes.

Example: Remote Monitoring for Diabetes Management

According to the International Diabetes Federation (IDF, 2019), approximately 463 million adults (aged 20–79) are living with diabetes worldwide. Diabetes can lead to various complications, including heart disease, stroke, kidney disease, vision impairment, and nerve damage. For instance, diabetes is a leading cause of blindness, kidney failure, and lower limb amputations. The economic burden of diabetes is substantial. The IDF estimated that diabetes accounted for $760 billion in healthcare expenditures globally in 2019. Diabetes places a significant burden on healthcare systems. It requires ongoing monitoring, treatment, and management. A substantial portion of healthcare resources is allocated to diabetes care.

Managing diabetes is an ongoing process that requires continuous monitoring of blood glucose levels, medication adherence, lifestyle factors, and regular communication with healthcare providers. In the absence of remote monitoring, patients often need to make frequent clinic visits for check-ups, leading to inconveniences and potential gaps in care. Healthcare organizations that are taking on increasing accountability for the total cost of care and broader populations can maximize technology investments to elevate clinical teams to working top of license while promoting patient engagement and self-management techniques that are easy to adopt.

Remote Monitoring Solutions

- **Continuous Glucose Monitoring (CGM) Devices**: Patients with diabetes can wear CGM devices, which continuously measure their blood glucose levels throughout the day and night. These devices transmit real-time data to mobile apps or web platforms.
- **Smart Insulin Pens and Medication Adherence Apps**: Smart insulin pens can record the dose and timing of insulin injections. Medication adherence apps can send reminders and track medication usage, improving adherence.
- **Connected Health Platforms**: Patients' data from CGM devices, smart insulin pens, and other sources is integrated into connected health platforms. These platforms can be accessed by patients and their healthcare providers.

Value-Based Benefits of Remote Monitoring for Diabetes Management

- **Timely Intervention**: With real-time data, healthcare providers can identify glucose level fluctuations and intervene promptly, adjusting treatment plans as needed. This prevents extremely high or low blood sugar episodes, reducing the risk of complications.
- **Patient Empowerment**: Patients can actively participate in their care, making informed decisions based on real-time data. They can see how their lifestyle choices impact their glucose levels and adjust accordingly. Self-management techniques are elevated with the complement of technology.
- **Reduced Clinic Visits**: Remote monitoring reduces the need for frequent clinic visits, making healthcare more convenient for patients. They only need to visit their healthcare providers when necessary, such as for significant issues or treatment adjustments.
- **Improved Adherence**: Medication adherence apps help patients stick to their treatment regimens, resulting in better disease management and reduced risk of complications.
- **Quality of Life**: Patients experience an improved quality of life as they can better manage their condition with less disruption to their daily activities.
- **Prevention of Complications**: By proactively managing blood glucose levels and making timely adjustments, the risk of

diabetes-related complications, such as kidney disease, nerve damage, and vision problems, is significantly reduced.

■ **Cost Savings**: Fewer acute care visits, hospitalizations, and complications can result in cost savings for both patients and healthcare systems.

Remote monitoring of chronic conditions like diabetes empowers patients, enhances the quality of care, and ultimately improves outcomes while reducing the burden on acute care facilities. It also showcases the potential for remote monitoring to transform the management of chronic diseases and promote a more patient-centered approach to healthcare.

Care and Business Delivery Transformation

Care and Business Delivery Transformation in the context of VBC from a provider wellness viewpoint is a multifaceted approach that not only focuses on enhancing patient outcomes but also recognizes the well-being and satisfaction of healthcare professionals as a critical component of successful care delivery. The integration of patient-centered care, education, shared decision-making, and telehealth services into healthcare models represents a business transformation for healthcare organizations. It requires investments in technology, staff training, and changes in operational processes. VBC models should promote self-care as an integral part of healthcare provider wellness. Encouraging providers to prioritize self-care activities, hobbies, and relaxation techniques is essential to avoiding provider burnout. The pressure to meet performance metrics, often accompanied by increased administrative burdens, may contribute to provider burnout. This, in turn, can affect the quality of care and patient satisfaction. The increased emphasis on data collection and analytics may lead to information overload for healthcare providers, as well. Sorting through vast amounts of data can be overwhelming and counterproductive if not managed effectively. Identifying internal structures, workflows, and processes to address these challenges will position organizations to be sustainable in the value journey transformation. For every $1 invested in improving the health of the population, the United States stands to gain almost $4 in economic benefit. When healthcare providers are supported, engaged, and fulfilled, they are better positioned to deliver high-quality, patient-centered care.

Provider Well-Being as a Priority

VBC acknowledges that the well-being of healthcare providers, including physicians, nurses, and other care team members, is crucial for the sustainability and effectiveness of healthcare delivery. Burnout and stress among healthcare professionals can negatively impact the quality of care. Provider wellness is closely linked to a patient-centered approach. When providers can focus on patients and build meaningful relationships, they often experience greater job satisfaction. Training programs that teach emotional resilience can be integrated into VBC models. These programs equip providers with tools to cope with the emotional challenges of their work. One specific example of training providers is psychological first aid. These tools can be valuable, as they equip them to provide initial emotional support to colleagues and patients in times of crisis. A technical advancement to be considered is AL-Powered Chatbots. AI-driven chatbots and virtual assistants can be used to provide immediate mental health support. They can engage in conversations, offer emotional support, and direct providers to appropriate resources.

Mental Health Support

Mental health support for healthcare providers in the context of VBC is a crucial component of ensuring the well-being and resilience of the healthcare workforce. Providers often face intense pressures, emotional challenges, and high-stress environments, which can take a toll on their mental health. VBC models should begin with the acknowledgment that healthcare providers, like anyone else, can experience mental health challenges. Creating a culture of awareness and open communication around mental health is the first step. Encouraging peer support and mentorship programs within healthcare organizations can help providers navigate the emotional demands of their work. Experienced colleagues can provide guidance and a safe space for sharing experiences. There is a growing market for mental health apps designed to reduce stress and promote emotional well-being. These apps may include meditation and mindfulness apps, mood-tracking tools, and virtual support groups. VBC models should offer easy access to counseling services. Confidential counseling, both in-person and through telehealth, can provide healthcare providers with a space to discuss and manage their mental health concerns. Wearable devices and sensor technology can monitor real-time physiological indicators of stress. These devices can provide healthcare providers with alerts and recommendations when stress levels are elevated. Virtual reality (VR) therapy can be used to create immersive environments for relaxation and stress reduction. Providers can use VR headsets to escape calming virtual settings, promoting relaxation. Organizations should also promote educational initiatives. Mental health education can help providers recognize the signs of stress and burnout in themselves and their colleagues. By understanding the importance of mental health, providers can be more proactive in seeking support.

Balancing Clinical and Administrative Work

Provider wellness in VBC involves streamlining administrative tasks and reducing the burden of paperwork. VBC models aim to minimize the administrative workload of healthcare providers by streamlining documentation and reporting processes, reducing the time spent on non-clinical tasks. Technology and support staff can be leveraged to handle administrative duties, allowing providers to focus more on patient care. Examples that have shown promise include assigning billing and coding responsibilities to dedicated personnel rather than providers, which can reduce the administrative workload and ensure accurate and timely claim submissions. Working top-of-license is a key tenant to achieving the quintuple-aim. Ensuring that EHR systems are optimized to support clinical workflows can streamline administrative processes. Customized EHR configurations can prioritize clinical data entry and reduce redundancy.

Leveraging data analytics can help identify areas where administrative processes can be made more efficient. Analyzing workflow data can lead to process improvements that drive improved adoption for the system overall.

Interdisciplinary Care Teams

Collaborative and interdisciplinary care teams are promoted in VBC. This approach fosters a sense of community and support among healthcare professionals, reducing the isolation that some providers may experience. Interdisciplinary teams aim to provide seamless and coordinated care. They collaborate to develop and execute care plans that address all aspects of the whole person's health, from physical, emotional, mental, social, and spiritual care needs. Organizations must consider care across the continuum and the ability to scale these care teams as populations change or grow. Interdisciplinary care teams must be focused on providing consistent care across various healthcare and community settings, including hospitals, primary care practices, community health centers, schools, and even the patient's home, ensuring continuity of care. The interdisciplinary care model can be scaled to meet the needs of different patient populations, making it adaptable to various healthcare scenarios. Ongoing training in teamwork, communication, and collaboration is essential for the success of interdisciplinary care teams. Healthcare organizations should invest in team-building exercises and education.

Interdisciplinary care teams are a cornerstone of VBC, aligning with the overarching goal of improving patient outcomes and the patient experience. By bringing together healthcare professionals from diverse backgrounds, VBC ensures that patients receive well-rounded, comprehensive care that addresses all aspects of their health. This approach benefits both patients and healthcare providers, creating a more fulfilling and supportive work environment while enhancing the quality of care.

A provider wellness viewpoint in Care and Business Delivery Transformation within a VBC model recognizes that a healthy and engaged healthcare workforce is essential for achieving positive patient outcomes and ensuring the sustainability of healthcare systems. By addressing the well-being and job satisfaction of healthcare providers, VBC can create a more supportive and fulfilling work environment, ultimately benefiting both patients and the healthcare professionals who care for them.

Conclusion

In conclusion, the road ahead for VBC transformation is marked by a commitment to delivering high-quality, cost-effective care, fostering collaboration, and embracing the ever-evolving landscape of healthcare regulations and technology. The journey to VBC is one of continuous improvement and adaptation, driven by a shared commitment to improving patient outcomes and population health while reducing the overall cost of care. Success in this endeavor will position healthcare organizations as leaders in the delivery of patient-centric, value-driven healthcare services.

USE PEOPLE WITH IT | USE PEOPLE IN IT TO DRIVE AI INNOVATION IN HEALTHCARE | *BY SAKSHIKA DHINGRA*

Introduction

AI has emerged as a transformative force in healthcare, promising to enhance diagnostics, treatment, and operational efficiency. However, the successful integration of AI into healthcare systems is not solely dependent on advanced algorithms and data; it requires the skilled and strategic involvement of IT professionals. This essay explores the critical role of IT professionals in driving AI innovation in healthcare, highlighting their contributions, challenges, and impact on patient care. The case study of the Cleveland Clinic's AI initiatives serves as a real-life example of how leveraging IT expertise can lead to groundbreaking advancements in healthcare.

Too often, well-intentioned practitioners embark on AI initiatives on their own. This lack of collaboration may speed things up initially but often become the reason why projects come to a screeching halt or are otherwise sub-optimized. Similarly, when AI initiatives become "IT projects," poor outcomes are likely to follow. Below we summarize why IT professionals should be included upfront with two material case studies to prove the point.

The Role of IT Professionals in AI Innovation

Data Management and Integration

Data is the lifeblood of AI. Healthcare generates vast amounts of data, from EHRs to imaging and genetic information. IT professionals are essential in managing, integrating, and ensuring the quality of this data. Their expertise enables the seamless flow of data across different systems, making it accessible for AI algorithms to analyze.

- ■ **Data Cleaning and Preprocessing**: IT professionals are responsible for cleaning and preprocessing data, removing inaccuracies, and ensuring consistency. This process is crucial for training AI models, as high-quality data leads to more accurate and reliable outputs.
- ■ **Data Integration**: Healthcare data often resides in disparate systems. IT experts facilitate the integration of these data sources, creating comprehensive datasets that AI can use to generate insights. This integration is vital for holistic patient care and advanced analytics.

Infrastructure Development and Maintenance

Robust and scalable infrastructure is essential for deploying AI solutions. IT professionals design and maintain the infrastructure that supports AI applications, ensuring they run efficiently and securely.

- **Cloud Computing and Storage**: The vast amount of data required for AI necessitates scalable storage solutions. IT professionals implement and manage cloud computing resources, providing the flexibility and capacity needed for AI projects.
- **Computational Power**: AI algorithms, particularly those involving deep learning, require significant computational power. IT teams set up and optimize high-performance computing (HPC) environments to handle these demands.

Cybersecurity and Compliance

The sensitive nature of healthcare data makes cybersecurity a top priority. IT professionals implement robust security measures to protect data from breaches and ensure compliance with regulations such as HIPAA (Health Insurance Portability and Accountability Act).

- **Data Encryption and Access Controls**: IT teams deploy encryption technologies and access controls to safeguard data. This ensures that only authorized personnel can access sensitive information.
- **Regulatory Compliance**: Compliance with healthcare regulations is mandatory. IT professionals ensure that AI solutions adhere to regulatory standards, mitigating legal and financial risks.

Software Development and Customization

AI applications often require custom software development to meet the specific needs of healthcare providers. IT professionals design, develop, and customize software solutions, integrating AI capabilities into existing systems.

- **Application Development**: IT experts develop applications that incorporate AI algorithms, making them user-friendly for healthcare professionals. This involves creating interfaces that allow clinicians to interact with AI tools seamlessly.

■ **System Integration**: Integrating AI solutions with existing healthcare systems, such as EHRs, is crucial for smooth operation. IT professionals ensure that AI applications work harmoniously with other software, enhancing their utility and adoption.

Case Study: Kaiser Permanente

Introduction

Kaiser Permanente, one of the largest and most integrated healthcare systems in the United States, has successfully utilized the expertise of IT professionals to drive AI innovation in healthcare. This case study explores how Kaiser Permanente's IT team has been instrumental in developing and implementing AI-driven solutions to enhance patient care, operational efficiency, and clinical outcomes.

Overview of Kaiser Permanente

Kaiser Permanente serves over 12 million members across multiple states, providing a comprehensive range of healthcare services. The organization is renowned for its integrated care model, which combines health insurance and healthcare services under one umbrella. This structure provides a unique advantage for leveraging data and technology to improve healthcare delivery.

Role of IT Professionals in AI Innovation

At Kaiser Permanente, IT professionals play a crucial role in driving AI innovation through various key functions, including data management, infrastructure development, cybersecurity, and software development. Their expertise ensures that AI technologies are effectively integrated into clinical workflows, enhancing the quality of care provided to patients.

Data Management and Integration

Data is fundamental to AI in healthcare, and IT professionals at Kaiser Permanente are responsible for managing and integrating vast amounts of patient data from different sources.

■ **Data Cleaning and Preprocessing**: IT teams clean and preprocess data to ensure it is accurate and ready for AI analysis. This involves removing duplicates, correcting errors, and standardizing data formats.

- **Data Integration**: By integrating data from EHRs, lab results, imaging systems, and wearable devices, IT professionals create comprehensive datasets that enable robust AI analytics.

Infrastructure Development and Maintenance

AI applications require robust infrastructure, and IT professionals at Kaiser Permanente are tasked with developing and maintaining this infrastructure.

- **Cloud Computing**: The IT team leverages cloud computing to provide scalable storage and computational power necessary for AI applications.
- **HPC**: IT professionals set up and optimize HPC environments to support complex AI algorithms, ensuring they run efficiently and effectively.

Cybersecurity and Compliance

Ensuring the security and privacy of patient data is paramount in healthcare. IT professionals at Kaiser Permanente implement rigorous cybersecurity measures to protect data and ensure compliance with regulatory standards.

- **Encryption and Access Controls**: IT teams deploy encryption technologies and strict access controls to safeguard sensitive patient information.
- **Regulatory Compliance**: IT professionals ensure that AI solutions adhere to healthcare regulations such as HIPAA, mitigating legal and financial risks.

Software Development and Customization

IT professionals at Kaiser Permanente develop and customize software solutions to integrate AI capabilities into existing systems, making them user-friendly and accessible to healthcare providers.

- **Application Development**: The IT team creates applications that incorporate AI algorithms, enabling clinicians to use these tools seamlessly within their workflows.

■ **System Integration**: By integrating AI solutions with existing health-care systems, IT professionals ensure that these tools enhance clinical processes and improve patient outcomes.

AI Innovations at Kaiser Permanente

AI-Powered Predictive Analytics for Chronic Disease Management

One of Kaiser Permanente's significant AI innovations is the use of predictive analytics for chronic disease management, particularly for conditions such as diabetes and heart disease.

■ **Data Integration and Analytics**: IT professionals integrated patient data from EHRs, lab results, and wearable devices into a unified platform. This data was then analyzed using AI algorithms to predict disease progression and identify patients at risk of complications.

■ **Infrastructure Development**: The IT team developed a scalable cloud infrastructure to handle the large datasets and complex computations required for predictive analytics.

■ **Cybersecurity**: Advanced encryption and access controls were implemented to ensure the security of patient data and compliance with HIPAA regulations.

■ **Software Customization**: Custom applications were developed to deliver predictive insights to clinicians in real-time, enabling proactive interventions and personalized care plans.

AI-Driven Radiology and Imaging

Kaiser Permanente has also leveraged AI to enhance radiology and imaging services, improving diagnostic accuracy and efficiency.

■ **Data Preprocessing and Integration**: IT professionals preprocessed and integrated imaging data from various sources, creating a comprehensive dataset for AI analysis.

■ **HPC**: The IT team established HPC environments to support AI algorithms capable of analyzing large volumes of imaging data rapidly.

■ **Security Measures**: Robust cybersecurity measures were implemented to protect sensitive imaging data and ensure compliance with regulatory standards.

■ **Application Development**: Custom AI applications were developed to assist radiologists in detecting anomalies in medical images, enhancing diagnostic accuracy, and reducing the workload on healthcare providers.

Impact of IT-Driven AI Innovations

The involvement of IT professionals in driving AI innovation at Kaiser Permanente has had a profound impact on patient care, operational efficiency, and clinical outcomes.

Improved Patient Outcomes

AI-powered predictive analytics have significantly improved the management of chronic diseases at Kaiser Permanente. By identifying patients at risk of complications, healthcare providers can intervene earlier, preventing disease progression and reducing hospitalizations. For example, AI algorithms used in diabetes management have helped identify patients at risk of developing complications, leading to timely interventions and better health outcomes.

Enhanced Diagnostic Accuracy

AI-driven radiology and imaging tools have enhanced diagnostic accuracy at Kaiser Permanente. AI algorithms can detect subtle anomalies in medical images that may be missed by human radiologists, leading to earlier and more accurate diagnoses. This has improved the quality of care provided to patients and increased the efficiency of radiology departments.

Operational Efficiency

The integration of AI solutions has streamlined workflows and increased operational efficiency at Kaiser Permanente. Predictive analytics tools have optimized resource allocation, reducing wait times and improving patient throughput. AI-driven imaging analysis has decreased the time required for radiologists to review medical images, allowing them to focus on more complex cases.

Increased Patient Engagement

AI tools have also increased patient engagement by providing personalized care plans and real-time health insights. For example, patients with chronic diseases can use mobile applications to monitor their health and receive personalized recommendations, improving adherence to treatment plans and overall health outcomes.

Challenges and Solutions

While Kaiser Permanente has achieved significant success in leveraging IT professionals to drive AI innovation, several challenges have been encountered and addressed.

Data Silos and Interoperability

- **Challenge**: Data silos and lack of interoperability between different healthcare systems posed a significant challenge.
- **Solution**: IT professionals implemented data integration solutions, such as health information exchanges (HIEs) and application programming interfaces (APIs), to facilitate seamless data exchange and create unified datasets for AI analysis.

Scalability and Performance

- **Challenge**: AI applications require significant computational resources, leading to scalability and performance challenges.
- **Solution**: The IT team leveraged cloud computing and HPC clusters to provide the necessary scalability and computational power for AI applications.

Data Privacy and Security

- **Challenge**: Protecting sensitive healthcare data from breaches was a constant challenge.
- **Solution**: IT professionals implemented advanced cybersecurity measures, such as multi-factor authentication, encryption, and continuous monitoring, to safeguard data and ensure compliance with regulatory standards.

User Adoption and Training

- **Challenge**: Ensuring user adoption and providing adequate training for AI tools were critical challenges.
- **Solution**: IT professionals developed user-friendly interfaces and comprehensive training programs to promote adoption. Involving clinicians in the development process ensured that AI tools met their needs and were easy to use.

Conclusion

Kaiser Permanente's success in leveraging IT professionals to drive AI innovation highlights the critical role of IT expertise in transforming healthcare. By managing and integrating data, developing robust infrastructure, ensuring cybersecurity, and customizing software solutions, IT professionals have enabled the effective integration of AI technologies into clinical workflows. The impact of these innovations has been significant, leading to improved patient outcomes, enhanced diagnostic accuracy, operational efficiency, and increased patient engagement.

As AI continues to evolve, the collaboration between IT professionals and healthcare providers will become increasingly important. By recognizing and harnessing the skills of IT experts, healthcare organizations can fully realize the potential of AI, transforming patient care and creating a more efficient and effective healthcare system. Kaiser Permanente's case study serves as a powerful example of how leveraging IT expertise can drive AI innovation and improve healthcare delivery.

Case Study: Cleveland Clinic

The Cleveland Clinic, a renowned healthcare institution, has successfully leveraged IT professionals to drive AI innovation. The following sections detail how IT expertise has been pivotal in their AI initiatives, focusing on data management, infrastructure, cybersecurity, and software development.

AI-Powered Diagnostic Tools

One of the Cleveland Clinic's significant achievements in AI innovation is the development of AI-powered diagnostic tools. These tools assist clinicians in diagnosing diseases more accurately and efficiently.

- **Data Management and Integration**: IT professionals at Cleveland Clinic have integrated vast amounts of patient data from EHRs, imaging systems, and lab results into a unified platform. This comprehensive dataset enables the training of AI models that can identify patterns and anomalies indicative of diseases.
- **Infrastructure Development**: To support AI diagnostics, the Cleveland Clinic's IT team has implemented scalable cloud infrastructure. This infrastructure provides the necessary computational power and storage, allowing AI algorithms to process large datasets quickly.
- **Cybersecurity**: Ensuring the security of patient data is paramount. The IT department has implemented advanced encryption and access control measures to protect data, ensuring that AI applications comply with HIPAA and other regulations.
- **Software Development**: Custom AI applications have been developed to integrate diagnostic tools into clinicians' workflows. These applications provide real-time analysis and decision support, enhancing the accuracy and speed of diagnoses.

Predictive Analytics for Patient Outcomes

The Cleveland Clinic has also employed AI for predictive analytics, helping to forecast patient outcomes and improve care management.

- **Data Cleaning and Preprocessing**: IT professionals clean and preprocess patient data, ensuring it is suitable for predictive modeling. This involves standardizing data formats and removing inconsistencies.
- **Infrastructure**: HPC environments have been established to support the complex computations required for predictive analytics. This infrastructure enables the rapid analysis of large datasets, providing timely insights for clinical decision-making.
- **Cybersecurity and Compliance**: The IT team ensures that predictive analytics tools comply with regulatory requirements. This includes regular audits and updates to security protocols, safeguarding patient information.

- **Application Development**: Predictive analytics tools are integrated into the Cleveland Clinic's care management systems. These tools provide healthcare providers with actionable insights, such as identifying patients at high risk of readmission and allowing for proactive interventions.

Challenges and Solutions

Data Silos and Interoperability

One of the primary challenges in healthcare AI is the existence of data silos, where information is stored in disparate systems that do not communicate effectively.

- **Solution**: IT professionals can address this challenge by implementing data integration solutions, such as HIEs and APIs. These solutions facilitate the seamless exchange of data across different systems, creating a unified dataset for AI analysis.

Scalability and Performance

AI applications require significant computational resources, which can strain existing infrastructure.

- **Solution**: Leveraging cloud computing and HPC clusters can provide the necessary scalability and performance. IT professionals play a critical role in designing and maintaining these infrastructures, ensuring they meet the demands of AI applications.

Data Privacy and Security

Protecting sensitive healthcare data from breaches is a constant challenge.

- **Solution**: Implementing advanced cybersecurity measures, such as multi-factor authentication, encryption, and continuous monitoring, can mitigate risks. IT professionals ensure that AI solutions comply with regulatory standards, maintaining patient trust and confidentiality.

User Adoption and Training

For AI solutions to be effective, healthcare providers must be willing and able to use them.

■ **Solution**: IT professionals can develop user-friendly interfaces and provide comprehensive training programs. Involving clinicians in the development process ensures that AI tools meet their needs and are easy to use, promoting adoption.

Impact on Patient Care

The strategic involvement of IT professionals in AI innovation has profound implications for patient care. The Cleveland Clinic's initiatives provide concrete examples of these impacts.

Improved Diagnostic Accuracy

AI-powered diagnostic tools at the Cleveland Clinic have improved the accuracy of disease detection. For instance, AI algorithms can analyze medical images with high precision, identifying early signs of conditions such as cancer. This enables earlier interventions, improving patient outcomes.

Enhanced Predictive Capabilities

Predictive analytics tools help healthcare providers anticipate patient needs and outcomes. At the Cleveland Clinic, these tools have been used to predict patient deterioration, allowing for timely interventions that prevent complications and reduce hospital readmissions.

Operational Efficiency

The integration of AI into operational processes has streamlined workflows and increased efficiency. For example, AI-driven scheduling systems optimize resource allocation, reducing wait times and improving patient throughput. This allows healthcare providers to deliver care more effectively and efficiently.

Personalized Treatment Plans

AI enables the development of personalized treatment plans based on individual patient data. At the Cleveland Clinic, AI algorithms analyze genetic, clinical, and lifestyle data to recommend tailored treatments. This approach enhances the effectiveness of care and improves patient satisfaction.

Conclusion

The successful integration of AI into healthcare is heavily dependent on the expertise and strategic involvement of IT professionals. Their roles in data management, infrastructure development, cybersecurity, and software customization are crucial for the development and deployment of AI solutions. The Cleveland Clinic's AI initiatives exemplify how leveraging IT expertise can drive innovation, leading to improved patient care, operational efficiency, and predictive capabilities.

As healthcare continues to evolve, the collaboration between IT professionals and healthcare providers will become increasingly important. By recognizing and harnessing the skills of IT experts, healthcare organizations can fully realize the potential of AI, transforming patient care and creating a more efficient and effective healthcare system. The future of healthcare innovation lies in the seamless integration of technology and human expertise, and IT professionals are at the forefront of this transformation.

Never begin an AI initiative without significant collaboration, a topic we tackle with greater emphasis on "Collaborate & Listen."

Note: The author leveraged ChatGBT3 to source additional documented examples of AI in healthcare to compliment the others used in the article. We leveraged AI the same way we would search for examples using traditional methods such as Google or a public library for basic research.

USE PEOPLE WITH IT | ENHANCING PATIENT-CENTERED CARE: THE ROLE OF ADVANCE CARE PLANNING AND DATA ANALYTICS IN HEALTHCARE | BY WINIFRED TEUTEBERG, MD, JACK GUO-QING ZENG, PH.D., BRITHTHA SEEVARATNAM, M.S., KELLY KNIGHT, LISA TSERING, AND MICHAEL A. PFEFFER, MD

Introduction

In healthcare, promoting person-centered care for those living with severe illnesses involves more than just medical intervention. At its heart, this comprehensive strategy encourages open conversations about prognosis, life goals and values. This not only enables patients to work with clinicians to make well-informed decisions but also respects their autonomy and promotes their dignity.

Recognizing the pivotal importance of these conversations, Stanford Medicine has implemented an evidence-based program aimed at optimizing the timing and quality of advance care planning (ACP) discussions. Upon completion of the Ariadne Labs Serious Illness Care Program learning collaborative in 2018, our teams took the work to the next level by leveraging groundbreaking data analytics and innovative technological solutions. This innovative implementation of the Serious Illness Care Program at Stanford Medicine represents a paradigm shift toward earlier, more frequent, and higher-quality ACP conversations.

The Evolution of Advance Care Planning at Stanford Medicine

The bedrock of this transformative initiative is the ACPMed app, a sophisticated dashboard designed to capture crucial components of ACP discussions such as illness understanding, prognosis, patient values, and treatment preferences. These elements are documented in a streamlined form within the EHR and visualized within ACPMed, which allows program leaders, executive sponsors and clinical champions to view progress and identify areas of opportunity. Development of the documentation tools and dashboard was supported by our Serious Illness Care Program. The program has witnessed significant traction since its inception in 2018, having touched over 12,000 patients across the enterprise.

The Significance of Quality Conversations in Advance Care Planning

A core tenet of the program lies in the emphasis on conducting quality conversations at the appropriate juncture of a patient's illness trajectory. This underscores the imperative of ensuring thorough and meaningful discussions, wherein clinicians navigate the intricacies of ACP with precision and empathy.

By standardizing the documentation process through the ACP form in the EHR, providers are empowered to cover essential topics while obviating the need for redundant discussions in subsequent encounters. Moreover, the program endeavors to shift the discourse upstream in the continuum of care, affording patients greater agency and decision-making autonomy during their healthcare journey and improving the range of options over their care in the time they have left.

The program also addresses how often these conversations happen; improved prevalence of ACP helps account for ongoing changes in patients' disease progression and provides clinicians with information to adjust goal-concordant care as needed.

The Role of Technology and Data Analytics

Central to the success of the Serious Illness Care Program is the symbiotic relationship between technology and data analytics. The ACPMed app serves as a conduit for aggregating vast amounts of clinical data, thereby enabling program leaders to monitor progress, track programmatic outcomes, and identify areas for improvement. By harnessing the power of data visualization and trend analysis, the program has garnered actionable insights, driving continuous quality improvement initiatives.

Machine Learning and Patient Selection for Advance Care Planning

A cornerstone of the program's success lies in its ability to effectively identify patients who would benefit from ACP discussions by leveraging machine learning to create predictive models that help identify patient need for ACP. These advanced algorithms clarify information for the clinical team, enabling them to engage more proactively with patients, thus fostering a more active, patient-focused approach to care.

The Integration of the Serious Illness Conversation Guide

A pivotal component of the program is the integration of the "Serious Illness Conversation Guide," a structured framework comprising open-ended questions categorized into five main sections. The interactive form in the EHR serves as a dynamic tool accessible to clinicians across various care settings, thereby ensuring consistency and comprehensiveness in ACP documentation.

The Implications for Clinical Practice and Quality Improvement

Beyond its immediate clinical applications, the program holds far-reaching implications for enhancing patient outcomes and quality of care. By leveraging the ACP form as a central repository for documentation, clinicians can seamlessly integrate ACP discussions into their practice, thereby promoting continuity of care and patient-centered decision-making. Moreover, the program's emphasis on data-driven quality improvement initiatives underscores its commitment to ongoing refinement and optimization of clinical workflows. Through the generation of run charts and feedback mechanisms, stakeholders are empowered to iteratively enhance programmatic effectiveness, thereby fostering a culture of continuous learning and innovation.

Conclusion

The integration of ACP into clinical practice represents a watershed moment in the evolution of patient-centered care. The innovative initiatives spearheaded by Stanford Medicine, including the ACPMed app and the Serious Illness Care Program, exemplify a proactive approach toward addressing the complex needs of patients with serious illnesses. By harnessing the synergistic potential of technology, data analytics, and interdisciplinary collaboration, these initiatives hold immense promise for transforming the delivery of healthcare, one quality conversation at a time. As we navigate the complexities of modern medicine, let us remain steadfast in our commitment to placing patients at the heart of healthcare delivery, ensuring dignity, compassion, and autonomy throughout their healthcare journey.

Bibliography

Albano, D., Galiano, V., Basile, M., Di Luca, F., Gitto, S., Messina, C., Cagetti, M. G., Del Fabbro, M., Tartaglia, G. M., & Sconfienza, L. M. (2024). Artificial intelligence for radiographic imaging detection of caries lesions: A systematic review. *BMC Oral Health*, *24*(1), 274. https://doi.org/10.1186/s12903-024-04046-7

Anil, S., Porwal, P., & Porwal, A. (2023). Transforming dental caries diagnosis through artificial intelligence-based techniques. *Cureus*. https://doi.org/10.7759/cureus.41694

Bayraktar, Y., & Ayan, E. (2021). Diagnosis of interproximal caries lesions with deep convolutional neural network in digital bitewing radiographs. *Clinical Oral Investigations*, *26*(1), 623–632. https://doi.org/10.1007/s00784-021-04040-1

Grand View Research. (2021, April). Remote Patient Monitoring System Market Size, Share & Trends Analysis Report By Product (Vital Sign Monitors, Special Monitors), By Application (Cancer, Cardiovascular Diseases, Diabetes), By End-use, By Region, And Segment Forecasts, 2021–2028. Retrieved from https://www.grandviewresearch.com/industry-analysis/remote-patient-monitoring-devices-market

Khanagar, S. B., Alfouzan, K., Awawdeh, M., Alkadi, L., Albalawi, F., & Alfadley, A. (2022). Application and performance of artificial intelligence technology in detection, diagnosis and prediction of Dental Caries (DC)-A systematic review. *Diagnostics, 12*(5), 1083. https://doi.org/10.3390/diagnostics12051083

Merriam-Webster. (2021). Revolution. In Merriam-Webster.com dictionary. Retrieved from https://www.merriam-webster.com/dictionary/revolution

Mertens, S., Krois, J., Cantu, A. G., Arsiwala, L. T., & Schwendicke, F. (2021). Artificial intelligence for caries detection: Randomized trial. *Journal of Dentistry, 115*, 103849. https://doi.org/10.1016/j.jdent.2021.103849

Musri, N., Christie, B., Ichwan, S. J. A., & Cahyanto, A. (2021). Deep learning convolutional neural network algorithms for the early detection and diagnosis of dental caries on periapical radiographs: A systematic review. *Imaging Science in Dentistry, 51*(3), 237. https://doi.org/10.5624/isd.20210074

Pérez De Frutos, J., Holden Helland, R., Desai, S., Nymoen, L. C., Langø, T., Remman, T., & Sen, A. (2024). AI-Dentify: Deep learning for proximal caries detection on bitewing X-ray - HUNT4 oral health study. *BMC Oral Health, 24*(1), 344. https://doi.org/10.1186/s12903-024-04120-0

Saeedi, P., Petersohn, I., Salpea, P., Malanda, B., Karuranga, S., Unwin, N., Colagiuri, S., Guariguata, L., Motala, A., Ogurtsova, K., Shaw, J., Bright, D. & Williams, R. (2019). Global and regional diabetes prevalence estimates for 2019 and projections for 2030 and 2045: Results from the International Diabetes Federation Diabetes Atlas, 9th edition. *Diabetes Research and Clinical Practice, 157*, 107843.

Schwendicke, F., Cejudo Grano De Oro, J., Garcia Cantu, A., Meyer-Lueckel, H., Chaurasia, A., & Krois, J. (2022). Artificial intelligence for caries detection: Value of data and information. *Journal of Dental Research, 101*(11), 1350–1356. https://doi.org/10.1177/00220345221113756

Schwendicke, F., Golla, T., Dreher, M., & Krois, J. (2019). Convolutional neural networks for dental image diagnostics: A scoping review. *Journal of Dentistry, 91*, 103226. https://doi.org/10.1016/j.jdent.2019.103226

Schwendicke, F., Rossi, J. G., Göstemeyer, G., Elhennawy, K., Cantu, A. G., Gaudin, R., Chaurasia, A., Gehrung, S., & Krois, J. (2021). Cost-effectiveness of convol for proximal caries detection. *Journal of Dental Research, 100*(4), 369–376. https://doi.org/10.1177/0022034520972335

U.S. Bureau of Labor Statistics. (2020, September 1). Employment Projections—2019-2029. Retrieved from https://www.bls.gov/news.release/archives/ecopro_09012020.pdf

World Health Organization. (1948). *Constitution of the World Health Organization.* Geneva: WHO. Retrieved from https://www.who.int/about/governance/constitution

Zanini, L. G. K., Rubira-Bullen, I. R. F., & Nunes, F. D. L. D. S. (2024). A systematic review on caries detection, classification, and segmentation from X-Ray images: Methods, datasets, evaluation, and open opportunities. *Journal of Imaging Informatics in Medicine.* https://doi.org/10.1007/s10278-024-01054-5

Chapter 4

Create Roadmaps

Develop A Plan For The Functions Required to Innovate and Encourage Effective Communication Between Functional Experts For Strategic Clarity.

There is an unsubstantiated fear that plans and orders run counter to the innovation spirit. Effective roadmaps actually serve as beacons or markers that help innovators navigate their way without being distracted and thrown off course. Plans do not stifle innovation but rather provide necessary guardrails to ensure focus and completion. Too many great ideas were never realized as resources and passion dwindled from an unnecessarily long journey.

CREATE ROADMAPS | CREATING ROADMAPS FOR A TRUE AI-DRIVEN SIEM FOR HEALTHCARE OF TOMORROW | *BY INDERPAL KOHLI AND KANNAN SRINIVASAN*

Executive Summary

The secure exchange of sensitive information across extensive networks is of utmost importance in the healthcare sector. However, the digital landscape also introduces significant cybersecurity vulnerabilities, including the threat of cyberattacks, data breaches, and unauthorized intrusions, which

DOI: 10.4324/9781032715155-4

can have far-reaching consequences, ranging from financial losses and concerns about patient safety to regulatory fines. Traditional security information and event monitoring (SIEM) systems often prove insufficient, lacking the essential threat visibility and early detection capabilities needed to combat modern threats in the healthcare industry effectively. Outdated technology and a lack of advanced analytics hinder legacy solutions from addressing these challenges effectively.

Englewood Health (EH), a leading healthcare system in New Jersey, wanted to strengthen our defenses in light of the increasing cyberattack trend. We relied on a third-party SIEM tool, functioning predominantly as a log aggregator. Recognizing the imperative of real-time security threat detection, EH partnered with GS Lab | GAVS to bolster our security posture. Together, we decided to move to a new SIEM product, which would be fine-tuned into a solution for the healthcare requirements of tomorrow. The new product also brings true AI/ML capabilities to bolster the security landscape further. This transformation not only addressed the critical security gaps but also provided multiple benefits (Figure 4.1).

Key learning from this collaboration emphasizes the importance of phase-wise implementation, prioritizing quality over quantity, and the versatile applications of this solution across various healthcare security domains. EH's successful collaboration with GS Lab | GAVS showcases the power of partnership in addressing complex cybersecurity challenges and underscores the critical need for advanced SIEM solutions in healthcare cybersecurity.

Figure 4.1   Benefits Achieved with AI-Driven SIEM Solution.

The Need for Change: Challenges that Stood between Englewood Health and Their Goals

Englewood relied on a SIEM solution primarily serving as a log aggregator. However, this system lacked advanced analytics driven by AI/ML technology, leaving a potential gap in our security posture. Without the AI/ML-powered threat detection model, identifying anomalies related to Indicators of Compromise (IoCs) was a challenge. This gap meant the system might miss or misinterpret crucial signs of potential security breaches, carrying substantial risks.

Recognizing the critical need for real-time security threat detection and response, we acknowledged the necessity for an AI-based SIEM solution, a capability deficit in our existing system. Apart from identifying the right solution, we faced numerous other challenges.

Complexity

Networks in enterprises consist of various security elements, like firewalls, routers, web security tools, and intrusion detection and protection systems, among other solutions crucial for network security. These components produce a significant volume of events and alerts. To effectively coordinate log collection, data analysis, and threat detection across a diverse range of security elements, meticulous discovery, planning, policy evaluation, and precise adjustments were necessary to ensure the SIEM solution met the desired objectives.

Compatibility

The presence of varied network devices and applications in most organizations can lead to compatibility issues and security gaps in SIEM implementation. Seamless integration with existing network security tools, including endpoint protection, was vital to enhancing SIEM efficiency. However, integrating SIEM with outdated legacy systems and generating logs in proprietary formats further complicated the implementation process.

The Solution

Enabling a True AI/ML-Driven SIEM

Leveraging AI, Seceon's advanced SIEM solution, aiSIEM™, promised robust threat detection, automated incident response, and real-time security analytics. After successful proof-of-concept demonstrations, EH decided to deploy Seceon aiSIEM™, thereby strengthening our security measures and ensuring proactive threat management.

Seceon aiSIEM™ was able to differentiate itself from legacy and modern SIEM solutions with

- **Automated Threat Containment and Remediation**: Seamlessly integrates with IT infrastructure for swift action.
- **Comprehensive IT Infrastructure Visibility**: Offers insights into inventory, applications, users, and their interactions.
- **Continuous Real-Time Compliance**: Ensures ongoing adherence to standards.
- **MITRE ATTACK Framework-Based TTP Insights**: Identifies suspicious processes and behaviors.
- **True SaaS Model**: Delivered with NIST-defined characteristics.
- **Multi-tier and Multi-tenancy Support**: Ideal for managed service providers.
- **Scalability and Ease of Management**: Designed for effortless expansion and administration.

Challenges the AI/ML-Driven SIEM Solution Overcame

- **Real-time monitoring for rapid detection**: While time to detection is crucial, it could take hours for the correlation engine to sift through static events stored in a database. This can cause unwanted delays in raising alerts and notifications for a SOC analyst to take action in halting kill chain propagation. Consequently, we have to live with the reduced effectiveness of a security solution in minimizing harm to the assets and operations of a business, organization, or enterprise.

  Our SIEM is designed to process security events and flow data sourced from various network devices, hosts, endpoints, and security tools in real-time. This allows for threat indicators to be identified early enough for a malware's progression to be thwarted or for unusual user behavior to be flagged before further damage is inflicted.
- **Enrichment with threat intelligence feeds for better accuracy**: Threat intelligence data provides crucial insights about an attacker or attack, often confirming harmful intent. Legacy SIEM tools relying solely on security events needed more means and motions to gather threat intelligence information for the benefit of business or enterprise.

Seceon's aiSIEM™ platform, however, takes a big step forward in realizing the value of data gathered from the dark web and clear web through independent sources. Specific pointers relating to a destination IP address—such as the reputation, geo-location, and association with malware—can be concurrently fed into the processing engine to improve the confidence score of a potential threat. The AI-based SIEM platform gathers threat intelligence from 50+ sources.

■ **User entity behavior analysis with machine learning for improved anomaly detection**: When tracked properly, the interaction between users and various entities of the IT infrastructure (servers, applications, and databases) can serve as strong evidence for insider and outsider threats. Legacy SIEM solutions would allow queries relating to a specific user while the results had to be manually interpreted and correlated further (again manually) to construct an evidence chart. Missing big time was an insider's interaction with specific types of data that could constitute a significant breach.

Seceon's aiSIEM™ takes user and entity interaction very seriously by establishing identity based on the Active Directory log and recognizing attempts by malicious actors to escalate privilege. Also, an internal user's attempt to upload data to an external site or cloud storage can be tracked, and an alert can be raised for further investigation. Users' behavior is compared with a baseline of known behavior using machine learning, thus facilitating anomaly detection. The result is an SIEM solution that automatically synthesizes strong evidence for identifying zero-day malware (with unknown threat vectors).

■ **Advanced analytics and correlation with AI/ML**: Advanced analytics can be used to develop comprehensive models. This allows an organization to conduct risk assessments of users and systems and alert all entities that may pose a potential threat. It sifts through large amounts of data, correlating events to identify non-conforming patterns and anomalies (e.g., compromised credentials, rogue users on the network, unwarranted escalation of user privileges, and transmission of sensitive corporate information across unsolicited channels).

While traditional SIEM would require a security analyst to write hundreds of correlation rules, subject to trial and error over a lengthy period, the self-learning SIEM processes event data, traffic flows, user information, threat intelligence, and other data feed in real-time, applying dynamic threat models to an advanced analytics engine running on artificial intelligence (AI). The result is a time-sequenced aggregation of threat indicators threaded together to raise an alert—critical, significant, or minor severity.

■ **Network traffic analysis and network detection and response**: As adversaries modify their tactics to avoid detection and often work their way through IT assets with pre-deployed trusted tools and legitimate credentials, it becomes challenging for organizations to identify malicious intent proactively. Network traffic analysis brings broad visibility across all network communications in real time—traditional TCP/IP style packets, traffic crossing a virtual switch (vSwitch), traffic from cloud workloads, and API calls to SaaS applications or serverless computing instances. This level of network traffic analysis and rich insights were grossly deficient in traditional SIEM.

Seceon aiSIEM™ embraces the essence of NTA by applying machine learning to create a baseline of evolving behaviors while mapping out entities and their relationships. Specifically, entities on a network are the devices, hosts, users, applications, destinations, IP addresses, ports, etc. Also, by extracting the metadata (TLS version, Length of Public Key, etc.) from encrypted traffic (HTTPS) and attributes (URL, DNS hostname, etc.) from Initial Data Packet, NTA based solution (like Seceon aiSIEM™) can detect anomalous behavior without the need for decryption that is computed intensive and disruptive for user experience. It should be noted here that Packet Captures are rarely effective, as more than 70% of web traffic is encrypted, including those used by malicious actors, thus emphasizing the significance of network traffic analysis.

■ **Alert effectiveness for reduction in operational backlog**: There has never been a dull moment with a deluge of events flowing into legacy SIEM and other security monitoring tools. However, if we were to heed all the alerts bubbling up on the dashboard, we would run out of resource capacity quite quickly and leave a good portion unattended. This is a classic situation many IT organizations and CISO-led teams have been facing for years, painstakingly clearing the backlog of false alarms (false positives). In contrast, true positives remain hidden and unidentified in the mess.

By design, AI-based SIEM has automated threat detection with machine learning, dynamic threat models, and built-in correlation. Days, weeks, and months of tuning effort through custom correlation rules can be avoided. Also, the variability of threat detection outcomes based on the level of human expertise (security analyst) is eliminated in this approach. The benefits are quite staggering—qualitatively enhanced and prioritized alerts (only a handful) with validated Threat Indicators. As a runoff, we get a reprieve from alert fatigue, elimination of human errors, and reduced time to analysis.

■ **Automated and semi-automated response to incidents (security orchestration automation and response (SOAR))**: Response and remediation make up the final yet most crucial stage of cybersecurity in the event of a breach, attack, or compromise. It often takes a while to carve out a remediation plan and execute it accordingly. Using traditional SIEM, this would be a manual process orchestrated across various security systems, each requiring specific configuration changes instrumented through separate interfaces/consoles. Considering the importance of limiting damage through containment and countermeasures to block kill chains, the response and remediation must be quick.

Enter the world of SOAR, and you have a new paradigm looking at reducing human touchpoints and expediting the response stream through predefined workflows, integrations, and countermeasures. Seceon aiSIEM™ incorporates this model through automation, semi-automation, and manual modes of threat remediation without the need to invest effort in building playbooks. Remediation-related actions can be configured against particular alerts on the aiSIEM portal, with the option of automating a specific countermeasure. For example, a firewall policy can be altered to drop any connection to a suspicious URL or block outbound connections from an endpoint to prevent malware propagation.

Collaborating for Success

A seamless cross-functional collaboration involving IT, networking, and security experts from all organizations was needed to bring the envisioned solution to life.

■ **Tool Selection**: The EH team collaborated with the GS Lab | GAVS team to assess the existing ecosystem. Together, we identified the deficiencies of the current platform and outlined the requirements for the new platform. This served as the foundation for evaluating several

SIEM platforms, ultimately leading us to select a platform tailored precisely to address these challenges to create an incident-free environment.

■ **Tri-party Collaboration**: Once the appropriate tool was identified, all three stakeholders—the product company, the implementation partner, and the customer—joined forces to facilitate a seamless transition from the old SIEM tool to the new one without disrupting operations. Daily synchronization meetings between all parties ensured the effective resolution of obstacles in a short timeframe.

■ **Deep Tech Collaboration**: The implementation process encountered a standstill when significant issues arose in synchronizing Windows and Linux-based operating system logs with the new SIEM tool. Proactive involvement from the EH team facilitated access to disparate systems, substantially reducing implementation time.

■ **Reducing Noise**: Immediately after the go-live phase, considerable noise was generated as data began to flow into the system. Minimizing this noise required extensive collaborative efforts to identify false positives and exceptions within the new system.

Key Outcome Highlights

■ Since implementing Seceon aiSIEM™ at EH by GS Lab | GAVS, the tool has analyzed over 1.16 billion events, flagging 80 million threat indicators.

■ The seamless integration of the MITRE framework with every alert triggered by the solution empowers the SOC team to identify and address MITRE attack techniques swiftly. This integration streamlines alert triage, prioritizing and mitigating critical threats promptly.

■ Implementing Seceon aiSIEM™'s advanced "Behavior Analytics," Engelwood cyber security team gained precise insights into user and host-level anomalous behavior. This capability enables SOC associates to effectively discern genuine threats from false positives, ensuring that resources focus on critical security issues.

■ This AI-based SEIM has SOAR capabilities, allowing EH to craft playbooks to automate alert responses. This automation significantly reduced response times, enabling rapid and efficient incident resolution.

Key Learning

A phased approach to SIEM implementation is a prudent strategy for healthcare organizations when migrating sensitive information. This method entails a systematic and gradual transition, beginning with critical devices and progressively expanding to encompass additional ecosystem components. This approach aims to ensure a smooth and controlled migration process while gaining a comprehensive understanding of how the monitoring tool integrates and functions within the healthcare environment.

The key benefits of adopting a Phased Approach are as follows:

- **Risk Mitigation**: By starting with critical devices, healthcare organizations can minimize the potential risks associated with data transfer. This allows them to focus on safeguarding the most vital aspects of their operations.
- **Requirement Assessment**: As the migration progresses, the organization can continually assess its evolving requirements. This ongoing evaluation ensures that the monitoring tool aligns with the organization's changing needs and objectives.
- **Operational Clarity**: A phased approach provides the opportunity to gain insights into how the monitoring tool operates within the healthcare environment. This operational clarity is crucial for fine-tuning the system, optimizing performance, and enhancing overall security.
- **Resource Allocation**: Gradual migration allows for efficient allocation of resources. Healthcare organizations can allocate resources judiciously based on the specific needs of each phase, optimizing budget utilization.
- **Adaptation and Learning**: The phased approach facilitates a learning curve for staff. As the monitoring tool is implemented in stages, teams can adapt to its functionalities progressively, reducing the potential for disruptions and ensuring a smoother transition.

In summary, a phased approach to implementation in healthcare minimizes risks. It provides the flexibility to adapt to changing requirements, gain operational clarity, optimize resource allocation, and facilitate a more seamless learning and adoption process for the organization.

CREATE ROADMAPS | REVOLUTIONIZING CLINICAL TRIALS | *BY TATYANA KANZAVELI*

Introduction

In the rapidly evolving landscape of healthcare, the integration of AI is not just an innovation; it's a necessity. At Open Health Network, we are at the forefront of this transformation. I am Tatyana Kanzaveli, the Founder and CEO, and I am excited to introduce TrialSphere, our groundbreaking generative AI solution for clinical trial protocol development. In this essay, I will discuss how TrialSphere is revolutionizing the way we create roadmaps for clinical trials, making the process faster, more efficient, and more reliable.

The Need for a Roadmap in Clinical Trials

Clinical trials are the backbone of medical advancements, yet the traditional process of protocol development is fraught with complexities. It's time-consuming, costly, and often riddled with inefficiencies. Creating a clear, strategic roadmap is crucial to navigating these challenges. A well-defined plan ensures that all stakeholders are aligned, resources are optimally utilized, and objectives are clearly outlined. TrialSphere steps in to streamline this process, offering a structured approach that leverages the power of generative AI.

The traditional approach to clinical trial protocol development often involves extensive manual effort, multiple iterations, and lengthy approval cycles. This cumbersome process can significantly delay the initiation of clinical trials, which in turn delays the delivery of potentially life-saving treatments to patients. The inefficiencies in this process are not just logistical but also financial. The high costs associated with protocol development can limit the scope of research and innovation, as resources are tied up in lengthy administrative processes.

Moreover, the lack of a standardized approach to protocol development can lead to inconsistencies and errors, further complicating the approval process. These challenges highlight the need for a more efficient and reliable method to create clinical trial protocols. This is where TrialSphere comes into play, offering a comprehensive solution that addresses these pain points and transforms the way clinical trials are conducted.

How TrialSphere Creates Effective Roadmaps

Automated Draft Creation

One of the most significant hurdles in clinical trial protocol development is the sheer amount of time it takes to draft a protocol. TrialSphere uses generative AI to automate this process, drastically reducing the time required. By analyzing vast datasets from previous trials, medical guidelines, and current research, TrialSphere generates a comprehensive draft protocol in a fraction of the time it would take manually. This automation not only speeds up the process but also ensures consistency and adherence to regulatory standards.

The automation capabilities of TrialSphere extend beyond mere drafting. The system is designed to learn from each iteration, continuously improving its accuracy and efficiency. By leveraging machine learning algorithms, TrialSphere can predict potential issues and suggest optimizations, ensuring that the draft protocols are of the highest quality. This level of automation not only reduces the workload for clinical trial teams but also minimizes the risk of human error, leading to more robust and reliable protocols.

Intelligent Data Integration

The integration of relevant data is critical for the accuracy and comprehensiveness of clinical trial protocols. TrialSphere excels in this area by intelligently integrating data from multiple sources. Whether it's historical trial data, current medical guidelines, or real-time research findings, TrialSphere assimilates this information seamlessly. This capability ensures that the draft protocols are not only comprehensive but also reflect the latest scientific and regulatory developments.

Intelligent data integration also facilitates better decision-making. By providing a holistic view of all relevant data, TrialSphere enables clinical trial teams to make informed decisions based on the most current and accurate information available. This not only improves the quality of the protocols but also enhances the overall efficiency of the clinical trial process. The ability to integrate and analyze data from various sources is a game-changer in the field of clinical trials, paving the way for more effective and timely research.

Regulatory Compliance Checks

Regulatory compliance is a significant concern in clinical trial protocols. Non-compliance can lead to costly delays and even trial terminations. TrialSphere incorporates built-in compliance checks that align with various regulatory standards, reducing the risk of non-compliance. This feature ensures that protocols meet all necessary requirements before they are submitted for approval, streamlining the regulatory review process.

The compliance checks in TrialSphere are designed to be comprehensive and adaptive. The system is continuously updated with the latest regulatory requirements, ensuring that the protocols generated are always in line with current standards. This proactive approach to compliance not only reduces the risk of regulatory issues but also accelerates the approval process. By ensuring that all protocols meet the necessary regulatory standards from the outset, TrialSphere minimizes delays and facilitates smoother, more efficient clinical trials.

Collaborative Review Platform

Effective communication and collaboration among stakeholders are essential for the success of clinical trials. TrialSphere offers a collaborative review platform that allows multiple stakeholders to review and refine protocols in real-time. This feature enhances communication, reduces errors, and ensures that all feedback is incorporated efficiently. The result is a streamlined approval process that accelerates the start of clinical trials.

The collaborative review platform in TrialSphere is designed to foster a more inclusive and participatory approach to protocol development. By enabling real-time collaboration, the platform ensures that all stakeholders, including clinical researchers, regulatory bodies, and trial sponsors, can provide input and feedback throughout the process. This not only improves the quality of the protocols but also builds consensus and alignment among all parties involved. The result is a more efficient and effective clinical trial process, with fewer delays and higher success rates.

Sample Use Case: TrialSphere in Action

Imagine a Phase II oncology trial where the traditional protocol development process typically takes 16 weeks and involves five full-time equivalents (FTEs). Using TrialSphere, the same protocol could be drafted in just three weeks, requiring only two FTEs. This significant reduction in time and resources would not only save costs but also allow the trial to start three months earlier than projected. The potential benefits are clear: faster initiation of the trial, reduced operational costs, and quicker delivery of potentially life-saving treatments to patients.

This sample use case highlights the transformative potential of TrialSphere in clinical trial protocol development. By automating and optimizing the process, TrialSphere enables clinical trial teams to focus on higher-value activities, such as patient recruitment and data analysis, rather than being bogged down by administrative tasks. The result is a more efficient and effective clinical trial process, with faster timelines and better outcomes for patients.

The Future of Clinical Trial Protocol Development

The implications of using generative AI in clinical trials extend far beyond speed and cost savings. TrialSphere represents the future of protocol development, where adaptive trials can modify protocols in real-time based on emerging data. This flexibility allows for more responsive and effective trial designs, ultimately leading to better patient outcomes and accelerated medical innovations. As we continue to refine and expand the capabilities of TrialSphere, we foresee a landscape where clinical trials are not only faster but also more adaptive and precise.

Phase One of a Larger Vision

It's important to note that TrialSphere is just the first phase in our broader vision for transforming the entire clinical trial process. Our future plans include integrating generative AI capabilities into other phases of clinical trials, from patient recruitment to data analysis and reporting. This holistic approach will ensure that every aspect of clinical trials benefits from the efficiencies and insights provided by AI, driving even greater improvements in speed, cost, and quality.

Adaptive trials represent a new frontier in clinical research, where protocols can be adjusted in real-time based on interim results and emerging data. This approach not only improves the efficiency of clinical trials but also enhances their scientific validity and relevance. By leveraging the power of generative AI, TrialSphere is well-positioned to lead this transformation, driving more effective and timely medical research.

Moreover, the continuous improvement capabilities of TrialSphere ensure that the system remains at the cutting edge of clinical trial protocol development. As new data and insights become available, TrialSphere can quickly incorporate them into its processes, ensuring that the protocols generated are always based on the latest and most accurate information. This ability to adapt and evolve is critical in the fast-paced world of medical research, where new discoveries and innovations are constantly emerging.

Conclusion

Generative AI, exemplified by TrialSphere, is revolutionizing clinical trial protocol development. By automating and optimizing the creation of protocols, we are reducing the time and costs associated with clinical trials, ensuring higher quality and compliance, and facilitating seamless collaboration. These advancements are not just theoretical; they are being realized in real-world applications, driving significant improvements in the speed and efficiency of clinical trials.

The impact of these advancements extends beyond the clinical trial process itself. By accelerating the development and approval of new treatments, TrialSphere is helping to bring life-saving therapies to patients faster. This has profound implications for public health, as faster access to new treatments can improve patient outcomes and save lives. Moreover, the cost savings associated with more efficient clinical trials can free up resources for further research and innovation, driving continued advancements in the field of medicine.

Invitation to Collaborate

We invite healthcare organizations, research institutions, and industry leaders to join us in this revolution. By partnering with Open Health Network, you can leverage the power of TrialSphere to enhance your clinical trial processes, accelerate medical breakthroughs, and bring innovative treatments to patients faster. Together, we can transform the future of healthcare.

The potential for collaboration is vast. Whether you are looking to streamline your clinical trial processes, improve regulatory compliance, or enhance collaboration among stakeholders, TrialSphere offers a comprehensive solution that can help you achieve your goals. By working together, we can drive innovation and make a lasting impact on healthcare.

CREATE ROADMAPS | GET READY FOR THE NEXT GENERATION OF AI: QUANTUM TECHNOLOGIES | *BY GREG SKULMOSKI AND ASHKAN MEMARI*

A new form of AI is on the horizon that will transform healthcare and other industries in unimaginable ways. The purpose of this book chapter is to foreshadow the next generation of quantum technologies that are ideally suited to healthcare AI applications. Early adopters, innovators, and other thought leaders in healthcare can champion actions today (regarding technology, processes, and people) to guide their organizations to a quantum technologies ecosystem to optimize caregiving.

Introduction

AI is a suite of technologies like the Internet of Things (IoT), big data, machine learning, and deep neural networks used collectively to mimic human intelligence to assist people in various ways, like improved decision-making and problem-solving. Our current generation of technologies (e.g., classical computing based on bits and bytes) powers AI applications to provide staggering capabilities at home and work.

But wait! Powerful quantum technologies are emerging to propel AI applications to offer capabilities never before imagined. Quantum technologies are rapidly advancing and will be implemented to solve some of the world's most challenging problems that are tough to solve within a reasonable time, even with the most sophisticated classical supercomputers. Not only will copious computing power be available, but the *way* quantum computing is performed is radically different (e.g., quantum bits, superimposition, and entanglement, as described by Rietsche et al., 2022). A quantum computing ecosystem is like racing a car against a helicopter: The helicopter is faster and can lift you off the ground and fly you to Mt. Everest Base Camp! Thus, quantum computing applied to AI technologies will transform healthcare decision-making and problem-solving. Healthcare leaders, early adopters, disrupters, tinkerers, innovators, and other quantum champions can play a role today in bringing quantum technologies into healthcare, including the next generation of AI. In this context, it is essential to understand the potential of quantum technologies and how they can be leveraged to create value. In this chapter, we explore the latest insights into quantum technologies and how they are expected to shape the future of AI in healthcare systems.

Quantum Technologies: The Next Generation of AI

Before looking at quantum technologies in healthcare and the transformational change on the horizon, we review how AI can deliver improved problem-solving and decision-making capabilities, which is different from popular generative AI technologies used to create data in the form of images, songs, text, manuals, poetry, and so forth.

Problem-Solving and Decision-Making with AI

While AI technologies are impressive, what they promise to do in health-care is transformational. Healthcare involves considerable problem-solving and decision-making, whether clinical or non-clinical. AI can help answer four key problem-solving and decision-making questions (Gartner, 2017) for caregivers:

1. **Descriptive**: What happened? A description of basic facts, patterns, and characteristics about something that happened in the past.
2. **Diagnostic**: What did happen? Go beyond descriptive analysis and determine why particular events or patterns occurred.
3. **Predictive**: What will happen? Use historical data (e.g., big data) and mathematical algorithms (machine learning) to forecast future trends or sevents.
4. **Prescriptive**: What should I do? The highest level of analysis, where recommendations are provided based on descriptive, diagnostic, and predictive analyses.

To answer these questions, AI uses a collection of technologies like machine learning, big data, and IoT (Figure 4.2) powered with classical central processing units (CPUs) and, shortly, more powerful quantum CPUs and associated technologies. Machine learning includes technologies that support mathematical models (algorithms) to predict and learn from data where the model's accuracy improves over time. Big data is data, but with i) massive volumes of data (structured and unstructured), ii) in a wide variety of forms, and iii) can be processed at a sufficient rate (velocity) to be helpful. Big data can be inputs to machine learning mathematical models (e.g., quantum neural networks). Machine learning models may also use data from IoT

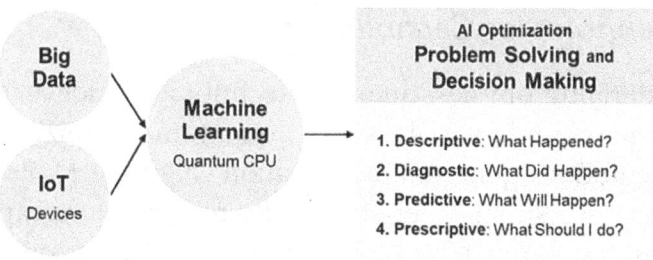

Figure 4.2 Quantum AI Technologies.

devices (e.g., medical devices like those used for remote patient monitoring). Connecting IoT devices to the internet to exchange data can be inputs to machine learning systems used by caregivers for decision-making and problem-solving.

Quantum CPUs will power machine learning models in the future at speeds unseen before to provide revolutionary AI capabilities. As described in this *Voices of Innovation* book, AI capabilities have already transformed healthcare, and more innovation is emerging, made possible with formidable quantum CPUs and supporting technologies.

Quantum Technologies 101

Early adopters pursue quantum computing because of the ability to process large volumes of data at unparalleled speed; at the time of writing, an early quantum computer with the *Sycamore* quantum CPU developed by Google was "156 million times faster than the world's fastest supercomputer" (France, 2023, p. 1) even without full error correction. The Google quantum computer can accomplish in four minutes what a supercomputer would take 10,000 years to complete. Such speeds can provide new opportunities and digital capabilities.

Quantum technologies are based on quantum mechanics, which is a fundamentally different way of computational computing. For example, in classical computing, bits can either be a 1 or 0, while in quantum computing, we use qubits that simultaneously can be both! This multidimensionality allows a quantum computer to calculate all the combinations *simultaneously* rather than *sequentially*, as in classical computing. For emphasis, simultaneous rather than sequential calculations will transform AI in healthcare. We leave it to the reader to more fully explore the mechanics of quantum computing while we examine the capabilities that quantum technologies can deliver.

Quantum Technologies Capabilities

Due to the underlying physics, quantum technologies deliver four types of capabilities: i) quantum linear algebra, ii) quantum optimization, iii) quantum simulation, and iv) quantum factorization (Figure 4.3). Early in our quantum journey, we should identify the desired quantum capabilities (e.g., optimization or simulation) we wish to bring to our organization (e.g., the target state). For example, do we want to optimize a workflow (e.g., minimize or maximize targets) or develop a new molecular

1. Quantum Linear Algebra*

A diverse field of quantum linear algebra techniques (e.g., neural networks) often used in AI and machine learning (e.g., speedy matrix multiplications) to exponentially decrease the model training time

2. Quantum Optimization*

Applying quantum algorithms to find the best solution (maximize or minimize) including combinatorial optimization (finding the best solution from a finite number of permutations/combinations), and algorithms to speed up searches (Grover's algorithm to search unstructured databases)

3. Quantum Simulation

Simulation techniques to mimic and model quantum molecular systems and processes that are intractable for classical computers allowing new insights such as drug discovery and new materials

4. Quantum Factorization

The process of using quantum computers and algorithms (e.g., Shor's algorithm for integer factorization) to factor very large integers into their prime components that is problematic for classical computers

*Our focus in "Quantum Technologies: The Next Generation of AI"

Figure 4.3 Quantum Technologies Key Capabilities.

compound (e.g., quantum simulation to model molecular systems)? They require different skill sets and technologies for which we can begin planning. While we focus on optimization through AI quantum technologies (e.g., quantum linear algebra and quantum optimization with heavy box outline in Figure 4.4), we marvel at the simulation capabilities in healthcare that quantum technologies can bring (Biondi et al., 2021)

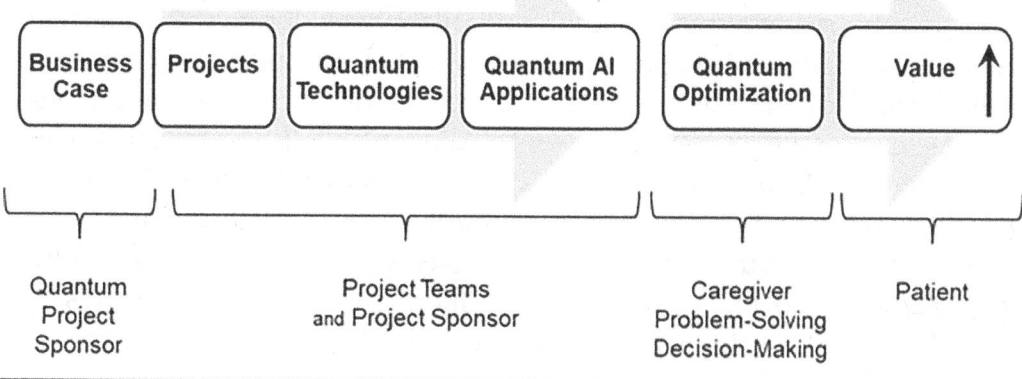

Figure 4.4 Quantum AI Value Proposition.

and recommend action to manage the encryptogeddon threat of quantum factorization in the hands of cyber threat actors (Deloitte, 2022).

As AI is a collection of technologies, one can use these technologies in combinations to aid problem-solving and decision-making:

1. Apply quantum linear algebra to machine learning models for faster processing (e.g., the quantum technologies speed up principle component analysis in machine learning algorithms).
2. Apply quantum optimization to machine learning models to find multiple optimal solutions.
3. Apply quantum search algorithms to machine learning models to optimize decision-making using unstructured databases.
4. Apply Monte Carlo Simulation techniques to quantum machine learning models to speed up probability sampling.

Therefore, organizations are well-served to document in their business case the type of quantum capabilities to implement (Figure 4.4). The project sponsor develops a business case that outlines the quantum use case (e.g., minimizing the clinical pathology diagnosis workflow times). A project is initiated to leverage the quantum technologies available in the cloud as a customized quantum AI application. The project is planned, designed, built, tested, implemented, stabilized, and closed out. Caregivers use the quantum AI application, followed by continual improvement initiatives. Clinical pathologists use the quantum application to minimize diagnosis time, which patients and caregivers value.

This end-to-end process is a common way an IT department manages technology and is detailed in the Information Technology Infrastructure Library (ITIL) framework. Notice that the process begins and ends with the end user who requests new technology, collaborates during the project (e.g., requirements elaboration and user acceptance testing), and then derives value from the digital product or service as outlined in the quantum business case and technical use case. ITIL guides the IT and business teams to add new products and services like quantum technologies to the IT strategy (Axelos, 2020). Together, the clinical and non-clinical quantum champions proceed through a series of projects with technology teams to bring quantum capabilities to the organization. The ITIL process begins with a business case that includes the specific technology use case: the quantum AI use case.

Six Notional Quantum AI Use Cases

The service owner (e.g., project sponsor) prepares the detailed business case as taught in MBA programs. The business case may include market and financial analysis and strategy, risk analysis, service management plan, and resourcing. A use case is more specific and identifies the specific scenario, problem, or workflow the technology addresses.

Quantum AI technologies can be applied to clinical and non-clinical problem-solving and decision-making tasks (Figure 4.5). The quantum AI application can help answer the prescriptive question: "What should I do to optimize the workflow?" (Figure 4.2). The quantum AI application will process massive amounts of data (structured and unstructured) through the machine learning model using quantum neural networks to quickly find optimum solutions to the problem (e.g., simultaneous rather than consecutive calculations). The six notional use cases optimize process flows to minimize certain variables while maximizing other variables in the quantum machine learning model. These use cases are based on the early generations of quantum technologies appropriate for "easier" and less complex calculations represented in the quantum use case.

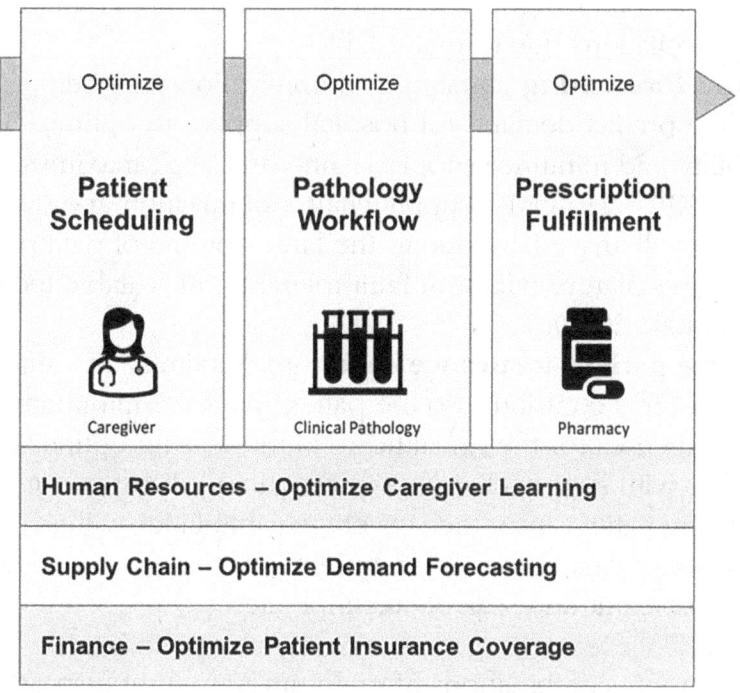

Figure 4.5   Notional Quantum AI Use Cases in Healthcare.

Following are three clinical and three non-clinical quantum use cases:

1. **Patient scheduling**: Quantum-powered AI applications will be able to maximize the utilization of appointment slots and hospital beds with the appropriate clinical and supporting caregivers (e.g., competency-based scheduling) and medical equipment while minimizing waiting times as the patient progresses through their care journey.

2. **Pathology workflow optimization**: Quantum-driven AI applications in the lab will maximize the use of clinical pathology equipment and specialists and minimize waiting times for the patient and ordering physician as specimens progress through the clinical pathology workflows (e.g., simultaneous quantum searches of many clinical pathology databases to analyze and interpret data).

3. **Prescription fulfillment**: Quantum AI applications will maximize the utilization of the pharmacy team and minimize patient waiting times for the prescription fulfillment process.

4. **Learning optimization**: Quantum AI applications can optimize caregiver learning so that certifications (e.g., intubation skills and procedures) do not lapse and just-in-time training is scheduled and completed, optimizing resourcing capabilities and minimizing appointment cancellations due to unavailable caregivers.

5. **Demand forecasting**: Quantum AI applications can help supply chain specialists predict demand for hospital supplies to optimize inventory availability and minimize supply chain costs (e.g., maximize inventory turnover KPIs). However, supply chain optimization and disruption modeling will arrive later due to the large volume of data processing that requires mature quantum fault-tolerant and scalable technologies (Biondi et al., 2021).

6. **Maximize patient insurance coverage**: Maximize the amount of money insurers contribute so the patient pays the minimum out-of-pocket expenses for their healthcare journey using optimization algorithms. As with supply chain optimization and disruption modeling, maximizing patient insurance coverage capabilities will arrive later due to heavy-duty data processing requirements that require mature quantum fault-tolerant and scalable technologies.

Thus, we can apply combinations of quantum AI, neural networks, and machine learning technologies to optimize (minimize and/or maximize) objectives, workflows, and resources on both the clinical and non-clinical side of healthcare to benefit patients and staff. Notice that we often want to optimize the flow through a process and maximize and minimize objectives. We can apply these quantum AI technologies outside healthcare, such as air traffic control and garbage collection.

- **Air traffic control**: Quantum AI applications will help maximize airport resource utilization (e.g., people and equipment) and passenger throughput and minimize waiting times.
- **City garbage collection**: Quantum AI applications will be able to maximize garbage collection workers and equipment usage and minimize garbage can overflow incidents.

These non-healthcare use cases are also based on AI technologies like combinatorial optimization and machine learning and are powered by quantum technologies. Therefore, we expect quantum computing to have broad applicability within and outside of healthcare; however, there are enormous entry barriers (e.g., high costs and specialized skill sets), and we leave the economics and public policy considerations for others.

Implementing Quantum AI Technologies

There are three main ways organizations will adopt quantum technologies:

1. **In-house computing**: Implement quantum technologies in a dedicated space in your organization (e.g., your server rooms), as did Cleveland Clinic in 2023 to advance biomedical research combining high-performance computing, quantum computing, and AI (Cleveland Clinic, 2023). In-house computing is the traditional approach to enterprise computing and is supported by an internal computer department. The organization will need specialists who can use a quantum programming language like Qiskit and follow software engineering best practices to create specialized healthcare applications (e.g., clinical pathology process optimization).
2. **Quantum Computing-as-a-Service**: Where organizations lease time and services to connect to a vendor's quantum computing infrastructure in the cloud rather than having the quantum computing system on their premises (in-house). The organization can experiment and develop quantum applications to address unique problems and opportunities.

3. **Quantum applications in the cloud**: Your favorite software vendors will transition to quantum-ready and quantum-secure applications in the cloud. Quantum technologies will be applied to standard and high-value workflows (e.g., clinical pathology specimen analysis and reporting, financial year-end close-out process, program scheduling, and supply chain disruption modeling) to optimize the movement through processes. Expect top clinical and business application vendors to introduce quantum use cases and technologies into their software platforms in the cloud.

Quantum-driven AI in healthcare begins with customized software written to complete specific tasks; commercially available quantum applications from your favorite vendors will follow. The developing Quantum-as-a-Service technical approach allows organizations to learn and experiment as they develop their IT and business strategies to transition to quantum technologies.

Radwin and Hussein (2020) wrote *Quantum Computing as a Saviour* to explain quantum computing and AI opportunities and threats. While quantum computing might appear as a technological savior, it also brings the potential for great harm: the dual potentialities of technology.

Dual Potentialities of Quantum Technologies

We know that technologies are inherently neutral; they can be used in a good way (e.g., use a word processor to write a quantum use case) or a negative way (e.g., use a word processor to write extorting ransomware letters). The dual potentialities of quantum computing include promises of transformational capabilities like finding a cure for cancer, yet hackers may use powerful quantum computing algorithms to break current encryption algorithms. Hackers using quantum technologies can quickly and effortlessly break existing encryption (e.g., RSA algorithm) and take whatever they want: personally identifiable information, health information, financial information, intellectual property, and more like nuclear system launch codes. Therefore, to avoid *encryptogeddon*, organizations should be planning their transition to post-quantum cryptography to replace existing technologies (e.g., operating systems, hardware, middleware, application software, and IoT devices) with new, quantum-resistant algorithms to keep healthcare systems data secure.

The implication for healthcare leadership is that there will be a decade or so of projects to secure systems and data from quantum attacks. Healthcare leaders will prepare their organizations for transformative quantum AI capabilities and participate in post-quantum cryptographic transition projects to safeguard their data. Unfortunately, it may already be too late for some organizations, as threat actors may steal sensitive data today and wait until they have quantum technologies to break its classical encryption (also known as "steal now, decrypt later").

Leading the Quantum AI Transition

Quantum computing is nascent, and we can use this lead time to prepare our organizations to manage its arrival. Quantum champions can work in three areas to prepare for the next generation of AI technologies: technology, people, and processes.

Technology

Continue learning about quantum technologies in general (e.g., quantum bits, superimposition, and entanglement) and, specifically, their capabilities (Figure 4.2) as they pertain to your organization and professional discipline. Monitor quantum application and workflow development from your favorite vendors (hardware and software).

Quantum computing will change the cyber threat landscape, and your data will be at risk and needs to be protected by updating the cryptographic algorithms. Therefore, learn about post-quantum cryptography and cryptographic agility, two other complex quantum technology programs your IT teams will undertake, and may request your involvement. Ensure your medical device equipment manufacturers have a quantum upgrade path.

Process

Identify processes in your organization and unit that are promising candidates for optimization (minimize or maximize). The Lean Six Sigma approach is ideally suited for process optimization, with a certification program to boost competency in this approach. Indeed, you can find free online Lean Six Sigma courses. Ask your favorite software vendors how quantum AI technologies can improve workflows (e.g., how can quantum

AI improve clinical pathology workflows like managing orders, results, test records, auto-verification quality control, specimen storage, tracking, reporting, and billing?). Process improvement projects using the Lean Six Sigma approach can begin before implementing quantum technologies. Improving processes are known as "no-regret projects."

People

Finally, we can enhance our quantum journey by developing quantum-related competencies for tomorrow's opportunities and challenges. Encourage hands-on quantum experience in your organization and unit; increasingly, there are opportunities to learn quantum programming languages and to experiment with quantum technologies. Major technology providers (e.g., IBM, Microsoft, Amazon, and Google) offer quantum technologies training and certifications. Review job descriptions for new positions and revise them for AI and quantum-related competencies (e.g., look for people who like Python programming).

Quantum technologies are on the horizon and are making their way into our technical strategies. Quantum technologies may arrive suddenly, like the arrival and disruption of ChatGPT in 2022, or more gradually and linearly. Whatever trajectory, we must prepare our people, technologies, and processes ahead of the dual potentialities of a quantum-relevant computer (Mosca and Piani 2022).

Conclusion

We are inspired by the term "Quantum as a Savior' as we appreciate the transformative capabilities promised by the next generation of quantum AI. Whether simulating new drug compounds or optimizing workflows, quantum computing is *the next big thing*. When we pair quantum computing with AI, we will see more process automation, fewer manual steps, reduced administrative burden, and increased quality. Problem-solving and decision-making are enhanced with the descriptive, diagnostic, predictive, and prescriptive capabilities enabled by new technologies like quantum machine learning and neural networks (Figure 4.1).

However, our technological savior also has a dark side; quantum technologies in the wrong hands threaten all organizations and people. Therefore, astute organizations are planning their transition to post-quantum cryptography solutions to protect sensitive and critical data. Since clinical (e.g., imaging) and non-clinical departments (e.g., finance) produce and use data, they will be invited to participate in quantum readiness projects. Therefore, we recommend forward-thinking leaders to become quantum champions to bring the next generation of quantum AI technologies into their organizations.

CREATE ROADMAPS | NLP IN IMAGING TECHNOLOGY CAN IMPROVE THE DIAGNOSIS OF LUNG CANCER | BY DURGA MALLESWARI

Background

Lung cancer, ranked second globally in cancer incidence and foremost in cancer-related mortality, poses challenges in timely diagnosis and treatment. Despite advancements like low-dose computed tomography (LDCT) screening, accurately discerning malignant from benign nodules remains a critical hurdle.

This study examines the integration of Natural Language Processing (NLP) in radiology reports, leveraging its capacity to extract insights from unstructured text. NLP not only aids in distinguishing between normal and cancerous nodules but also facilitates the identification of early symptoms, potentially revolutionizing lung cancer diagnosis and improving patient outcomes.

For the year 2023, lung cancer is projected to be responsible for an estimated 238,340 new cases and 127,070 deaths (Lung Cancer Research Foundation, 2023). Its prognosis is contingent on timely and accurate diagnosis, which informs the choice of treatment, be it surgery, radiotherapy, or systemic drug therapy, and ultimately patient outcomes (L. Wang et al., 2019). Imaging plays a pivotal role in the diagnosis and staging of lung cancer, standing as the most prevalent oncological cause of death (Nobel et al., 2021).

Introduction

NLP is an AI technology that has immense potential to revolutionize lung cancer diagnosis and care. By enabling computers to understand, process, and extract valuable insights from unstructured medical data like radiology reports, clinical notes, and electronic health records, NLP can significantly enhance diagnostic accuracy, efficiency, and early detection capabilities. Given the complexity, high mortality rate of lung cancer and the critical importance of timely diagnosis, NLP offers a promising solution to improve diagnostic practices and patient management.

Methodology

This comprehensive study evaluated the role of NLP in tackling the challenges of lung cancer diagnosis through an extensive review of relevant peer-reviewed research articles published between 2018 and 2024. The rigorous methodology involved systematically searching major medical databases, including CINAHL, MEDLINE, PubMed, and IEEE Xplore, and carefully screening the results to select studies directly relevant to NLP applications for analyzing unstructured radiology data in lung cancer diagnosis.

Results

The findings are organized into three primary themes that highlight NLP's transformative impact. First, NLP demonstrably improves diagnostic accuracy by effectively distinguishing between benign and malignant pulmonary nodules on imaging scans. Crucially, studies showed NLP models achieved a remarkable sensitivity of 0.99 and specificity of 0.94 in detecting concerning nodule characteristics indicative of lung cancer during internal validation (Hunter et al., 2021). This level of accuracy can significantly reduce misdiagnoses and ensure timely interventions.

Second, NLP vastly enhances diagnostic efficiency by automating the extraction of critical data elements from unstructured radiology reports. Techniques like the Temporal Tagger achieved an F1-score of 0.93 for accurately identifying date expressions within clinical documents (Najafabadipour et al., 2020). This ability to swiftly parse and structure unstructured data can streamline diagnostic workflows, saving valuable time and resources for healthcare providers.

Third, and perhaps most crucially, NLP demonstrates remarkable potential in aiding early lung cancer detection by identifying key symptoms and risk factors from electronic health records. Studies highlighted NLP's ability to flag high-risk indicators like finger clubbing, lymphadenopathy, hemoptysis, and others, enabling earlier diagnosis when combined with screening programs (Prado et al., 2023). Given lung cancer's high mortality rates and the importance of early treatment, this application of NLP could significantly improve patient outcomes.

Discussion

The study underscores the transformative potential of NLP in lung cancer diagnosis. By analyzing unstructured radiology reports, NLP significantly improves diagnostic accuracy, efficiency, and early detection capabilities. These advancements can substantially reduce diagnostic errors, streamline clinical workflows, and enable data-driven medical decisions, ultimately enhancing patient outcomes. For example, the high sensitivity and specificity of NLP models in identifying malignant nodules can assist radiologists in making more accurate diagnoses, thereby minimizing missed or misinterpreted cases.

Moreover, integrating NLP with existing screening programs, such as LDCT, offers a powerful complementary approach. NLP can extract critical information from unstructured data, enhancing the efficacy of LDCT screenings and facilitating earlier detection of lung cancer when it is most treatable. This could lead to significant reductions in mortality rates and improved prognoses for patients.

The study exemplifies the immense potential of combining cutting-edge AI with healthcare data to drive precision medicine. By enabling more accurate and timely diagnoses, NLP can improve the quality and efficiency of lung cancer care delivery. These findings highlight the importance of continued research and development in NLP technologies to further enhance their impact on healthcare.

Significance

The implications of these findings are profound for the fields of healthcare, informatics, and public policy. By reducing diagnostic errors, streamlining clinical workflows, and enabling data-driven medical decisions, NLP integration can drive substantial improvements in the quality and efficiency of lung cancer care delivery. Moreover, when coupled with existing screening initiatives like low-dose CT scans, NLP offers a complementary solution to enhance early detection efforts, potentially saving countless lives and significantly improving patient outcomes.

From an informatics perspective, this study exemplifies the immense potential of blending cutting-edge AI with healthcare data to extract valuable insights and drive precision medicine. It underscores the transformative impact such technologies can have on clinical practice and patient outcomes while highlighting avenues for future innovation.

Limitations

However, the study also acknowledges certain limitations that must be addressed through further research. These include the reliance on existing datasets for model training, which may not capture the full diversity of clinical scenarios, the potential for biases within these datasets to propagate into NLP systems, and the inherently limited scope of focusing exclusively on radiology reports rather than a comprehensive multi-modal diagnostic approach.

To build upon these findings, there is a need for expanding and diversifying NLP model training datasets, implementing rigorous debiasing techniques, and exploring the integration of NLP with other diagnostic tools and data sources for a nuanced, multifaceted lung cancer screening and diagnosis solution. Overcoming these challenges through continued research and development could unlock NLP's full potential as a core component of precision oncology.

Conclusion

In conclusion, this study presents compelling evidence of NLP's ability to revolutionize lung cancer diagnosis and care delivery. By harnessing AI to extract insights from unstructured medical data, NLP demonstrates remarkable prowess in enhancing diagnostic accuracy, efficiency, and early detection capabilities—three pillars critical to improving treatment outcomes for this deadly disease. While challenges remain, the transformative potential of integrating NLP into healthcare systems is undeniable, paving the way for a future of data-driven, personalized cancer care that could save countless lives. The introduction of NLP is expected to reduce diagnostic times, lower healthcare costs by minimizing unnecessary procedures, and improve patient outcomes through earlier and more precise diagnoses (C. Li et al., 2023; Huang et al., 2023). This innovative approach holds significant potential for revolutionizing lung cancer diagnosis, resulting in earlier and more precise detection of the condition (Rawat et al., 2023).

Future Directions

Future research should aim to address the current limitations by expanding NLP model training datasets to include a broader and more diverse range of clinical scenarios. Additionally, efforts should be made to mitigate potential biases in these datasets to ensure equitable and accurate diagnostic outcomes across different patient demographics.

Furthermore, the integration of NLP with other diagnostic tools, such as imaging technologies and genomic data, could provide a more comprehensive approach to lung cancer diagnosis and treatment. This multi-modal strategy would leverage the strengths of various diagnostic modalities, enhancing the overall accuracy and effectiveness of lung cancer screening and early detection efforts. Ultimately, these advancements could significantly improve patient outcomes and reduce lung cancer mortality rates.

CREATE ROADMAPS | NAVIGATING THE PATH, TURNING VISION INTO SUCCESSFUL ANALYTICS, THROUGH SIMPLICITY, CLARITY, AND COLLABORATION | *BY SHAUN GARCIA*

Introduction

> Traveler, there is no path,
> The path is made by walking.
> By walking the path is made,
> And when you look back
> You'll see a road never to be trodden again.

> **—Antonio Machado**
> *(Spanish Poet)*

In healthcare, we embark on a journey like a traveler in Antonio Machado's poem, navigating an uncharted path shaped by our steps. This journey is not predefined but crafted through our relentless pursuit of innovation, efforts to unravel the complexities of our systems, and endeavors to enhance patient care through the lens of analytics.

As a clinician, I have experienced firsthand the frustration of navigating this landscape while providing the best possible care for patients. And as an operator and analytics leader, I've seen how this complexity can hinder our efforts to drive meaningful change and innovation.

Consider the challenges healthcare organizations face when dealing with multiple health plans, each with unique data-sharing processes and formats. One health plan uses its own acronyms and terminology to represent distinct areas they are focusing on, while another provides data in Excel sheets. Some plans may require you to access their proprietary portal to retrieve data, while others offer widgets to integrate with your EHR. Now, imagine navigating this complexity across eight different health plans, each with its own requirements and processes. This multifaceted environment compelled us to take a foundational approach.

In this initial stage, our focus was on descriptive analytics. By examining historical data, we uncovered patterns that would inform our strategies. By reviewing historical patient data, we discerned patterns in chronic disease management and identified a notable trend in hypertension medication adherence. This valuable insight spurred us to create personalized patient education sessions, significantly improving our medication adherence rates and patient outcomes. Depending on the location within the United States, healthcare delivery organizations often work with more than eight health plans, which further amplifies the complexity and challenges.

Tech-enabled healthcare delivery partners may expect you to work within their portals, adding another layer of complexity to an already fragmented data landscape and further complicating matters. Despite these hurdles, we recognized the necessity of a strategic framework to navigate through the noise.

But what if I told you that the key to transforming healthcare analytics lies not in more complexity but in simplicity? By focusing on clear road-maps, human-centered design, and a people-first approach, we can unlock the true potential of data-informed decision-making.

Throughout my career, I've had the privilege of serving in various roles that have given me a unique perspective on the challenges and opportunities facing healthcare today. As a General Practitioner, I experienced the challenges of delivering high-quality patient care in a complex and often fragmented system. As a Business Operations Manager and Health Plan Liaison, I gained a deep understanding of healthcare organizations' operational and financial complexities and the importance of aligning incentives and goals across stakeholders.

During my tenure as Chief Quality Officer at Brevard Health Alliance, I navigated the complexities of value-based care (VBC) as both the architect and strategist of our healthcare system. Our community health center uniquely addresses medical, dental, and behavioral health, pushing the envelope in areas often sidelined in traditional VBC models. This broad approach underscores the power of data and analytics in enhancing care and highlights the importance of simplicity, clarity, and a patient-centered focus in transforming healthcare delivery.

Creating a Roadmap for Success

One of the most critical factors in driving successful analytics initiatives is having a clear roadmap that defines your vision and priorities over a specific timeframe. Given the rapid pace of change in healthcare analytics, a 2–3-year horizon strikes the right balance between long-term strategic thinking and short-term agility.

When faced with the challenge of transitioning our organization from fee-for-service to VBC, we knew that analytics would be critical to our success. We engaged stakeholders from across the organization to create a comprehensive 2–3-year roadmap outlining our key objectives, milestones, and metrics. This ensured our plan was grounded in the realities of patient care and aligned with our strategic goals.

To prioritize initiatives based on impact and feasibility, we started by looking at our organization's vision: where did we want to be in 3–5 years? This long-term perspective provided the foundation for our roadmap, allowing us to identify the incremental steps needed to achieve our goals from an analytics and informatics standpoint. This practical, phased approach was integral to our forward momentum.

We recognized that analytics data comes from disparate sources, including EHRs and other systems, each with varying levels of data quality. To ensure the success of our initiatives, we needed to be prepared to work with each data set in its current state, which required tedious and detailed work but was essential for achieving our objectives.

Key elements of our roadmap included:

■ A phased approach to implementation, prioritizing initiatives based on impact and feasibility over the 2–3-year timeframe.
■ Clear communication and accountability with both internal and external stakeholders.
■ Regular check-ins and progress reports to keep everyone informed and aligned.

By clearly communicating our roadmap to external stakeholders, we had more productive conversations about how their offerings could support our efforts rather than getting sidetracked by one-off initiatives that didn't align with our strategy. This proactive approach helped us stay focused, build stronger partnerships, and successfully navigate the transition to VBC while laying the foundation for a more data-informed, patient-centered approach to care delivery.

The Case for Simplicity

As we worked to implement our analytics roadmap, one of the biggest challenges we faced was the constant pressure from external stakeholders to adopt the latest tools and solutions. It's easy to get caught up in the allure of these shiny new objects, but it's crucial to recognize that only some new tools are the right fit for your organization, not all. In such situations, it's essential to have the courage to say no and stay focused on your company's strategic objectives.

It's important to acknowledge that health plans and healthcare delivery organizations may have different priorities and time horizons. As a not-for-profit healthcare delivery organization, we have the flexibility to prioritize long-term objectives and the well-being of our patients. However, we can still work together effectively. We can build strong partnerships with health plans and other stakeholders by communicating clearly and transparently about our strategic goals and the reasoning behind our decisions. Being a good business partner means not only saying no when necessary but also explaining our rationale and exploring alternative solutions that align with our shared objectives. This is especially critical during the healthcare delivery transformation phase, when collaboration and mutual understanding are essential for success.

One particularly challenging example came when a large health plan approached us with a widget that would bolt onto our EHR. However, we realized that the widget only supported their specific plan, and we worked with at least eight others. Implementing it would have meant excluding other partners or adding a confusing array of plan-specific tools to our already complex EHR environment, causing chaos and frustration for our clinicians at the point of care. To make matters worse, even our EHR vendor came to us with a widget that worked with only a handful of health plans. Had we implemented both widgets, the distraction and frustration for our clinicians and staff would have been compounded.

Drawing on my clinical experience and understanding of the constraints these widgets can place on clinicians and staff, we carefully evaluated the potential impact of implementing these tools. We considered factors such as the additional cognitive load they would put on our care teams, the time it would take to navigate between different widgets, and the potential for confusion and errors that could arise from juggling multiple plan-specific tools.

Ultimately, despite the pressure, we made the difficult decision to say no to both widgets. We recognized that they would create more complexity and friction for our clinicians, detracting from their ability to deliver their fundamental role of patient-centered care. This deliberate focus on simplicity paved the way for a more human-centric perspective. This decision allowed us to stay focused on our roadmap and avoid a situation where our EHR became a confusing patchwork of plan-specific tools.

The key lesson here is that simplicity isn't always easy, but it's essential for driving meaningful, sustainable change. Saying no and staying focused on your priorities, goals, and vision is crucial. By keeping analytics initiatives focused on core priorities and considering the impact on end-users, you can avoid the pitfalls of over-complexity and ensure your efforts deliver real value. While it's important to consider new tools and solutions, it's crucial to be intentional and strategic about how and when you integrate them into your roadmap.

Putting People at the Center

Throughout my career, I've learned that the most powerful analytics tools are only as effective as those using them. If your solutions meet the needs of your clinicians, staff, and operational teams, they can deliver real impact.

Putting people at the center of your analytics initiatives is critical. By understanding the day-to-day realities and challenges of those on the front lines, you can design solutions that make a meaningful difference in their work and the lives of our patients.

During my time as a practicing physician, I saw how the lack of human-centered design in our EHR caused frustration and burnout among my colleagues. This experience stuck with me, so I can reach back to it. To drive change, I worked closely with our IT team and an experienced informaticist to identify pain points and workflow challenges, designing targeted solutions to streamline processes and reduce cognitive load.

We engaged representatives of the clinical staff, including medical assistants, nurses, and clinicians, to review the proposed changes on a weekly or monthly basis, depending on the size and scope of the initiative. This iterative process allowed us to gather valuable feedback, identify potential issues early on, and refine our solutions to better meet the needs of our end-users. It's crucial to note that when compromises need to be made in human-centered design, prioritizing the needs of clinicians and clinical staff should always come first. Administrators can often find alternative ways to understand and work with data, but clinicians need tools that seamlessly integrate with their workflows as they make critical decisions every minute. By ensuring that data works for clinicians, we can maintain a patient-centered focus and ultimately improve outcomes.

Of course, this human-centered approach applies to stakeholders across your organization. To drive impact, you must engage and empower everyone, from frontline staff to executive decision-makers.

We did this by establishing cross-functional teams and governance structures that brought together diverse perspectives and expertise, creating forums for collaboration and knowledge-sharing to break down silos. We also invested heavily in training and education to ensure our staff had the skills and knowledge to leverage analytics effectively in their work.

Navigating Change and Complexity

Implementing analytics in healthcare involves navigating change and managing multiple stakeholders with competing demands. Focusing on simplicity and a clear roadmap can help you successfully manage these complexities.

When building our data governance framework, we faced differing opinions from various departments on implementation. Rather than getting bogged down in these competing visions, we focused on finding the simplest, most pragmatic solution that met our core requirements while allowing for flexibility and adaptation over time.

By taking a phased approach to implementation and demonstrating early wins, we were able to build momentum and support for our governance efforts, even as we continued to refine and expand our policies over time.

The key to navigating change and complexity is to stay focused on your core principles, communicate clearly and consistently with your stakeholders, and be willing to make tough choices to serve your larger goals. You can cut through the noise and drive meaningful, measurable impact by embracing simplicity, building a clear roadmap, and maintaining alignment with your organizational priorities.

Outcomes and Benefits

By following the principles of simplicity, clear roadmaps, and human-centered design, we've not only adhered to the core tenets of VBC but also achieved significant outcomes and benefits across multiple dimensions through our data analytics initiatives. These initiatives have yielded impressive results, which serve as a powerful testament to what we can achieve across our entire organization.

In our first two years, we made modest but meaningful wins, such as increasing cervical cancer screening rates by 8.2%, colorectal cancer screening rates by 15%, and improving the percentage of patients with controlled blood pressure by 12.1%. These foundational achievements reflect our commitment to a data-informed approach to quality improvement and population health management.

Leveraging our analytics has enabled us to identify variations in care processes and outcomes, developing standardized best practices that improved consistency and quality across all care sites. Fundamentally, we transformed our organizational culture to embrace a data-informed, human-centered approach, fostering collaboration and innovation.

Brevard Health Alliance's data-informed approach has enabled us to deliver more patient-centered care, manage population health more effectively, control costs while maintaining quality, support provider well-being, and foster a collaborative and inclusive care team environment. As a primary care delivery organization, this matters profoundly.

The financial and operational efficiency metrics highlighted here represent only one health plan, demonstrating the impact of our analytics-driven strategies at a micro-level. The Health Benefits Ratio (HBR) decreased by 2.7 percentage points, moving from 81.3% to 78.6%, while the surplus saw a significant increase, from $9.28 per member in 2022 to $19.15 per member in 2023. This improvement is not merely a near doubling of savings; it also anticipates a larger surplus payout for risk-bearing contracts in 2023. The early wins we've achieved, such as significant reductions in inpatient expenses and targeted increases in primary care investments, signify our ability to optimize resources and point toward a scalable model for enhancing healthcare delivery across the board. As these wins compounded, they not only spoke to our achievements but also to our future aspirations. Importantly, this scalability hints at the broader impact achievable across multiple health plans and patient populations. Such robust financial health enables continued reinvestment in the organization to deliver whole-person care, aligning with our core values. As we gaze toward the horizon, we are eager to embrace emerging innovations, such as interoperability frameworks, that could dramatically enhance our analytic capabilities. These advancements hold promise for refining our current processes and unlocking new opportunities in patient care.

Alignment with the Institute of Healthcare Improvement's Quintuple Aim has been crucial in our transition to VBC and our continued efforts to develop a sustainable and equitable healthcare system. Our dedication to serving approximately 60,000 patients has boosted patient outcomes and organizational performance, affirming our status as a preferred employer, provider, and partner within our community. We have strengthened our community bonds by focusing on high-quality, patient-centered care and providing unwavering support to our staff. Equally important have been our partnerships with external stakeholders, which have enhanced our reputation and fostered trust.

Building on this strong foundation, we explore advanced data processing techniques and practical analytics tools to personalize care further. These strategic steps mark progress toward a more proactive healthcare paradigm. The path we carve today is setting the stage for a forward-thinking approach to healthcare that prioritizes each patient's well-being.

Lessons Learned and Best Practices

As we reflect on our journey to implement analytics in our previously data-naive organization, several key lessons and best practices stand out:

- Start with a clear vision and strategy that aligns with your organizational priorities and goals.
- Remain flexible and adaptable in the face of changing circumstances and new information.
- Balance simplicity with sophistication, focusing on solutions that are intuitive, easy to use, and aligned with end-user needs.
- Engage and empower stakeholders across your organization, fostering a culture of shared ownership and accountability.
- Always keep the human element at the center of your analytics efforts, designing initiatives with empathy and a deep understanding of the human experience.
- It's okay, in fact, important to say no! However, it's crucial to communicate thoroughly the reasons behind saying no.

By following these principles, you can unlock the true potential of data and technology to transform lives and improve outcomes in ways that truly matter.

Conclusion

At Brevard Health Alliance, we embrace the power of simplicity. By developing clear roadmaps and strategies and always keeping people at the center of your efforts, you can drive meaningful, measurable improvements in care delivery, patient outcomes, and organizational performance.

More than that, by harnessing analytics' transformative potential, you can fundamentally change the way we approach healthcare—from a reactive, episodic model to a proactive, preventive, and personalized approach that empowers patients, supports providers, and improves the health and well-being of entire populations.

CREATE ROADMAPS | CREATE ROADMAPS | *BY MALISSA MIOT*

Introduction

Hospitals and health systems are struggling to improve their financials and create operational efficiencies to better serve patients and retain staff in a heavy regulatory environment. Imagine a large physician practice or hospital inundated with hundreds of voicemails and messages daily from patients needing follow-ups, clarifications, or updates. This administrative burden leads to delays, missed communications, and frustrated patients.

Now envision a generative AI system that listens to these voicemails and reads messages, extracts the essential information, and routes them to the right departments within seconds. Additionally, visualize the AI system analyzing all incoming voicemails and messages, making recommendations for process improvements to reduce the volume of these communications and improve patient satisfaction. This scenario is no longer futuristic; it's a reality thanks to generative AI.

Generative AI is transforming healthcare by offering immediate benefits and a strong return on investment (ROI). Unlike traditional pre-generative AI models that require extensive data training and development time, generative AI can be deployed quickly and efficiently. Its ability to process NLP swiftly and accurately makes it indispensable in healthcare settings.

Beyond automating routine tasks, generative AI can enhance clinical decision-making, streamline administrative processes, and improve patient outcomes while enhancing the employee and patient experience. However, integrating AI into healthcare systems comes with challenges requiring strategic planning, robust governance, collaboration among leaders, prioritization alignment, and a clear understanding of the technology's capabilities and limitations.

This essay explores the transformative potential of generative AI in healthcare, focusing on high-value use cases that can be quickly and effectively implemented. We will examine real-world examples, discuss the strategic planning needed for AI adoption, and outline steps for healthcare leaders to leverage this technology for immediate impact. As organizations navigate regulatory challenges, cybersecurity concerns, and the need for efficiency, generative AI offers a promising path to improve patient care and operational excellence.

In the following sections, we will present key concepts of generative AI, highlight its practical applications in healthcare, and provide a roadmap for successful implementation that delivers results. Through insights and case studies, this chapter aims to equip healthcare leaders with the knowledge and tools to embark on their generative AI journey.

Understanding Generative AI

Generative AI is a new type of AI. Unlike traditional AI, which usually makes predictions or classifies data, generative AI can create text, images, audio, and even video, hence the "generative" name. The underlying technologies are large language models (LLMs), diffusion models (DM), and large vision models (LVMs). While the details of this are beyond the scope of this essay, an intuitive understanding is within reach of most people.

Advanced LLMs are trained on vast amounts of text from many different data sources. Through the training process, the LLM learns to recognize letters, words, idioms, expressions, and the flow of conversation. During the training process, humans provide feedback when the LLM makes mistakes, allowing it to improve. Eventually, the LLM can read, comprehend, and respond to different prompts accurately, much like a well-read and knowledgeable person can.

An LLM accessible via a chatbot interface is an expert in language understanding and generation and a subject matter expert on an unimaginable number of subjects, including healthcare knowledge. LLMs can also reason like humans and perform multi-step problem-solving tasks.

There are many "so-called" foundation models that are created by commercial (e.g., OpenAI, Anthropic, and Google) and open source (e.g., Meta, Mistral, Reka, and Cohere) organizations. Through a process called "fine-tuning," you can add your own data to the base training data of the foundation model, so you have an enterprise-aware LLM. This enterprise-aware LLM has "gone to college" and learned about your organization.

While generative AI is "the new kid on the block," traditional AI has been in use for many years. Traditional AI has mostly been used for predictive analytics and classification problems. The leap from traditional AI to generative AI represents a significant transformation, differing fundamentally in their core functionalities and applications.

Generative AI offers several significant advantages over traditional AI, particularly in healthcare:

1. **Faster Solution Development Cycles**: Traditional AI models, especially those based on supervised learning, require extensive data collection and considerable time and expense to train and validate. Generative AI, on the other hand, can be fine-tuned more quickly on much smaller datasets, accelerating the development process.

2. **Enhanced Data Processing and Understanding**: Generative AI models excel at understanding and generating human-like text, making them ideal for tasks such as medical documentation, chatbot interactions, and patient communication. They can synthesize information from multiple sources, providing comprehensive and coherent outputs.

3. **Versatility Across Applications**: The ability of generative AI to create new content allows it to be applied in diverse areas, from automating administrative tasks to aiding clinical decision-making. This versatility makes it a powerful tool for addressing various challenges within healthcare settings.

4. **Improved Accuracy and Personalization**: Generative AI models can generate personalized content tailored to individual patient needs, enhancing the patient experience and improving the quality of care. For instance, AI-generated patient education materials can be customized to the literacy level and preferences of each patient.

5. **Cost Efficiency**: By automating repetitive and time-consuming tasks, generative AI can significantly reduce operational costs. This efficiency is particularly beneficial in healthcare environments, where resources are often stretched thin.

Implementing Generative AI in Healthcare

Generative AI is a transformational technology and offers significant new capabilities to enterprises of all types. When ChatGPT was released by OpenAI in November 2022, it was the fastest application adoption by one hundred million users in history. In this case, first impressions matter, and some impressions we have heard from our customers are:

1. Generative AI = ChatGPT
2. ChatGPT makes stuff up (hallucinations), so I cannot trust it
3. My enterprise data is exposed, so I can't use it
4. Generative AI is going to cause the extinction of humanity

You might think that generative AI is synonymous with ChatGPT. However, this is not the case; ChatGPT is only the "tip of the iceberg" in terms of the capability of generative AI. The chatbot user interface is only one way of interacting with the underlying LLMs and LVMs.

It is true that ChatGPT does make stuff up, so this is a valid impression. However, there are approaches that can be applied to minimize this occurrence and to react if it does occur. It is a solvable problem and should not be a barrier to using generative AI.

In the initial rollout of ChatGPT, it was not clear where the data that was sent to the underlying LLM went. Since the initial release, generative AI providers have offered solutions to this problem, including private LLMs where your data is secured and cannot be shared and on-premises LLMs that are hosted inside the firewall.

While some of us who work in the field might find humor when we hear that people are worried about the end of humanity due to generative AI, it is a very real fear that a portion of people have. It is important to recognize that there may be a spectrum of perspectives within your organization, from those who worry about losing their jobs to those who see generative AI as a tool to improve work life.

So, how do you bring generative AI to your healthcare organization? We advocate for the process described in the following image (Figure 4.6).

The basis for this process is AI Governance. Effective governance and structure are vital for overseeing AI initiatives and ensuring they align with the objectives and ethical standards of the organization.

1. **Establish AI Governance Committees**: Form committees comprising cross-functional team members, including clinical, financial, IT, legal,

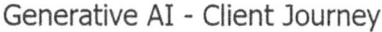

Generative AI - Client Journey

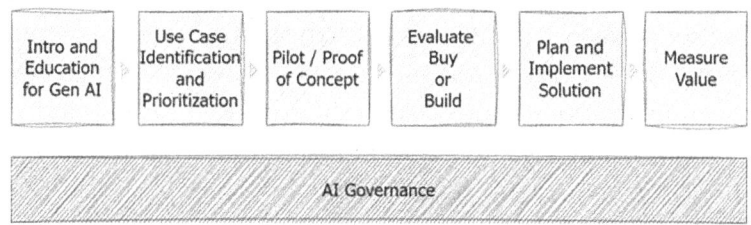

Figure 4.6   Generative AI - Client Journey.

and administrative representatives. These committees will oversee AI projects, set priorities, and ensure compliance with regulations and ethical standards while considering organizational goals and alignment with overall strategic plans, and they must have support from the leadership team to be effective.

2. **Create Policies and Procedures**: Develop comprehensive policies and procedures for AI adoption. These should cover data privacy, security, ethical considerations, and operational guidelines. Clear policies ensure consistency and mitigate risks.

3. **Regular Reviews and Audits**: Implement mechanisms for regular reviews and audits of AI systems. Continuous monitoring ensures that AI applications remain effective, secure, and aligned with organizational goals.

4. **Establish Internal AI User Groups**: Form internal AI user/working groups that include staff from various departments who will extensively use AI tools. These groups will serve as a platform for knowledge sharing, feedback, and collaboration on AI initiatives. They will help identify practical applications, promote best practices, and ensure that AI tools are used effectively and efficiently across the organization and in accordance with the overall governance structure and priorities.

Introduction and Education for Generative AI

Generative AI is NOT ChatGPT. It is essential for those wanting to utilize generative AI in their organization to understand the full breadth of capability offered. Beginning with educational workshops to raise awareness, clarity, and understanding of generative AI among staff is a suitable place to start. These sessions can include presentations, "hands-on" demonstrations, and preliminary discussions on potential applications and high-value use cases. It is normal for staff to be skeptical; the best way to deal with that is to show them by educating them with the facts. During this education, it is common for people to produce ideas for how generative AI can be used. We hear "Can it do this?" during our workshops frequently. Our answer is, "Let's try it now." In several cases, we can demonstrate at the moment to show the preliminary capabilities. More thought will be needed to go into developing a comprehensive solution that will meet the needs of your organization as described later in this essay.

Use Case Identification and Prioritization

Training and education generate ideas for potential high-value use cases that can create an immediate impact. We follow up with brainstorming sessions to identify specific use cases relevant to the organization. Use cases are discussed and scored along three dimensions.

1. Value to the organization
2. Complexity to implement
3. Risk to the organization

Use cases can be prioritized based on scoring with a focus on high-value, low complexity, and minimal risk.

Pilot/Proof of Concept

We recommend selecting a few high-priority use cases for pilot projects. Pilots or proof-of-concepts (POCs) allow you to verify your assumptions rapidly at a low cost. Generative AI allows for POCs to be created and validated in weeks rather than months or longer. We have found that sourcing and preparing data is the longest step in prototype development. Some programming capability is required from either inside or outside of your organization to make it happen.

Evaluate Buy or Build

There are many vendors developing and delivering solutions based on generative AI. Vendor selection in this space is similar to selecting other technology vendors, with two caveats.

■ **Caveat 1**. Generative AI is developing at a rapid pace. For example, consider the size of the context window for ChatGPT. The context window is the number of tokens (token is part of a word) that can be used in the prompt and response with a single "chat." GPT-3 is 4096 tokens and GPT-4 is 32,768 tokens. Several approaches to deal with limited context window sizes have been implemented by vendors. In the next 12 months, these approaches could be rendered obsolete.

■ **Caveat 2**. There is significant venture capital pouring into the generative AI startup field, offering many potential solutions to choose from. Performing due diligence on the vendors you are considering is critical. That due diligence should include the technology set on offer, which requires knowledge of what is inside the generative AI box of each vendor to be evaluated.

Plan and Implement Solution

The implementation of a generative AI solution follows the standard practices of a technology solution implementation. However, there are a few differences to be aware of.

Generative AI solutions rely heavily on data collection, cleaning, preprocessing, and feature engineering. Data is central to the project's success, and considerable time is spent on ensuring data quality.

Generative AI solutions require model validation both initially and then in an ongoing way. Generative AI solutions are non-deterministic, and the quality of output needs to be monitored to ensure that modes do not drift away from their initial performance. Therefore, developing a comprehensive project plan is important.

Measure Value

As with any undertaking that entails innovative technologies and demands cost and time commitment, there needs to be a quantitative and/or qualitative ROI.

A positive quantitative ROI is considered the goal, with a normal ROI of 5–7% often seen as a reasonable expectation. However, a strong general ROI is something greater than 10%. Qualatative ROIs are harder to measure but nevertheless just as important.

While the ROI for incorporating generative AI into your healthcare processes and workflows will vary, there should be clear definitions of how the ROI will be calculated. Quantitative—does it help reduce cost, time spent, or other measurable key performance indicators? Qualitative—does it enhance the patient experience; does it increase employee satisfaction by enhancing everyday repetitive tasks?

The final outcomes will vary depending on the workflow or process that is affected, and each result should be documented and tracked to fully understand and appreciate the value of the generative AI effort.

High-Value Use Cases in Healthcare

Triage and Communication

Efficient communication management is crucial in healthcare. Hospitals and clinics often face a large volume of voicemails and emails from patients seeking appointments, follow-ups, and information. This influx can overwhelm administrative staff, causing delays and missed communications. Generative AI can automate the triage of these messages.

Example: AI Triaging Voicemails and Emails

- **Process**: AI listens to voicemails and reads emails, transcribing the content and using NLP to determine the message's intent.
- **Routing**: The AI categorizes the messages and forwards them to the relevant department, such as scheduling, billing, or clinical support.
- **Follow-up**: Automated responses can be generated for routine inquiries, allowing staff to focus on complex issues.
- **Lessons Learned**: Quick analysis and recommendations for operational improvements can also be derived from voicemails and emails to aid leaders in making positive changes or to better train staff. This data analysis prior to generative AI would have been time consuming, and now with generative AI, the data can be analyzed and summarized to leverage in minutes.

Benefits:

1. **Efficiency**: Reduces the time spent listening to voicemails and sorting emails, allowing staff to focus on critical tasks.
2. **Patient Satisfaction**: Faster response times ensure patients receive timely and relevant information.
3. **Operational Insights**: Analyzing message patterns provides insights into common patient concerns and process improvement areas.
4. **Employee Satisfaction**: Allowing clinical staff to work at the "top of their licenses" to focus on patient care rather than mundane administrative

burdens enhances productivity and improves overall work satisfaction. With retention rates being a major concern for healthcare leaders, any improvements in administrative or clinical workflow are welcome.

Medical Coding

Accurate medical coding is essential for billing, regulatory compliance, and maintaining patient records. However, the process can be time-consuming and prone to errors, especially given the complexity of medical terminologies and coding systems.

AI Improving Medical Coding

Generative AI can assist medical coders by analyzing clinical documentation and automatically suggesting the appropriate codes for procedures, diagnoses, and treatments.

- **Process**: The AI reviews patient records, extracts relevant information, and maps it to the correct medical codes.
- **Validation**: Coders can review and validate the AI-generated codes, ensuring accuracy and compliance with regulatory standards.

Addressing the Shortage of Medical Coders

1. **Increased Speed**: Automating the coding process significantly speeds up the billing cycle, reducing the time between service delivery and reimbursement.
2. **Enhanced Accuracy**: AI systems minimize the risk of human error, ensuring that codes are accurate and consistent.
3. **Resource Allocation**: With AI handling routine coding tasks, experienced coders can focus on more complex cases, optimizing resource utilization.

Workflow Automation: Precertification

One of the main drivers of insurance denials is an incomplete or missing precertification process when patients are initially scheduled for visits or procedures. Precertification is a decision by your health insurer or plan that a health care service, treatment plan, prescription drug, or durable medical equipment is medically necessary.

The precertification process begins when orders from providers trigger the need for precertification. Non-clinical staff gather the required data from EMR systems and submit it to third-party vendors, predominantly through vendor portals, with faxing as a backup. There is often a high initial denial rate, often requiring multiple submissions. Denials can be appealed or resolved through direct physician-to-peer discussions with the vendors.

Generative AI can significantly enhance the pre-certification process through workflow automation. It can act as a comprehensive knowledge base for pre-certification rules, automatically ingesting rule changes from notification letters to stay current. By automating the workflow from order placement to submission, a generative AI solution streamlines data gathering, submission, and compliance with updated rules, reducing time and improving efficiency. Additionally, a generative AI solution can capture metrics throughout the process and analyze denials compared to approvals, identifying patterns and areas for improvement.

In Conclusion

If your organization is looking to utilize generative AI to improve patient experience and automate workflows to help staff be more efficient and lessen administrative burdens, we advocate for a crawl, walk, run, and fly framework. Crawl, walk, run, and fly is a framework for incremental development and improvement:

1. **Crawl**: Start small and simple, focusing on basic functionality and initial understanding.
2. **Walk**: Build on the basics, adding more features and improving stability.
3. **Run**: Expand capabilities significantly, optimizing performance and scalability.
4. **Fly**: Achieve advanced, innovative performance, pushing the limits, and setting new standards.

The first step is to educate your leaders on what is generative AI. What isn't generative AI? What is on the horizon for generative AI? The next step is to align your leaders and collaboratively determine high-value use cases and prioritize them. It is essential to have an AI governance structure to support these initiatives in accordance with the organization's strategic goals and mission. Collaborating with a strategic partner to assist in developing the pilot or proof-of-concept is important. A trusted and knowledgeable partner can help the AI committee determine whether to buy or build and why. The implementation planning and timeline come next, along with the actual implementation to follow. It is essential that the value is measured and tracked to learn and take the lessons into the next endeavor or use case.

By integrating generative AI, healthcare organizations can achieve a more patient-centric approach, reduce operational inefficiencies, and create a better work environment for their staff. This not only improves the quality of care provided but also ensures the financial health of the organization and its ability to retain skilled professionals.

Bibliography

American Cancer Society. (n.d.). Lung nodules | Is a lung nodule cancer? Retrieved from https://www.cancer.org/cancer/types/lung-cancer/detection-diagnosis-staging/lung-nodules.html

Axelos. *ITIL 4: Digital and IT Strategy*, Stationary Office, UK, 2020. ISBN 9780113316489.

Basílio, R., Carvalho, A.R., Rodrigues, R.S., Da Silva Conrado, M., Accorsi, S., Forghani, R., Machuca, T., Zanon, M., Altmayer, S., & Hochhegger, B. "Natural language processing for the identification of incidental lung nodules in computed tomography reports: a quality control tool." *JCO Global Oncology*, 2023, p. 9. 10.1200/go.23.00191

Bekbolatova, M., Mayer, J., Ong, C.W., & Toma, M. "Transformative potential of AI in healthcare: definitions, applications, and navigating the ethical landscape and public perspectives." *Healthcare*, vol. 12, no. 2, 2024, p. 125. 10.3390/healthcare12020125

Biondi, M., Heid, A., Ostojic, I., Henke, N., Pautasso, L., Mohr, N., Wester, L., & Zemmel, R. (2021). Quantum computing: An emerging ecosystem and industry use cases. McKinsey & Company. Retrieved from https://www.mckinsey.com/~/media/mckinsey/business%20functions/mckinsey%20digital/our%20insights/quantum%20computing%20use%20cases%20are%20getting%20real%20what%20you%20need%20to%20know/quantum-computing-an-emerging-ecosystem.pdf

Cavallo, J.J., De Oliveira Santo, I., Mezrich, J.L., & Forman, H.P. "Clinical implementation of a combined artificial intelligence and natural language processing quality assurance program for pulmonary nodule detection in the emergency department setting." *Journal of the American College of Radiology*, vol. 20, no. 4, 2023, pp. 438–445. 10.1016/j.jacr.2022.12.016

Centers for Disease Control and Prevention. (n.d.). Lung cancer statistics. Retrieved from https://www.cdc.gov/cancer/lung/statistics/

Cleveland Clinic News Room. *Cleveland Clinic and IBM Unveil First Quantum Computer Dedicated to Healthcare Research*, Cleveland Clinic, USA, 20 March 2023. https://newsroom.clevelandclinic.org/2023/03/20/cleveland-clinic-and-ibm-unveil-first-quantum-computer-dedicated-to-healthcare-research/

Deloitte. *Quantum Cyber Readiness*, 2022. https://www.deloitte.com/content/dam/assets-zone1/za/en/docs/services/risk-advisory/2023/risk-deloitte-quantum-cyber-readiness-perspective%20(1).pdf

Diamond, C.J., Laurentiev, J., Yang, J., Wint, A.J., Harris, K.A., Dang, T.H., Mecker, A., Carpenter, E.B., Tosteson, A.N., Wright, A., Haas, J.S., Atlas, S.J., & Zhou, L. "Natural language processing to identify abnormal breast, lung, and cervical cancer screening test results from unstructured reports to support timely follow-up." *In Studies in Health Technology and Informatics*, 2022. 10.3233/shti220112

Evers, M., Heid, A., & Ostojic, I. (2021). Pharma's digital Rx: Quantum computing in drug research and development. McKinsey & Company. Retrieved from https://www.mckinsey.com/industries/life-sciences/our-insights/pharmas-digital-rx-quantum-computing-in-drug-research-and-development

France, Jon. "The race against quantum: it's not too late to be the tortoise that beat the hare." *InfoSecurity Magazine*, 7 March 2023. https://www.infosecurity-magazine.com/opinions/race-quantum-tortoise-beat-hare/

Gartner. *A framework for applying ai in the enterprise* (Document ID: G00336031). Bern Elliot and Whit Andrews (analysts), Stamford, USA, 2017.

Hochheiser, H., Finan, S., Yuan, Z., Durbin, E.B., Jeong, J.C., Hands, I., Rust, D.M., Kavuluru, R., Wu, X., Warner, J.L., & Savova, G. "DeePPHE-CR: natural language processing software services for cancer registrar case abstraction." *JCO Clinical Cancer Informatics*, 2023, p. 7. 10.1200/cci.23.00156

Huang, S., Yang, J., Shen, N., Xu, Q., & Zhao, Q. "Artificial intelligence in lung cancer diagnosis and prognosis: current application and future perspective." *Seminars in Cancer Biology*, vol. 89, 2023, pp. 30–37. 10.1016/j.semcancer.2023.01.006

Hunter, B., Reis, S., Campbell, D., Matharu, S., Ratnakumar, P., Mercuri, L., Hindocha, S., Kalsi, H., Mayer, E., Glampson, B., Robinson, E., Al-Lazikani, B., Scerri, L., Bloch, S., & Lee, R.W. "Development of a structured query language and natural language processing algorithm to identify lung nodules in a cancer centre." *Frontiers in Medicine*, 2021, p. 8. 10.3389/fmed.2021.748168

Karunakaran, B., Misra, D., Marshall, K., Mathrawala, D., & Kethireddy, S. "Closing the loop — Finding lung cancer patients using NLP." *2017 IEEE International Conference on Big Data (Big Data)*, 2018. 10.1109/bigdata.2017.8258203

Kehl, K.L., Elmarakeby, H., Nishino, M., Van Allen, E.M., Lepisto, E.M., Hassett, M.J., Johnson, B.E., & Schrag, D. "Assessment of deep natural language processing in ascertaining oncologic outcomes from radiology reports." *JAMA Oncology*, vol. 5, no. 10, 2019, p. 1421. 10.1001/jamaoncol.2019.1800

Li, C., Zhang, Y., Weng, Y., Wang, B., & Li, Z. "Natural language processing applications for computer-aided diagnosis in oncology." *Diagnostics*, vol. 13, no. 2, 2023, p. 286. 10.3390/diagnostics13020286

Liu, S., McCoy, A.B., Aldrich, M.C., Sandler, K.L., Reese, T.J., Steitz, B.D., Bian, J., Wu, Y., Russo, E., & Wright, A. "Leveraging natural language processing to identify eligible lung cancer screening patients with the electronic health record." *International Journal of Medical Informatics*, vol. 177, 2023, p. 105136. 10.1016/j.ijmedinf.2023.105136

Lung Cancer Research Foundation. *Lung Cancer Facts 2023 - Lung Cancer Research Foundation.* 2023, January 17. https://www.lungcancerresearchfoundation.org/lung-cancer-facts/#:~:text=LUNG%20CANCER%20is%20the%20leading%20cause%20of%20cancer%20death%20worldwide.&text=AN%20ESTIMATED%20238%2C340%20PEOPLE%20will,in%202023%20in%20the%20U.S.&text=1%20IN%2016%20PEOPLE%20will,and%201%20in%2017%20women.&text=Approximately%20127%2C070%20AMERICAN%20LIVES%20are%20lost%20annually

Montazeri, M., Afraz, A., Farimani, R.M., & Ghasemian, F. "Natural language processing systems for diagnosing and determining level of lung cancer: a systematic review." *Front Health Inform*, vol. 10, no. 1, 2021, p. 68. 10.30699/fhi.v10i1.264

Mosca, M., & Piani, M. *Quantum Threat Timeline Report 2022.* Global Risk Institute, 2022. https://globalriskinstitute.org/publication/2022-quantum-threat-timeline-report/

Najafabadipour, M., Zanin, M., Rodríguez-González, A., Torrente, M., García, B.N., Bermúdez, J.L.C., Provencio, M., & Menasalvas, E. "Reconstructing the patient's natural history from electronic health records." *Artificial Intelligence in Medicine*, vol. 105, 2020, p. 101860. 10.1016/j.artmed.2020.101860

National Cancer Institute. (2018, October 10). Using artificial intelligence to classify lung cancer types. Retrieved from https://www.cancer.gov/news-events/cancer-currents-blog/2018/artificial-intelligence-lung-cancer-classification

Nobel, J.M., Puts, S., Weiß, J., Aerts, H.J., Mak, R.H., Robben, S.G.F., & Dekker, A. "T-staging pulmonary oncology from radiological reports using natural language processing: translating into a multi-language setting." *Insights Into Imaging*, vol. 12, no. 1, 2021. 10.1186/s13244-021-01018-1

Oken, M.M., Hocking, W.G., Kvale, P.A., Andriole, G.L., Buys, S.S., Church, T.R., Crawford, E.D., Fouad, M.N., Isaacs, C., Reding, D.J., Weissfeld, J.L., Yokochi, L., O'Brien, B., Ragard, L.R., Rathmell, J.M., Riley, T.L., Wright, P., Caparaso, N., Hu, P., … Team, F.T.P.P. "Screening by chest radiograph and lung cancer mortality." *JAMA*, vol. 306, no. 17, 2011, p. 1865. 10.1001/jama.2011.1591

Pabón, O.S., Torrente, M., Provencio, M., Rodríguez-González, A., & Menasalvas, E. "Integrating speculation detection and deep learning to extract lung cancer diagnosis from clinical notes." *Applied Sciences*, vol. 11, no. 2, 2021, p. 865. 10.3390/app11020865

Pabón, O.S., Torrente, M., Rodríguez-González, A., Provencio, M., Menasalvas, E., & Tuñas, J. M. "Lung Cancer Diagnosis Extraction from Clinical Notes

Written in Spanish." *2020 IEEE 33rd International Symposium on Computer-Based Medical Systems (CBMS)*, 2020. 10.1109/cbms49503.2020.00099

Palmer, E.L., Higgins, J., Hassanpour, S., Sargent, J.D., Robinson, C.M., Doherty, J.A., & Onega, T. "Assessing data availability and quality within an electronic health record system through external validation against an external clinical data source." *BMC Medical Informatics and Decision Making*, vol. 19, no. 1, 2019. 10.1186/s12911-019-0864-2

Park, H.J., Park, N., Lee, J.H., Choi, M.G., Ryu, J., Song, M., & Choi, C. "Automated extraction of information of lung cancer staging from unstructured reports of PET-CT interpretation: natural language processing with deep-learning." *BMC Medical Informatics and Decision Making*, vol. 22, no. 1, 2022. 10.1186/s12911-022-01975-7

Prado, M.G., Kessler, L.G., Au, M.A., Burkhardt, H.A., Suchsland, M.Z., Kowalski, L., Stephens, K.A., Yetişgen, M., Walter, F.M., Neal, R.D., Lybarger, K., Thompson, C.A., Achkar, M.A., Sarma, E.A., Turner, G., Farjah, F., & Thompson, M. "Symptoms and signs of lung cancer prior to diagnosis: case–control study using electronic health records from ambulatory care within a large US-based tertiary care centre." *BMJ Open*, vol. 13, no. 4, 2023, e068832. 10.1136/bmjopen-2022-068832

Radwin, M., & Hussein, A. *Quantum Computing as a Savior (QCaaS). Dell Technologies*, 2020. https://education.dell.com/content/dam/dell-emc/documents/en-us/2021KS_Radwan-Quantum_Computing_as_a_Savior_QCaaS.pdf

Rawat, D., Sharma, S., & Bhadula, S. "Natural Language Processing Techniques in Digital Diagnostic System for Lung Cancer Detection." *Second International Conference on Trends in Electrical, Electronics, and Computer Engineering (TEECCON)*, 2023. 10.1109/teeccon59234.2023.10335808

Rietsche, R., Dremel, C., Bosch, S., Steinacker, L., Meckel, M., & Leimeister, J.-M. "Quantum Computing." *Electronic Markets*, vol. 32, no. 4, 2022, pp. 2525–2536. 10.1007/s12525-022-00570-y

Sandler, K.L., Haddad, D., Paulson, A.B., Osterman, T., Scott, C., Poulos, E., & Deppen, S.A. "Women screened for breast cancer are dying from lung cancer: An opportunity to improve lung cancer screening in a mammography population." *Journal of Medical Screening*, vol. 28, no. 4, 2021, pp. 488–493. 10.1177/09691413211013058

Seesaghur, A., Egger, P., Warden, J.G., Abbasi, A.S., Levick, B., Riaz, M., McMahon, P., Thompson, M.D., & Cheeseman, S. "Assessment of bone-targeting agents use in patients with bone metastasis from breast, lung or prostate cancer using structured and unstructured electronic health records from a regional UK-based hospital." *BMJ Open*, vol. 13, no. 5, 2023, e069214. 10.1136/bmjopen-2022-069214

Siegel, R.L., Miller, K.D., Wagle, N.S., & Jemal, A. "Cancer statistics, 2023." *CA: A Cancer Journal for Clinicians*, vol. 73, no. 1, 2023, pp. 17–48. 10.3322/caac.21763

State of Lung Cancer 2023 Report. *American Lung Association.* 2023, November 14. https://www.lung.org/media/press-releases/solc-2023

Suchsland, M.Z., Kowalski, L., Burkhardt, H.A., Prado, M.G., Kessler, L.G., Yetişgen, M., Au, M.A., Stephens, K.A., Farjah, F., Schleyer, A.M., Walter, F.M., Neal, R.D., Lybarger, K., Thompson, C.A., Achkar, M.A., Sarma, E.A., Turner, G., & Thompson, M. "How timely is diagnosis of lung cancer? Cohort study of individuals with lung cancer presenting in ambulatory care in the United States." *Cancers*, vol. 14, no. 23, 2022, p. 5756. 10.3390/cancers14235756

U.S. Preventive Services Task Force. (2021, March 9). Lung cancer: Screening. Retrieved from https://www.uspreventiveservicestaskforce.org/uspstf/recommendation/lung-cancer-screening

Vachani, A., Zheng, C., Liu, I.A., Huang, B., Osuji, T.A., & Gould, M.K. "The probability of lung cancer in patients with incidentally detected pulmonary nodules." *Chest*, vol. 161, no. 2, 2022, pp. 562–571. 10.1016/j.chest.2021.07.2168

Wang, L., Luo, L., Wang, Y., Wampfler, J.A., Yang, P., & Liu, H. "Natural language processing for populating lung cancer clinical research data." *BMC Medical Informatics and Decision Making*, vol. 19, no. S5, 2019. 10.1186/s12911-019-0931-8

Yuan, Q., Cai, T., Hong, C., Du, M., Johnson, B.E., Lanuti, M., Cai, T., & Christiani, D.C. "Performance of a machine learning algorithm using electronic health record data to identify and estimate survival in a longitudinal cohort of patients with lung cancer." *JAMA Network Open*, vol. 4, no. 7, 2021, e2114723. 10.1001/jamanetworkopen.2021.14723

Zheng, C., Huang, B., Agazaryan, A.A., Creekmur, B., Osuj, T.A., & Gould, M.K. "Natural language processing to identify pulmonary nodules and extract nodule characteristics from radiology reports." *Chest*, vol. 160, no. 5, 2021, pp. 1902–1914. 10.1016/j.chest.2021.05.048

Chapter 5

Collaborate and Listen

Listen for ideas that will potentially solve a problem or present an opportunity to collaborate with stakeholders and galvanize your network.

Many innovations started by listening, observing and then communicating ideas and solutions to problems. When you listen, people are more likely to share ideas and provide encouragement. The more you engage others, the more ideas you are likely to catch. Great innovations are typically a result of multiple iterations by numerous individuals invited to participate in ideation and execution. Inviting others to share in your innovation will galvanize support and engagement necessary for success.

One is too small a number for innovation. Innovation is largely a result of a team of teams' approach to solving a problem or exploiting an opportunity. It can be an ego challenge to have a great innovation and allow others to modify and edit your dream. We can take innovation too personally and become captive to the potential and miss out on something greater. Leveraging others actually frees the innovation to grow and expand beyond what you initially envisioned. There is strength in seeking the wisdom of others.

DOI: 10.4324/9781032715155-5

COLLABORATE AND LISTEN | INNOVATION THROUGH COLLABORATION: THE JOURNEY OF ROOJH HEALTHCARE | *BY KAMAL MAHESHWARI*

A Case Study with All India Institute of Ayurveda

Introduction

What you have built or are selling is not exactly what the customer needs. You always have to tweak or pivot to satisfy the customer's needs. This agility in decision-making and product building is the key to successful implementation. One of the most compelling success stories under Roojh Healthcare's umbrella is the development and deployment of a queue management system for the All India Institute of Ayurveda (AIIA).

The Challenge

We approached AIIA with our product offering with practice management system (PMS), Ayushman Bharat Digital Mission (ABDM) compliance module, and personal health record (PHR). However, AIIA faced the daunting challenge of managing an overwhelming early morning patient influx. With up to 1,500 patients queuing from as early as 5 AM, the hospital gates would only open at 8:30 AM, followed by the lengthy process of token distribution for registration. This created significant stress and discomfort for patients and administrative burdens for the hospital staff. They were interested in the solution but also wanted a solution to this important problem. We said yes and worked with them tirelessly to build the solution despite slowing our product pipeline.

Listening to the Customer

Rooj Healthcare's approach began with a crucial first step: listening. By thoroughly understanding AIIA's specific pain points and requirements, Roojh crafted a custom solution tailored to alleviate their problems.

The Solution

The result was an innovative queue management system leveraging the ABDM framework. Roojh utilized QR-code-based tokens that patients could generate directly from their mobile phones, even while at home. This pre-emptive token generation system gradually improved the patient flow and reduced unnecessary early queues.

Additionally, Roojh began developing a predictive system to anticipate the likely times patients would be seen by doctors, allowing them to arrive at the hospital at appropriate times rather than waiting for hours.

Implementation and Impact

The new system was swiftly implemented, and the results were immediate and substantial. Within an hour from 8:30 AM, the system successfully generated and distributed 1,500 tokens using QR codes, facilitating both new and old patient registrations.

Patients no longer needed to endure long waiting periods, drastically improving their overall experience. By closely collaborating with AIIA and adhering to ABDM guidelines, Roojh Healthcare developed a scalable system that could be replicated across other government hospitals facing similar challenges. Not only did we solve a real-world problem, but doing this project helped raise our team morale, who were so proud to see the impact on hundreds of patient lives.

Continued Efforts and Test-Driven Development: A Parallel Approach

Rooj Healthcare's strategy of continuously listening to customer feedback and iteratively developing features to address the most acute pain points is remarkably akin to the principles of Test-Driven Development (TDD) in software engineering. In TDD, the desired outcome or functionality is first precisely defined through the creation of tests that fail initially. Following this, efforts are meticulously directed to develop and refine the solution until these tests are successfully passed. Similarly, by prioritizing feedback from the AIIA and other clients, Roojh Healthcare effectively sets clear, outcome-driven goals that directly respond to identified needs. Their methodical approach ensures that each development cycle focuses on tangible improvements and functionality that truly matter to users, thereby delivering a robust, user-validated system. This cyclical process not only ensures that the solutions are aligned with real-world requirements but also fosters a dynamic environment of continuous improvement and innovation.

Conclusion

Roojh Healthcare's journey is a testament to the power of innovation and the collaborative development of customer-focused solutions in the healthcare sector. By addressing specific needs and leveraging cutting-edge technology, Roojh not only solves immediate problems but also paves the way for a more efficient and compassionate healthcare environment. The work with AIIA exemplifies how thoughtful, technology-driven solutions can make a real difference in people's lives.

Key Lessons Learned

Our journey and interaction with various stakeholders reinforced that the digital health industry thrives on innovation, and fostering a collaborative environment is crucial for startups aiming to revolutionize healthcare. Here are ten key principles to remember:

1. **Diverse Expertise**: assemble a team with complementary skillsets. This could include doctors, data scientists, software developers, designers, and business professionals. We are proud to say that Roojh is built by doctors, and we are clear-eyed on hiring and collaborating with people with diverse expertise.
2. **Open Communication**: encourage transparency and information sharing across all departments and team members. This is especially hard when you are moving fast and when you are working with team members in different time zones. Utilize communication channels like project management tools and regular team meetings.
3. **Shared Goals**: ensure everyone understands the company's vision and mission. Clearly defined goals keep everyone working toward the same objective. This is especially true when you are making fast decisions with limited resources.
4. **Patient Focus**: collaborate with patients and healthcare providers to understand their needs and challenges. Integrate their feedback into product development. (e.g., many mental health startups collaborate with therapists to develop apps that address specific patient needs).
5. **Break Down Silos**: encourage cross-functional collaboration between departments. This fosters a more holistic approach to problem-solving.
6. **Embrace Feedback**: create a culture where constructive criticism is valued. Feedback from team members and external stakeholders helps refine ideas.

7. **Celebrate Successes**: recognize and reward collaborative achievements. This motivates teams and reinforces the value of working together.
8. **Utilize Technology**: leverage collaboration tools like video conferencing platforms and cloud-based document sharing to streamline communication, especially for geographically dispersed teams.
9. **Build Trust**: foster an environment where team members feel comfortable sharing ideas and taking risks. As leaders utilize all ways of communication, be it one-to-one meetings or group meetings, emails, or phone calls. There is no single way of communication which will fit all team members; there is no excuse for not knowing what is going on with the team.
10. **Conflict Resolution**: with diverse team members, it is sure that conflicts will happen. This is usually the biggest source of mental stress affecting team performance. Develop a process for addressing disagreements constructively. Effective conflict resolution prevents roadblocks and fosters better solutions.

About Roojh Health

Roojh Health was started to empower patients and doctors with the best technology, especially in developing countries, for the highest impact. There are numerous challenges, including poor health education and awareness, lack of digitization, and lack of resources, to name a few. Nonetheless, we wanted to be part of the solution and took on this huge challenge. Going down the problem-solving path, we realized that it is not the artificial intelligence (AI)-based guidance which will solve the problem. Creating a PHR for patients should be the first step. Without basic health information about the people, any other solution will be incomplete. Once we have information, we can provide guidance to improve health. While it seems simple in theory, the execution is difficult; however, we are committed and on track to deliver. We strive to be a beacon of innovation and excellence in the healthcare software development space, particularly in resource-poor settings. We started with India, the most populous nation in the world. Fortunately, our effort of empowerment through digitization was aligned with a new government initiative called ABDM with the goal of digitizing Indian health infrastructure. Roojh Health developed a mobile-based PHR to empower patients, a web-based PMS to empower doctors, and an ABDM compliance module to empower healthcare organizations to stay compliant with national initiatives.

Roojh Healthcare's Solutions

At its core, Roojh Healthcare offers a suite of solutions aimed at modernizing healthcare practices:

1. PHR: empowering patients. A digital repository for patients' medical records, ensuring easy access, management, and sharing of health information.
2. PMS: empowering doctors. Designed to streamline administrative tasks, improve patient management, and optimize overall operations.
3. ABDM Compliance: empowering healthcare organizations. Ensuring healthcare providers meet the rigorous standards set by the ABDM.

COLLABORATE AND LISTEN | REGISTRY AUTOMATION: SUCCESS STORY OF TRUE COLLABORATION | *BY DEBORAH GASH*

Leveraging AI to reduce administrative tasks in Healthcare

It's no secret that in today's busy health system environment, every minute is precious, and resources are stretched thin and in short supply – especially clinical resources. That environment is today's reality, and the challenges that every health system faces are daunting and ever-growing. However, amidst these challenges, literature suggests there is a beacon of hope: Artificial Intelligence (AI). The rapid progress of AI has made it a buzzword in healthcare; however, its tangible benefits and optimal use cases have proven to be elusive. Additionally, AI requires not only the right technical capabilities but specific skills to develop applications for its use. Not all healthcare provider organizations can bridge these capability gaps or innovate to generate tangible benefits.

With that in mind, the innovation team began to look for specific areas within the organization that made sense to be automated. The opportunities were focused on trying to find areas within the organization that could be automated specifically to take some of the burden off nurses. As the team dug into these questions, one of the biggest pain points that stuck out was the data abstraction and submission for clinical data registries (CDRs). Participation in CDRs is vital for hospitals, offering benefits in quality improvement, research, compliance, and cost reduction. However, the process of completing registry forms and submitting them to the proper data collection group is painstakingly manual and tedious. There were applications in place in the organization that were leveraged to help with quality data submission, but they did not fully automate the process. Even worse, due to the complicated nature of these registries and the knowledge that must go into them, the work is often performed by highly skilled clinical resources.

A team was created under the sponsorship of executive leadership in the quality areas to investigate and determine if the chart abstraction processes could be automated. It became clear very quickly after researching vendor solutions that this technology did not exist for the specialty registries – especially for the full automation that the team was seeking. The organization attempted to build a solution but learned it did not have the technology platform or technical skills necessary to create the solution. As the CIO, meeting with vendors and learning about their solutions is just part of the job. Experience has shown that partnerships with vendors to solve unique problems can be effective and speed innovation. It was in one of these meetings that a hypothesis for an application of a vendor solution to solve a unique challenge emerged.

Objectives

If the organization could Automate the abstraction and submission of these registries, it would allow the nurses performing this administrative work to be transitioned back into more of a clinical or bedside role. In an exploratory meeting with Trinisys, a leading healthcare software company based in Nashville, TN, a unique application of their capabilities emerged that could solve the objective the organization was seeking. Trinisys has specialized in data integration and process automation for over 20 years, making them an ideal partner for this ambitious project. They also weren't trying to sell consultants or remote abstractors to fix the problem; both organizations were aligned to fix this problem with software. To put it simply, both recognized this problem, and both wanted to solve it with technology.

The hypothesis was that together, both organizations could pull the necessary data out of the EHR and supporting technology platforms to populate the registry fields. With that as a starting point, the goal then became clear: automate the entire registry process without needing any human interaction. The potential impact would then be enormous. Not only would this partnership save time, money, and resources, but it would also standardize data entry, leading to improved performance, better patient outcomes, and easier paths to research and innovation. No matter how excellent the team was, the manual nature of abstraction lends itself to inconsistencies and/or mistakes. Looking at a patient chart that has mountains of pages and data, and then having to fill out a registry form that has hundreds of fields is something that will always be prone to errors.

Solution

Trinisys used their core software platform, Convergence, as the base for building "ClearWay," their registry automation product. They had a long history in archiving legacy data and therefore had already built an extensive set of rules for extracting and making sense of EHR data. The combined team started with the assumption that they would be able to leverage ETL to obtain discrete data that could be used to automatically fill in most of the registry fields. Natural Language Processing and AI technologies would then be layered on top to be the "icing on the cake" to interpret complex data and follow the coding instructions for each registry.

The innovation team also wanted to start with a specific group of registries for the automation. As they looked at the book of registries that the organization participated in, the cardiac area stuck out as a natural place to start. This was due to the complexity of the cardiac registries, the number of nurses that were dedicated to that area, and the clear need to have accurate data in those submissions. If this worked, it would free up the Abstraction resources tremendously. Instead of skilled clinical resources spending hours filling out and submitting one registry form, ClearWay would automate this process. The partnership with Trinisys would achieve significant time savings and resource reallocation.

Assumptions

At the start of the project, the team had a series of assumptions that guided the proof of concept and initial implementation. These were:

1. Natural Language Processing (NLP) is powerful enough to solve the problem of abstracting registry fields.
2. Many of the fields could be handled using discrete data elements, leaving only a subset of fields that require NLP processing.
3. Answering registry questions is straight forward - skills required in data mapping were sufficient to complete much of the task.

Reality

Scope

The sheer size and complexity of the problem was initially underestimated, stemming from a lack of clinical domain knowledge and registry experience within the technical team. Additionally, the subject matter experts were initially not able to fully convey all the challenges to the implementation team, which was understandable since this had never been done! The extensive data elements required for registries and the high percentage of fields needing complex reasoning over multiple data points presented numerous difficult-to-manage challenges.

Artificial Intelligence

Experimenting with AI technologies can be exciting, often yielding impressive results in proof-of-concept stages. However, this can also lead to over-confidence in operationalizing the technology for real-world problem-solving. If that is combined with a misunderstanding of the scope and complexity of the problem, it can result in unrealistic expectations regarding the capabilities and effort needed to solve it.

Incorporating AI across different domains also presents challenges in effectively leveraging it. Interpreting AI results can be a massive undertaking, and selecting the appropriate AI technique for each problem requires considerable effort. If one technique proves inadequate, adopting a new approach entails its own learning curve and integration effort, which may yield little to no gain.

Fine-tuning the 'creativity' or 'level of connection making' of an AI engine is another challenge. On one end of the spectrum, the engine may produce too many 'false positives,' while on the other, it may overlook relevant data. Both scenarios must be avoided. Too many 'false positives' can lead users to disregard valid evidence (like the boy who cried wolf), undermining the system's effectiveness.

Types of AI

Computer Aided Coding NLP

Computer Aided Coding (CAC) solutions have been well-established in the market for years, primarily focused on billing tasks such as generating ICD-10 codes. While these offerings are robust and effective for their intended purpose, they may have limited applicability for projects like registry automation or other similar initiatives.

Many of the established Natural Language Processing (NLP) engines in healthcare are designed with a focus on CAC, which may not align perfectly with the needs of projects requiring broader automation or analysis beyond coding.

Healthcare Specific NLP

Some healthcare-specific Natural Language Processing (NLP) engines prioritize SNOMED or the Unified Medical Language System (UMLS) over ICD-10, as they offer greater precision. However, these engines can sometimes be overly aggressive in making connections, leading to an increase in false positives.

Depending on the methodology employed, these engines may have issues with context understanding, being too inclusive and linking unrelated pieces of evidence, which can result in errors. Careful consideration of these factors is essential when leveraging these NLP engines for healthcare applications.

Large Language Models (LLMs)

Large Language Models (LLMs) have gained popularity, especially with the release of OpenAI's ChatGPT products. While these tools offer significant advantages in understanding unstructured text with high accuracy, they present challenges for HIPAA compliance, though these challenges are not insurmountable.

One strength of LLMs is their ability to comprehend language effectively. However, operationalizing the output can be challenging due to the often-longwinded nature of the responses, which can complicate result interpretation. This challenge can be addressed through prompt engineering, a concept that may be new to many technologists.

Two additional concerns with LLMs are false positives, often referred to as "hallucinations," and ensuring the LLM's understanding of medical jargon is comprehensive. Addressing these concerns requires careful consideration and potentially additional fine-tuning of the model.

Specific Challenging Examples

Registry submission involves answering questions using information from a patient's legal health record, a process known as abstraction. Some fields, like "first name" or "date of birth," are straightforward. Others, like determining the highest Creatine value between procedures or discharge, require more complex comparisons. Some fields even require understanding of the provider's decision-making process.

Abstraction often demands domain knowledge or experience with the Electronic Health Record (EHR). For example, a lab value could be documented in multiple places. Many fields have intricate rules dictating which evidence is relevant and when.

Here is an example of a relatively simple registry question along with the information you need to successfully answer it: *Has the patient experienced Atrial Fibrillation in the past week?*

If looking through the chart for terms such as 'Atrial Fibrillation', 'AFib' and other variations, you must also reduce your search to the week prior to the procedure due to the specific coding rules. However, documents from that week may contain historical references like 'History of Atrial Fibrillation' without indicating when it occurred. Using simple text searches could lead to false positives in such cases. To successfully answer this relatively simple question using AI, you must:

1. Have all the relevant documents, along with the appropriate meta data, such as document date.
2. Find relevant references, which could include synonyms, acronyms, and potential misspellings.
3. Understand the references and context surrounding a term to determine if the condition actually occurred, and, if so, when it happened. This can include looking for specific mentions of dates, events, or indicators that provide temporal information about the occurrence.
4. Once these are completed, then all the relevant evidence and related meta data must be processed. For instance, a patient may have experienced Afib, but if it occurred before the 7-day cutoff, it would be considered invalid.

HIPAA Concerns

When selecting tools for a project, it's important to consider various factors such as initial cost, ongoing support, and HIPAA compliance. The ability to comply with existing data governance policies and procedures is also crucial.

When working with a third party for Artificial Intelligence, there's an additional level of scrutiny required when executing Business Associates Agreements, especially when dealing with large datasets. This can add complexity to an already challenging project.

Overcoming Challenges

The key to success in a complex project involving new artificial intelligence-based technologies is to establish clear and concise goals that align with an overarching guiding principle. For this project, the guiding principle was to significantly reduce the time abstractors spent on registry automation while maintaining or improving accuracy. To achieve this, the team set specific accuracy measurement goals for each field. If a field did not meet the desired accuracy level, there had to be a mechanism to guide the user through manual review of the evidence for that field.

From a technical perspective, several factors were critical to overcoming this challenge. The team utilized a large dataset for testing and implemented a systematic approach to verify results. A user-friendly interface was essential, benefiting both abstractors and the implementation team for verification and mapping work. Although this required significant upfront and ongoing effort, the investment yielded substantial returns.

Central to our approach was a robust system framework developed by Trinisys, incorporating an ETL tool, interface engine, API management, workflow, process choreography, and security measures. This platform enabled the team to quickly adapt to new information and adjust course as needed.

Large Data Set

A crucial element of most AI projects is access to large datasets. The team transitioned from a proof of concept using a small set of examples with limited fields to leveraging a large dataset encompassing all fields for the initial registry. To achieve this, the ingested one to two years' worth of historically abstracted patient data into our system for each registry. This data served as test cases for our abstraction rules. Additionally, they analyzed how often a certain field was answered in a particular way, aiding in the creation of comprehensive test sets. The goal was to cover as many scenarios as possible.

However, this approach uncovered some unexpected challenges. The historical data was not always 100% accurate, partly due to human errors and partly due to changes in coding guidelines. These changes could result from updates from the registry provider or new understandings gained by abstractors for specific fields over time.

Systematic Verification

A detailed daily account of the system's accuracy not only helped the team focus and assess their performance but also provided leadership with a clear view of overall progress through measurable metrics, replacing reliance on anecdotal evidence and intuition. To achieve this, the team developed a systematic approach to evaluate our implementation against a large dataset of historically abstracted patient data. This involved running batches of test cases, reporting results, and the ability to delve into specific test cases to troubleshoot errors. As the project advanced, the team introduced a 'nightly build process' to run test cases for all registries under development, generating a morning report highlighting improved accuracy and potential regressions. Additionally, they integrated a drill-down feature in reports, leveraging abstraction review screens to test UI capabilities, resulting in valuable features that also proved useful during normal abstraction processes.

Strong User Interface

Implementing systematic verification was challenging but crucial for maintaining the implementation team's productivity and ensuring an accurate progress overview for a registry implementation. This capability allowed for tracking progress over time and swiftly delving into field details, significantly reducing the mental load on users by consolidating information sources. This mirrored the problem-solving approach for abstractors. The user interface needed to be sophisticated to manage a complex problem with numerous data elements effectively. The extra time dedicated to UI development proved worthwhile.

Despite this, the team faced complexities in feature development for our review process, needing to balance perceived time savings against development and testing efforts. The team also carefully considered any additional guardrails or structural changes in the system to avoid reducing flexibility, a common consideration in automation and applicable to our internal technical team's processes.

Framework

The system was designed as a flexible framework, which allowed the team to integrate new techniques and apply rules to results. Three separate AI technologies were utilized, as well as three more traditional techniques during implementation. The configuration UI allowed the team to set rules for each engine's results and enable or disable each engine per field, optimizing the use of engines for different types of fields. This significantly accelerated the implementation process.

A central concept in the approach was choreography, where the system orchestrates technology, data, and user input to create a cohesive solution. This involved not only the standard abstraction review process but also handling error conditions, validation warnings, and maintaining field mapping accuracy.

Lessons Learned

Upon completing our initial implementation, the team identified areas for improvement and keys to our success. The most impactful factors were our agile implementation approach and having a fully aligned, partnership approach.

Agile Approach

A large part of our success was driven by a measurable and adaptable approach, supported by a strong, cohesive team. Utilizing an appropriate framework and tools also enabled swift responses and turnaround times. As new challenges arose, the team's ability to adapt and try new approaches was crucial. Early end user involvement, while potentially challenging, allowed for quick adjustments based on new insights from those end users.

A successful agile approach depended on a fully aligned team. The Trinisys robust technology platform and a well thought out, flexible approach enabled us to react quickly as the team deepened their understanding of the problems faced.

Aligned Team

Progress in such a vast problem space required harnessing the expertise of subject matter experts, architects, and technologists, all working towards a clear end goal, or 'North Star'. A common challenge in technology projects is to stray from the original goal, despite the best of intentions. This can happen due to under-specification or misunderstandings among stakeholders, or a shift in goals as the project progresses. Projects can also be hindered by internal spin, with certain leaders painting an overly positive picture while actual results fall short from stakeholder expectations.

Ensuring alignment among end users is also crucial; concerns about job security or workload can lead to misalignment. Engaging the entire team in the project's mission, guided by a clear and transparent goal, was essential for the success of this complicated project.

Results

To avoid burying the lede, the team achieved immense success in this partnership. However, that success ended up being slightly different than the original hypothesis. The team realized throughout this process that some human interaction would still be needed. There are many times in a patient chart where the data shows conflicting evidence and judgement calls made by an Abstractor were still required.

The goal was changed to increasing efficiency by ~10x and to put every available tool right at the fingertips of the Abstractors. Through the use of the rules engines, NLP, and AI, Trinisys automated the population of all fields, with any conflicting evidence automatically flagged for review. With this result, Abstractors could now simply click through the fields (usually <10) that needed manual review, be taken directly to the evidence in the patient's chart and make the decision. This took our average time per chart submission from 60+ minutes to ~5 minutes. Not only were we now faster and much more efficient, but ClearWay was filling out all fields with a 95+ percent level of accuracy. Even though we determined that the organizations wasn't able to completely move away from human elements, the Trinisys partnership ensured that the abstraction team was now quicker, more accurate, and much more efficient. This also allowed the possibility to reallocate many of the highly valuable resources into more strategic work.

The Q/A process started proving one of the original theories correct, that ClearWay was proving to be more correct than the manual abstraction. 'Errors' would show up in ClearWay's results weren't errors at all. The team discovered that the previous manual submissions that ClearWay was run against for an initial quality baseline were the ones that were incorrect, with ClearWay's decision making proving to be technically correct. With all of the rules, NLP, and AI built in, ClearWay was able to process an immense amount of data instantly. With many of the fields previously requiring detailed manual research, it was easy to see why certain fields were so mentally taxing and more prone to mistakes.

In addition to the actual abstraction of the data, an unexpected but immensely impactful achievement was the automation of patient lists. Prior to ClearWay, our Abstraction teams spent countless hours (it wasn't officially measured) determining which patients were eligible for a particular registry. With ClearWay, Trinisys automated that process by having every eligible patient auto-populated onto the home screen when the Abstractor logs in to the platform. Daily feeds from the EHR allowed this possibility, showing all of the pre-requisites the eligible patients had met (or not), whether they were part of a research study, and whether or not they were ready for abstraction.

Conclusion

In conclusion, the partnership with Trinisys and the development of ClearWay have transformed the registry abstraction process, making it faster, more accurate, and significantly more efficient. While human judgment is still required in some cases, ClearWay has allowed us to reallocate valuable resources to more strategic work, ultimately improving patient care and outcomes.

COLLABORATE AND LISTEN | LIFEPOINT HEALTH. A MULTI-PRONGED APPROACH TO INNOVATION INCLUDING A UNIQUE PARTNERSHIP WITH 25M HEALTH | BY SAURABH BHATIA AND KAMAL MAHESHWARI

While LifePoint has always looked for innovative partnerships with 3rd party vendors, we have evolved significantly in the past 4 years. Two factors primarily drove this change in approach and attitude. First, LifePoint was acquired by a Private Equity (Apollo Global Management) firm in late 2018. With this acquisition came the ability and desire to invest capital into early-stage digital health companies as part of an investment strategy. This started as looking at strategic vendor partnerships that were already in the process of raising capital and making a few strategic investments. One of the primary drivers was a desire to "have a piece of the action" should we scale a small company and a desire to participate in the financial upside of helping a company achieve market success. With the success of many digital health companies over the years, this investment portfolio approach can yield a strong ROI. The second event was COVID-19. The pandemic caused us to look at our nimbleness and the need to be more digitally focused. Like all health systems, we had to react quickly to keep our facilities and clinics open in this new lockdown environment. Speed and innovative approaches were critical to keeping our operations open and running in the communities that we serve. Several successes in the digital health space during this trying time proved that we could be digital-first, could ideate through implementation in a streamlined manner, and in fact we needed to emphasize these types of digital-forward solutions in order to become a stronger competitor in our local markets. In essence, we built innovation muscle memory during COVID-19 that post-pandemic has continued to grow and strengthen.

The culmination of these activities led us to formally develop our LifePoint Forward innovation approach, where we take a multi-pronged approach to innovation. Our guiding principles are:

- **Build/Incubate solutions**: Approach to incubate new companies using LifePoint for ideation, testing, and the first partner to scale the solution. LifePoint has a unique partnership with 25madison—a Venture platform that builds new companies from scratch and/or invests in early-stage startup companies and propels them into their next phase of growth. Together, LifePoint, our PE firm, and 25madison have seeded 25m Health, the healthtech venture studio, with money to directly invest into early-stage digital health companies or be a creation platform that can build self-sustaining new companies that create solutions for LifePoint communities but also have the ability to scale beyond to become self-sustaining commercial entities. In the case of an incubated company, LifePoint serves as the design partner to help mature the company and make sure it is ready to stand up to the rigor that will be expected by other large health systems in terms of cyber security, scaling of sales, support, and implementation processes. As an acquisition company, LifePoint also has a disparity of core systems that allow these start-ups to try integration in a variety of ways to help them be ready for what they might find in the marketplace. If you can work with LifePoint, you are ready to work with just about any health system or hospital that you might encounter in the marketplace.
- **Buy/Invest**: Direct investment in early-stage digital health companies and help grow them. Usually, this entails an equity position in the company as well as some level of co-development of the product. Co-development affords LifePoint some influence in product direction to meet our strategic needs.
- **Partner**: A more traditional approach where we partner with vendors and scale them across the enterprise. Strategic partnerships to scale the company's solutions across our enterprise.

Launching 25m Health: A Unique Model for Collaboration

25m Health was born out of a belief that the best innovations in healthcare come from close collaboration between providers, technologists, and investors. We sought to combine 25madison's company-building principles, LifePoint's healthcare expertise (along with LifePoint-affiliated SCION Health), and Apollo's investing creativity to build a new platform that connects startups with timely feedback and support.

The 25m Health team is a Nashville-based group of former Product Managers, Engineers, General Managers, and Designers who have either previously founded businesses of their own or worked at healthcare startups. Through partnering with LifePoint and Scion, the 25m Health team has designed and optimized a healthcare-specific process that guides 25m Health Entrepreneurs-in-Residence (EIRs) through company creation. EIRs use templates and frameworks to navigate through "stage gates," unlocking additional resources, pilots, and commercial contracts along the way.

As a diverse and experienced healthcare services operator, LifePoint is an ideal partner for an early healthcare startup. LifePoint operates facilities ranging from primary care practices to critical access hospitals to level one trauma centers. There are a few problems within the healthcare ecosystem that LifePoint is not exposed to. The LifePoint and 25m Health partnership model focuses on connecting EIRs with the LifePoint operators that are most directly dealing with the "pain points" in the system. As a result, some of our most effective startup ideas have come directly from front-line operators. These early advocates are critical catalysts for making an incubation or investment partnership successful and driving adoption and meaningful change in LifePoint communities.

25m Health is structured as a holding company, so it can both incubate and invest. Importantly, 25m Health is managed day-to-day by 25madison, which enables it to experiment with new ideas and make decisions at start-up speed while still also having proximity to and the support of active healthcare operators.

LifePoint Forward Examples in Action: Success Stories

EON Health

EON was one of the first companies in the LifePoint Forward portfolio. EON started as an independent company, and then in 2018, EON and LifePoint joined together (along with several other health systems) to co-develop and scale a number of innovative solutions. EON's core competency in AI has been used to develop multiple algorithms as part of EON's Essential Patient Management (EPM) platform, which allows for the early identification and tracking of patients at risk for lung cancer, and subsequently launched similar applications to identify and track additional disease states, including thyroid, pancreas, and aortic aneurysms, among others. Using Computational Linguistics, a discipline of AI, EON extracts abnormal findings and clinically relevant information from radiology and other physician reports and automates redundant and burdensome tasks for low-risk patients while triaging high-risk patients for provider review. The result is more patients being captured within the system and longitudinally tracked per evidence-based guidelines.

LifePoint further leverages the EON Care Management platform and call center to proactively communicate to patients and physicians for follow-up care that can further diagnose if cancer is present and take the appropriate next steps. This unique blend of cutting-edge technology and the people and processes behind the technology to enable a full solution has been a great partnership, allowing LifePoint to be a leader in the early detection of certain cancers in the communities that we serve, increasing the chance of survival, doing the right thing for our patients, and capturing additional follow-on testing and services in our local markets.

Gratia Health

Founded in late 2022, Gratia Health is an incubation from 25m Health's first cohort. Gratia Health sought to address one of the most pressing issues facing Lifepoint and other health systems: nurse burnout and retention. Gratia is dedicated to redefining healthcare staffing by leveraging advanced data analytics and behavioral insights to optimize workforce management. Gratia was born out of an insight from a facility leader who constructed a small-scale but very successful incentive program to encourage employed nurses to pick up incremental shifts. Working closely with that site leader, Gratia first confirmed the beneficial impact of the program before working to build the idea into a product that could be scaled. After completing a three-LTACH pilot, leadership opted to offer the program more broadly. It is now being leveraged across dozens of facilities to help improve nurse satisfaction while saving millions in backfill and contract labor costs in the process.

In early 2024, the Gratia team announced a successful seed fundraise from Jumpstart Capital and the hire of experienced repeat founder Shawn

Dastmalchi as CEO. Gratia continues to operate across the LifePoint and Scion footprints and is in conversations with several other health systems about expanding to their sites of care.

Kouper Health

Launched in mid-2022, Kouper Health is an incubation focused on improving the transitions of care experience. Kouper is the product of close collaboration between EIR Salman Ali, the 25m Health team, and LifePoint discharge case management leader Dr Chris Frost. Working together, this group shaped the Kouper solution that was initially focused on helping more patients get seen for Transitional Care Management (TCM) visits following a discharge from an inpatient facility. After successfully deploying this solution at Paris Medical Center, Kouper received investment from General Catalyst to help scale their offering within LifePoint and beyond.

Since then, Kouper has expanded its offering to also support patients leaving the emergency room. Kouper leverages Large Language Models (LLMs) and automation to correspond with patients while building integrations to ensure patient data is shared appropriately and responsibly with their next site of care. Kouper and LifePoint continue to work together to support care transitions in communities across the country.

Lessons Learned for Innovation and Incubation

Over the past 3 years, there have been a number of lessons learned from our incubation efforts with 25m Health. First, fast triaging is critical in order to be efficient in the ideation and scoping phases. Quick market surveys for already established products leveraging 25m Health market intelligence as well as LifePoint knowledge and professional networks let us arrive at a Yes or No decision relatively quickly. Focus is critically important in order to make sure we don't waste capital and we have the energy and time to adequately devote to these efforts. We have found putting more effort behind fewer incubations and strategic investments is better, and connecting the investments/incubations to the core priorities of the organization helps with organizational alignment on the initiatives. Alignment and supporting existing LifePoint strategic efforts is critical to getting operational buy-in and the focus to scale these solutions. It may be a great idea, but if it does not directly support the operator's key strategic efforts, the needed energy to manage the implementation and local facility change management efforts will not materialize, and the initiative will fail.

Second, a new mindset that it's OK to fail and that not all of the solutions will work out. We have had several incubations, for example, that after the first field test did not deliver the value that we had expected. Having the courage to "fast fail" and know when to cut your losses and stop the initiative has been a new skill. Developing a culture that it's OK to fail on a small scale and then pivot to other initiatives has been a new paradigm for LifePoint.

Third, a combination of inside innovation (incubations) and outside innovation partners has worked best. Incubations take a lot of organizational care and feeding as well as LifePoint operations time to curate the ideas, assist in building the application, and then multiple iterations to mature the solution. The flexibility to dream it and it can happen is great, but the additional energy and time to see it through is a heavy burden. Having a mixed portfolio allows time for the incubations to mature but still get shovel-ready success in the innovation pipeline.

COLLABORATE AND LISTEN | THE INTERNATIONAL MEDICAL COMMUNITY (IMC) EXPERIENCE | *BY RAOUF HAJJI, ADDOBEA TWUM, LYNDSAY HERCULE, GABRIELLA MARCELJA, AND SHARENI DE LA ROSA XOCHITIOTZI*

"Collaborate and listen" emphasizes the importance of collaboration and active listening in driving innovation in healthcare. By working together and actively listening to each other's ideas, healthcare professionals, innovators, and entrepreneurs can identify new opportunities for innovation and develop more effective solutions to healthcare challenges.

Collaboration can bring together diverse perspectives and expertise, leading to more creative and effective problem-solving. Active listening, on the other hand, can help ensure that everyone's ideas are heard and considered, leading to more inclusive and equitable innovation.

We are a group of experts who had the opportunity to be mentors in different hackathons (MIT Hackathons, EUvsVirus) during the COVID-19 pandemic. Our experience during this globally challenging time in healthcare has altered our vision of healthcare and emerging technologies and shown us that improving universal access to high-quality healthcare worldwide needs strong collaboration between all the health stakeholders.

Seeing the importance of creating a healthcare innovation hub where young interns and imminent experts in different fields within MedTech (medical, legal, business, innovation, and technology) can meet and find guidance, mentoring, and assistance to develop their ideas, create their projects, and put their solutions in the marketplace, we established the International Medical Community (IMC).

Founded in 2020 in Rome, Italy, the IMC is a Non-Governmental Organization (NGO) that is legally incorporated and operates as a subsidiary of Sirius Global—Academic Diplomacy 4.0. 1. The IMC offers medical institutions, medical practitioners, academics and researchers, and public and private sector organizations focused on healthcare and healthcare innovation, with interdisciplinary support in the healthcare industry and in the field of medical technology.

We are dedicated to the implementation of Target 3 of the United Nations Sustainable Development Goals, 2030. With a special focus on supporting medical research and development for communicable and non-communicable diseases and achieving universal health coverage, we are equipped and positioned to support the medical community for the future of healthcare and MedTech intervention.

Our approach is based on listening to healthcare professionals, engineers, economists, and experts working on finding solutions for healthcare, social, economic, and political issues due to the pandemic and guiding them to conceptualize, create, and launch their projects.

The impact of the pandemic demands that our organization continues to work on the same strategy to cover the needs of academicians, researchers, medical practitioners, and entrepreneurs working on innovation in healthcare by offering them assistance and mentoring through the medical, legal, business, and innovation expertise of our organizational members.

Collaboration is set as the core of our internal teamwork and organization and also as an essential approach to developing our cooperation with individuals, groups, academic institutions, and healthcare and scientific communities.

We are working together and in collaboration with international teams and communities to offer the following:

■ **Healthcare Compliance Regulatory Support**: we aid individual, governmental, and non-governmental institutional clients with clear, concise, and timely healthcare regulatory advice, policy and procedure drafting, and healthcare compliance strategies across various jurisdictions under the international legal framework. We also aid clients in understanding and navigating developments in the administration of medical technology and medical devices in accordance with EU and USFDA In Vitro Diagnostic Medical Device Regulation (IVDR).

■ **Research and Development (R&D)**: we help design healthcare service delivery models through strategic partnerships with academic institutions, health policy think tanks, healthcare providers, and MedTech innovation firms. These partnerships support medical research processes and healthcare service delivery for optimal outcomes. We also create strategic alliances to support healthcare and MedTech R&D for healthcare industry clients who wish to outsource this function.

■ **Training and Professional Development**: we provide our individual and institutional clients access to a growing global database of medical providers, medical practitioners, and healthcare actors in the MedTech space. Our registered members are offered tailored knowledge tools through in-person and virtual training on key recurring and evolving areas within medical ethics, medical practice, and related MedTech fields.

Our team had developed the following:

1. **IMC Mentoring Program**: this initiative is set to act as an early-stage incubator for MedTech projects and startups, supporting them as they grow from an idea stage to a first prototype. In order to make healthcare sector services more accessible to everyone worldwide, we want all the projects to succeed and have a "maestro" guiding them during their first steps on a long entrepreneurship journey.

2. **IMC Internship Program**: this program is intended for young interns in medicine. Innovation, business, and legal fields, where they are trained to start biomedical research in emerging technologies in healthcare, develop their comprehension of the sector, and upscale their writing and analysis skills by creating monthly reports.

3. **IMC Monthly Reports**: these one- to two-page documents highlight some of the most relevant efforts in the healthcare sector. The monthly reports are divided into sections, namely medical, legal, technology, and innovation, which review the latest news in their respective fields related to health and the industry.

4. **IMC Training Courses**: with the collaboration of a team of international academicians, IMC plans to prepare training courses for its

different units (medical, innovation, business, and legal). This initiative aims to improve comprehension of MedTech development, its potential in the present and future of healthcare, and its challenges and solutions.

5. **IMC Spotlight**: IMC plans to launch a dedicated platform that shines a light on MedTech's remarkable advancements and breakthroughs. The forum will also feature interviews with experts in HealthTech, offering the opportunity to listen and understand the current situation, potential, and challenges of many healthcare solutions.

6. **IMC Publications and Research Projects**: led by a group of researchers and academicians in MedTech and close collaboration with other international teams, the IMC started publishing research papers and reference guides.

   a. The Physicians' Charter for Responsible AI is part of this project. As AI is developing rapidly, physicians must be explicit about what we expect from AI in patient care. It must be safe, accurate, and ethical. Physicians must be leaders in this field so we can shape AI's role in medicine. Together, we can responsibly leverage AI to enhance patient outcomes, reduce healthcare worker burnout, and transform healthcare for the better. With this approach, the IMC cofounder and medical lead, Dr Raouf Hajji, collaborated with nine other international experts to create an accessible, practical guide for the integration of AI into healthcare: The Physicians' Charter for Responsible AI (Executive Summary: https://lnkd.in/dBWnny4c / Full Charter: https://lnkd.in/d4P6f7Th / Website: https://lnkd.in/dSbzxAtk) to ensure that patient-centered care is always the focus of AI in medicine.

This document includes:

■ Our "10 Rules of the Road" for AI implementation, with a chapter for each rule using real clinical examples.
   – An executive summary offering a concise overview.
   – An accompanying website where you can download the PDFs, explore our core values, read the 10 Rules of the Road, and endorse the charter.

Multi-vortex Tornado Blueprint for Disruptive Global Co-Creation (Inspired by EUvsVirus): a chapter from the book Facilitation in Complexity: From Creation to Co-creation, from Dreaming to Co-dreaming, from Evolution to

Co-evolution, co-authored by IMC medical lead Dr Raouf Hajji and a group of imminent experts from diverse backgrounds and fields.

Academia Diffusion Experiment: trailblazing the Emergence from Co-creation: a chapter from the book: Facilitation in Complexity: from Creation to Co-creation, from Dreaming to Co-dreaming, from Evolution to Co-evolution: co-authored by IMC medical lead Dr Raouf Hajji and a group of imminent experts from diverse backgrounds and different fields

7. **IMC Healthcare Events**: since the first start of IMC, our team has been convinced by the role of sharing knowledge and expertise. So, with cooperation and partnerships with multiple scientific and expert communities worldwide, we organized a series of great, successful events about healthcare and emerging technologies.

   a. **Emerging Technology Conversations**: IMC's Co-Founder and Director, Lyndsay Hercule, speaks with Debby Lo-Dean, host of Emerging Technology Conversations, regarding the critical importance of innovation in the Medtech sector and the role IMC plays in bringing stakeholders together with the common goal of sharing ideas and resources globally.

   b. **ConV2X AI and Tech in Telehealth and Medicine 2023**: the last one was the collaboration of the IMC with Partners in Digital Health for the ConV2X AI and Tech in Telehealth and Medicine 2023, an event held at Loyola University in New Orleans, LA, on September 21 and 22.

   c. **AI in Healthcare: Potential and Challenges**: with the main idea of "Collaborate and Listen," we, the IMC, in collaboration with the Zealers Club from the Private International Polytechnic University of Tunis, Tunisia, had the opportunity to organize a successful online roundtable on "Artificial Intelligence (AI) in Healthcare: Potential and Challenges" held on 15th March 2023, 8 pm GMT, where international experts (USA, Uzbekistan, Belgium, China, and Tunisia) from diverse backgrounds were discussing AI in healthcare. We had the privilege to listen to the experts and understand their vision about AI in healthcare worldwide, figure out the crucial role of international collaboration in regulating and implementing this new technology in the healthcare system, and recognize how AI can improve and change the healthcare landscape.

   d. **Healthcare Summit 2021: RespiraCon II: Concept to Impact Conference: 29-30 January 2022**: was organized by The IMC with the partnership of Sirius Global Academic Diplomacy 4.0, Impact

Innovation Alliance, The Rice360 Institute of Global Health Technologies, Public Invention, and Every Breath Counts.

1. During the event, international experts participated in a critical global conversation on how to radically rethink the deployment of respiratory care technologies in the era of pandemics.
2. Engineers, healthcare professionals, innovators, and entrepreneurs were engaged in advancing the uptake of open-source technologies to benefit low-source healthcare settings worldwide. Using greater transparency, open-source techniques, and shared cooperative standards, we can build an open ecosystem of respiratory care medical devices, saving millions of lives in the next ten years.

e. **TechStars LUSAKA STARTUP WEEK: Theme: Embracing the 4th Industrial Revolution: 24th to 28th August 2020**: a Celebration of Tech Entrepreneurs in Lusaka: with the collaboration of the IMC team led by our Business Lead Gabriella Marcejla and our Medical Lead Raouf Hajji.

f. **Linz Impact Innovation Weeks 2020: Linz, Austria: Oct 1, 2020, 12:00 PM: Oct 15, 2020**: during two weeks starting from October 1st, the Impact Innovation Alliance, Sirius Global Academic Diplomacy, and IMC and its partners organized the Impact Innovation Week Linz 2020, showcasing a set of hybrid events, including press conferences, workshops, and meetups to sensitize and support major innovation breakthroughs "made in Europe," driving economic growth and fostering sustainable innovative infrastructures of tomorrow. On this occasion, two EUvsVirus program—winning impact-driven projects—Sophia Advisory and PolyVent—had launched their solutions in Linz, chosen as their starting point to fight the pandemic and the economic crisis affecting many small business owners in Austria and the world.

1. On 22 September 2020, during the Linz Impact weeks, an international panel hybrid event on "Reinventing Healthcare: from its Challenges to Opportunities" was organized in Linz, Austria.
2. Overall, "collaborate and listen" is a powerful strategy for driving innovation in healthcare because it encourages teamwork, open communication, and a focus on patient-centered solutions.
3. "Collaborate and Listen" remains one of the main strategies adopted by IMC. Thanks to this approach, we notice great success in developing new partnerships and upscale collaborations to benefit all and boost innovation in healthcare.

COLLABORATE AND LISTEN | UNLEASHING THE POWER OF TEAM INNOVATION | *BY CARIG KWAITKOWSKI*

> The best way to have a good idea is to have lots of ideas.
>
> *Linus Pauling (1961)*

Innovation is a driving force behind the advancement of society. From the wheel to AI, innovations have shaped the world, and every innovation started with a simple idea. Consider Linus Pauling, whose pioneering research in chemistry and molecular biology revolutionized our understanding of the atomic world. Just as Pauling's ideas left an indelible mark on science, each innovative leap, no matter its scale, contributes to our collective progress and evolution.

Yet true innovation rarely occurs in isolation. It thrives when people listen, observe, and communicate ideas and solutions to problems. The act of listening creates a space for people to share their thoughts and encouragement, paving the way for great innovations. This collaborative approach often results in multiple iterations, involving numerous individuals who contribute to the ideation and execution process. Inviting others to share in innovation galvanizes support and engagement, essential for success.

The importance of seeking the wisdom of others cannot be overstated. This essay explores the significance of ideation and collaboration in fostering innovation, emphasizing the power of teamwork in the healthcare industry, and embracing a philosophy of listening, sharing, and engaging to drive progress.

A Journey of Collaborative Innovation

The rise of generative AI tools marks a revolutionary leap in the world of technology, with unprecedented potential across a multitude of sectors. These advanced algorithms are not just creators; they can ideate, design, and predict in ways that are reshaping industries. Healthcare stands at the forefront of sectors poised to be transformed. Imagine AI systems that can generate personalized treatment plans based on an individual's genetics, tools that assimilate tens of thousands of data elements from a patient's chart into a concise update within seconds, virtual health assistants that can engage with patients to ease their healthcare journey, or software that can create simulations of a patient's response to specific medications.

As we stand at the cusp of these transformative innovations, a collaborative approach is critical to further progress. Harnessing the true potential of these tools requires that we work together with the very people we are meant to serve: patients, clinicians, caregivers, and staff. Their insights and experiences will not only inform the direction of these tools but ensure their relevance and efficacy. By integrating the voices of those most affected, we can navigate the integration and adoption of generative AI in a way that is not only innovative but ethical, safe, and truly beneficial for all involved.

Cedars-Sinai's Approach to Idea-Thons

The adage "nothing about me without me" encapsulates a profound call for inclusivity, emphasizing the indispensability of firsthand perspectives in decision-making and design processes. In the realm of innovation, this sentiment underscores the necessity to truly listen to those for whom we design solutions. It's not merely about crafting advanced technologies or pioneering novel strategies; it's about ensuring that these innovations solve real-world problems.

Cedars-Sinai has a long history of innovation in healthcare and in the practice of medicine, boasting a legacy of groundbreaking research and translational medical advances where ideas have transformed the health of our communities. Cedars-Sinai has consistently demonstrated a profound recognition of the value that frontline staff bring to the innovation process and that the road to innovation is built on collaboration. Those with hands-on experience and intimate knowledge of patient care intricacies are an invaluable resource in ideation and solution formulation. This collaborative ethos ensures that these voices are heard and remain integral to the design and execution of healthcare strategies. This philosophy has given birth to a new approach to AI technology innovation known as "Idea-Thons."

These Idea-Thons are the embodiment of the belief that by listening to its experts, Cedars-Sinai can unlock the potential of AI technology to create innovative solutions for patient care and healthcare operations. Idea generation sessions are far more than mere meetings; they are collaborative efforts where diverse voices harmonize to generate innovative ideas. However, these Idea-Thons also serve a pragmatic purpose. Given the vast potential of generative AI solutions, there is a palpable need to channel the flood of ideas in a direction that concentrates on what can be most beneficial in their applied use. To achieve this, the sessions involve not only physicians, specialists, nurses, pharmacists, therapists, and staff but also AI experts, data scientists, prompt engineers, and other tech-savvy professionals. The goal? To harmonize medical, clinical, operational, and technological expertise, ensuring that innovation remains holistic, grounded, and impactful. Through this multidisciplinary approach, Cedars-Sinai strives to bridge the gap between what AI can do and what the healthcare community truly needs.

The Idea-Thons, steered by Cedars-Sinai's AI Council, are emblematic of the institution's commitment to innovation that is both forward-thinking and grounded. At the heart of these sessions lie three foundational pillars that shape every phase of the process, ensuring a holistic approach to harnessing the potential of AI.

The first pillar, "investing and planning," serves as the compass for these brainstorming sessions. Recognizing that innovation without direction can often lead to dispersed efforts, this pillar emphasizes the need for strategic focus. By investing in areas of utmost significance and ensuring meticulous planning, the Idea-Thons channel the collective energies of participants toward challenges that are both pressing and aligned with the institution's priorities. It's not only about generating ideas but ensuring these ideas resonate with what is fundamentally important for Cedars-Sinai.

The second pillar, "transitioning innovation into adoption," underscores the idea that innovation in a vacuum holds little value. For an idea to truly make an impact, it must transcend the ideation phase and find its place in the real world. This pillar ensures that the Idea-Thons remain grounded in practicality, pushing teams to go beyond ideation to consider the trajectory of their ideas in real terms. It instills a perspective that weighs the feasibility of implementation, the potential for adoption, and the broader impact of an idea within the healthcare ecosystem.

The final pillar, advocating for the "ethical, responsible, and scientifically sound" use of AI, is the conscience of the Idea-Thons. As participants explore the vast expanse of what AI can achieve, this pillar serves as a constant reminder to proceed responsibly. It emphasizes that innovation must be underpinned by ethical considerations, ensuring equitable development and deployment. Beyond mere functionality, it necessitates a contemplation of broader societal implications, ensuring that the tools developed are effective, just, and equitable.

In weaving together these three pillars, the Idea-Thons at Cedars-Sinai ensure a comprehensive approach to innovation—one that is strategic, pragmatic, and sound.

Impacts on Patient Care and Beyond

Idea-Thons at Cedars-Sinai are structured events designed to harness the collaborative intellect of its participants over an intense three-hour session. Each event kicks off with a comprehensive 45-minute introduction to generative AI. This segment isn't just a theoretical overview; it delves into the mechanics of how LLMs function. To ensure participants gain a tangible understanding, live demonstrations are conducted, showcasing these AI models in action. This hands-on approach is intended to equip participants with a vision of the technology's potential, laying the groundwork for the brainstorming to follow.

Following the introduction, attendees are organized into teams, each typically consisting of 5–6 individuals. The groupings are designed with intention; each team is paired with a facilitator—an individual well-versed in the intricacies of generative AI. The facilitator's role is pivotal, offering real-time guidance, addressing queries, and ensuring the team remains focused on the task at hand. With the clock ticking, teams are afforded 75 minutes of intense brainstorming. Afterward, they are expected to distill their discussions into three concrete ideas.

Once the brainstorming concludes, it's time for each team to take center stage. Teams are allocated 10 minutes each to pitch their trio of ideas to a judging panel comprising members from the AI Council. This presentation phase is as much about the quality of the ideas as it is about articulation and potential impact.

After all teams have presented, the judges convene for what is perhaps the most challenging part of the Idea-Thons: deliberation. Their task is twofold: to identify the standout idea from each team and, from among these, when possible, to select the singular idea that shines brightest overall for the session. Through this quick yet rigorous and collaborative process, the Idea-Thons serve as a crucible for innovation, melding diverse perspectives with leading-edge technology to chart the future course of healthcare at Cedars-Sinai.

Cedars-Sinai has so far held three Idea-Thons. The first, involving a diverse group of physicians and specialists, generated innovative solutions in areas such as care coordination, triage, medication management, communications, and clinical trial recruitment. The second, tailored to non-physician clinical staff, resulted in proposals aimed at improving the delivery of healthcare. These proposals ranged from staffing optimization to enhancing patient interactions and streamlining the hiring process. The diverse group of participants showcased the extent of innovation that could be harnessed through collaboration.

In another Idea-Thon session, Cedars-Sinai expanded its horizons by inviting administrative and operational staff from various domains. These administrative teams presented ideas related to billing and authorization workflows, supply chain information assimilation tools, privacy and compliance screening, and project triage, among others. This diversification of perspectives illuminated the potential for profound efficiencies in processes that often remain behind the scenes but are fundamental to the smooth functioning of any healthcare institution. The insights from this cohort underscored the promise of AI in improving productivity and substantially decreasing operational costs. These enhancements, though typically less visible to the patient's eye, are paramount in streamlining the foundational aspects of healthcare delivery, ensuring that clinicians can focus on patient care without administrative burdens.

The Journey Continues

Cedars-Sinai's journey with Idea-Thons is a testament to the boundless potential of collaboration. Having amassed a wealth of ideas from these collaborative endeavors, Cedars-Sinai is charting a thoughtful path forward. Each winning idea, and many of the non-winning but highly valuable ideas, undergoes a rigorous assessment process to gauge its strategic alignment with the institution's overarching goals, its potential impact on both patient care and operations, its feasibility given current resources and technological landscape, and its originality, ensuring that it brings a fresh perspective or solution to the table.

Ideas that excel in these criteria enter a more intensive discovery and design stage. Here, the feasibility of these concepts is further tested, prototypes may be developed, and strategies for implementation are fleshed out. It's a phase that transforms raw, innovative thoughts into actionable projects, maintaining the institution's commitment to evolving patient care and operational excellence.

Cedars-Sinai remains dedicated to rigorous testing and impact assessments to ensure that these solutions align with its mission to deliver the highest quality care. The process underscores the importance of refining and tailoring AI solutions to meet the unique needs of both patients and the organization. This structured and inclusive approach is designed to ensure that the future of patient care is technologically advanced, deeply human-centric, and efficient.

Conclusion

The emergence of generative AI represents a transformative juncture in our technological evolution, with its potential paralleling the sweeping changes of the Industrial Revolution. Just as the industrial age redrew the contours of society, employment, and daily life, generative AI promises to usher in a similarly profound shift across a myriad of sectors. However, a notable distinction lies in our collective foresight. While the ramifications of the Industrial Revolution were perhaps not immediately evident to its contemporaries, today we possess a heightened awareness of the transformative power of AI. This affords us a unique vantage point—an opportunity not only to witness but to proactively harness and shape our shared trajectory. Through ideas, innovation, and collaborative efforts, we stand poised to adapt, embrace, and mold a future filled with possibilities.

"Collaborate and Listen" is a call to action, a reminder that innovation thrives in the fertile ground of ideation. By leaning into the wisdom of others, we can harness the full potential of generative AI, using it to tackle the most pressing challenges in healthcare. It's my hope that our experience, as showcased through Cedars-Sinai's Idea-Thons, exemplifies the transformative power of listening, sharing, and engaging with diverse voices—and that our journey inspires others to emphasize the significance of teamwork in cultivating AI-driven solutions for the healthcare community.

COLLABORATE AND LISTEN | TACKLING PANCREATIC CANCER WITH TEAMWORK AND AI | *BY LOGAN NYE*

Introduction

As a physician turned computer scientist at Carnegie Mellon, my journey into the intersection of healthcare and AI has been filled with experiences emphasizing the need for diverse skillsets and perspectives in innovation. When innovation sits at the nexus between two technical disciplines, such as computer science and medicine, communication and collaborative efforts become paramount. The inception of Galen Health, a startup I founded with my colleague Kushagra Agarwal, underscores this point. It was spurred by a shared ambition to harness AI in tackling some of healthcare's most daunting challenges. Among these, pancreatic cancer stands out as a particularly dire adversary, with pancreatic ductal adenocarcinoma (PDAC) claiming the lives of approximately 90% of the 500,000 patients diagnosed each year within less than 12 months. The story of Galen Health illustrates the importance of collaborative innovation that led to the creation of OncoSight, an AI platform for early detection of pancreatic cancer.

Background: The Genesis of Galen Health

The inception of Galen Health can be traced back to a moment of serendipitous collaboration between Kushagra and myself during a hackathon at Carnegie Mellon University. Our shared aspiration to leverage AI for the betterment of healthcare converged on one of the most formidable adversaries in the medical field: pancreatic cancer. The disease's bleak outlook, primarily due to the absence of effective early detection methods, presented a daunting challenge that was both critical and unresolved. Driven by a deep-seated commitment to make a tangible difference with AI, we set our sights on devising a solution that could potentially alter the trajectory of pancreatic cancer diagnosis and treatment.

Identifying the Need: Listening to the Frontlines

Our journey began with a foundational step: engaging directly with those at the frontline of pancreatic cancer treatment. We initiated discussions with specialists at the UPMC Hillman Cancer Center, an institution not just geographically close to CMU but also at the forefront of oncological research and treatment. These early interviews were revelatory; they not only confirmed our hypothesis that early diagnosis was the critical juncture at which the battle against pancreatic cancer could be swayed but also illuminated the nuanced challenges inherent in detecting the disease at its nascent stages. Pancreatic cancer's notorious subtlety in symptomatology, coupled with the absence of a viable screening mechanism, conspired to delay diagnosis until cancer had progressed to advanced, and often untreatable, stages. The main reason that pancreatic cancer has a 1-year survival rate of just around 10% is the lack of early diagnoses. If patients could be diagnosed just a little earlier, then approximately 1/3 of them would be effectively saved. This insight was pivotal, guiding our resolve to pioneer a solution based on concrete details. We then decided to start creating a solution that could intercept the disease early, thereby enhancing patient outcomes and survival rates.

Building the Team: A Multidisciplinary Approach

Acknowledging the multifaceted nature of the challenge at hand, we began assembling a team equipped with a diverse array of expertise fit for the challenge. This included healthcare practitioners from UPMC, adept in the clinical realities of pancreatic cancer; computer scientists from CMU, including Kushagra and myself, armed with the technical skills required to develop AI and machine learning technologies; and IT architects and data engineers from UPMC headquarters, who provided the essential infrastructure and data management insight regarding the local patient population of greater Pittsburgh. This multidisciplinary team was more than just a team of experts; it was a key enabler. Only by getting all personnel together did we cross traditional disciplinary boundaries enough to begin developing something like an AI platform for early detection of pancreatic cancer.

During this process, it became evident that the IT team was eager to work on AI solutions for their patients but lacked the medical expertise and connections to begin anything worthwhile. Simultaneously, physicians were often interested in developing AI for improving patient outcomes but lacked the technical skills to do so and were unaware of how health data management worked within their enterprise. Only by getting everyone together in a room at the same time did they realize they held the keys to each other's setbacks. Each voice was valued, and every insight was considered as we discussed how to successfully harness the potential of computer science practicals with the realities of healthcare system infrastructure. It was here, in this melting pot of expertise and experience, that the foundations for OncoSight were laid. Through iterative dialogue, direct conversation, and shared learning, we began to assemble the tools and resources that would underpin our AI-driven approach to early pancreatic cancer detection.

It is clear that the challenges we faced were too complex for any single discipline to solve in isolation. We only gained traction when all disciplines gathered together to identify who needed what to solve the problem of pancreatic cancer AI. It was the interplay of medical insight, computational innovation, and systems thinking that paved the way for a breakthrough. In this collaborative endeavor, we were guided by a shared vision: to transcend the limitations of current diagnostic timelines and chart a new course in the fight against pancreatic cancer. That was sufficient to break down barriers.

Developing OncoSight: Iteration and Integration

The evolution of OncoSight from a concept to a clinical tool was a journey marked by rigorous iteration and deep integration of multidisciplinary insights. At the heart of this process was our ongoing collaboration with the medical experts at UPMC, who provided critical feedback at every stage of development. This iterative cycle was not a mere back-and-forth but a nuanced dialogue, where each refinement of our AI algorithms was informed by clinical insights into the early markers of PDAC.

The complexity of pancreatic cancer, with its elusive early signs, demanded that our technology not only be precise but also adaptable to the subtleties of individual patient data. We dove into the granular details of clinical histories, imaging data, and biomarker profiles, calibrating our AI to discern the faint signals of early-stage cancer amid a sea of normal variations. This painstaking process of iteration and integration was driven by a singular aim: to craft an AI tool that was not just sophisticated in its technology but truly attuned to the realities of clinical practice.

With each iteration, OncoSight grew more refined, its algorithms increasingly capable of detecting the subtle patterns that signify the onset of pancreatic cancer. This progress was not merely technical; it was a series of breakthroughs that brought us closer to our goal of transforming pancreatic cancer diagnosis, making early detection a tangible reality with the potential to save countless lives.

Engaging Stakeholders: Expanding the Ecosystem

The development of OncoSight was paralleled by an expansive effort to engage a broad spectrum of stakeholders within the healthcare ecosystem. Beyond the confines of algorithm development, we ventured into discussions with potential users, healthcare administrators, and specialists at leading cancer centers. Each conversation was an opportunity to glean insights, understand needs, and anticipate the challenges of implementing a new diagnostic tool in varied clinical environments.

These engagements were far more than informational exchanges; they were collaborations in their own right, providing us with invaluable perspectives that shaped the evolution of OncoSight. From the practical concerns of primary care physicians to the strategic considerations of healthcare executives, every interaction was a piece of the puzzle, guiding us in refining OncoSight to meet the multifaceted demands of the healthcare landscape.

This expansive stakeholder engagement was instrumental in ensuring that OncoSight was not just a technological marvel but a solution grounded in the practicalities and intricacies of real-world healthcare delivery. It was a process that underscored the importance of looking beyond the technology itself to the ecosystem in which it would operate, ensuring OncoSight's relevance and utility in the hands of those who would ultimately use it to combat pancreatic cancer.

Overcoming Challenges: The Power of Collaboration

Our journey with OncoSight was not without its share of obstacles. The challenges we encountered ranged from initial skepticism within the medical community to the intricate regulatory pathways governing healthcare innovations, not to mention the daunting task of integrating a new AI tool into established healthcare workflows.

Each of these hurdles could have stymied our progress, yet the collaborative foundation upon which Galen Health was built turned these potential roadblocks into avenues for further innovation. The skepticism we faced prompted us to delve deeper into validating our algorithms, strengthening OncoSight's clinical credibility. Regulatory complexities became opportunities to engage in dialogue with policymakers, advocating for a framework that recognized the potential of AI in healthcare while ensuring patient safety and privacy.

Integrating OncoSight into existing healthcare systems was perhaps the most tangible challenge, requiring us to not only fine-tune our technology but also to understand and adapt to the complex ecosystems of hospitals and clinics. This effort was a testament to the power of collaboration, as we worked hand in hand with healthcare providers, IT specialists, and administrators to ensure that OncoSight could seamlessly complement existing workflows, enhancing rather than disrupting the vital work of cancer detection and treatment.

In facing these challenges, the collaborative ethos that had characterized our entire venture proved to be our greatest asset. It was through the strength of our partnerships, the diversity of our team, and the shared commitment to our mission that we were able to navigate the complexities of bringing a groundbreaking innovation like OncoSight to fruition.

Conclusion

The journey of Galen Health, from its inception at a Carnegie Mellon hackathon to the deployment of OncoSight in the clinical setting, epitomizes the transformative power of collaboration, listening, and teamwork in healthcare innovation. At every turn, the development of our AI tool for the early detection of pancreatic cancer was enabled by a commitment to multidisciplinary partnership, an openness to diverse perspectives, and the pursuit of a shared vision. The collaboration between physicians, computer scientists, data engineers, and a myriad of other stakeholders was not merely a strategy but an absolute necessity that guided Galen Health's mission.

This story underscores a fundamental truth: in the complex and ever-evolving landscape of healthcare, innovation cannot thrive in isolation. It is through the confluence of varied expertise, the willingness to listen and adapt, and the collective effort of dedicated individuals that solutions like OncoSight come to life. The impact of such innovations extends far beyond the technological domain, offering hope and the promise of improved outcomes to patients facing life-threatening diseases. As OncoSight begins to make its mark in the fight against pancreatic cancer, it stands as a testament to the idea that, in the pursuit of meaningful change, collaboration is not just beneficial—it is indispensable.

COLLABORATE AND LISTEN | EMPOWERING MEDICAL PROFESSIONALS WITH TAILORED EDUCATION FOR EFFECTIVE AI INNOVATION IN HEALTHCARE | *BY AVNEESH KHARE*

Throughout the world, AI is impacting almost every industry, including healthcare, which is one of the most promising areas for its application. AI holds great promise for enhancing healthcare, be it by increasing diagnostic accuracy or optimizing treatment for better patient outcomes. This potential, however, will be realized only when practitioners understand and effectively integrate AI into their practices. AI implementation in healthcare is no longer a pipe dream; it is already a reality in fields such as radiology and pathology. However, the rate at which these AI technologies advance has outpaced the methods by which current medical professionals are educated, resulting in a knowledge gap. Despite all of the excitement about the transformative potential of AI, a large part of the healthcare workforce still lacks a thorough understanding of the technology. This discrepancy highlights the urgent need to close the gap between current educational practices and technological advancement, ensuring that medical professionals are well-prepared to capitalize on AI's benefits while addressing its challenges.

Understanding the Need for Tailored AI Education in Healthcare

It is critical to understand that a paradigm shift in medical education is mandatory for effective AI application in healthcare. The traditional medical education methods focus on medical knowledge and clinical skills. In contrast, AI education necessitates a thorough understanding of data science, machine learning methodologies, and ethical issues. To successfully use AI technologies and critically analyze the results and consequences, medical practitioners must also develop critical thinking and knowledge management skills. Medical professionals need to develop competencies in various AI-related domains, including:

- **Foundational Knowledge**: medical professionals must understand how AI systems function, including the underlying concepts of algorithm development, data processing, and the numerous accessible machine-learning approaches. This is required to make judgments concerning the use and implementation of AI technology in healthcare contexts. Without it, medical practitioners may struggle to critically assess the reliability and validity of instruments, perhaps over-relying on such systems.
- **Critical Evaluation**: medical professionals must be taught to challenge the AI system's interpretations if they are to supplement human judgment rather than replace it. They must always consider the patient's entire clinical picture, in addition to other elements that AI-powered systems may miss. This is especially crucial when employing AI technology to aid in the diagnosis of diseases. The capability to critically appraise the outputs of AI avoids cases of misdiagnosis, thus ensuring safety and quality care.
- **Clinical Integration**: the successful application of AI technologies by medical professionals in real-world clinical situations is critical to AI's effectiveness in healthcare. This entails incorporating AI technology to improve, rather than disrupt, routine clinical workflows. Medical professionals should be trained in practical applications, such as using AI for diagnostic imaging, predictive analytics, and crafting personalized treatment plans. Furthermore, they must be able to skillfully control the interface between the AI systems and other health technologies to ensure smooth flow and optimal performance.
- **Communication and Collaboration**: medical professionals should have the ability to effectively share knowledge about AI with different

stakeholders. They should be ready to answer any questions patients may have regarding the use of AI in their care, as well as to describe how it works in medical decision-making, what risks it includes, and what benefits are expected. Furthermore, they need to be able to bridge the gap between clinical and technological domains to foster multidisciplinary collaboration in the development and use of successful AI solutions for healthcare.

Risks of Poor Education

Failure to deliver tailored AI education to medical professionals poses serious risks. AI technology may be used ineffectively, resulting in misdiagnosis, incorrect treatment decisions, or jeopardizing patient safety. Not recognizing the bias embedded in the AI system may increase current gaps in healthcare delivery. Biased data sets, for example, might provide skewed outcomes, placing specific patient groups in danger. This has the potential to damage trust in both AI technology and the medical professionals who employ it. Furthermore, a provider's inability to apply AI effectively may reduce patient trust in the entire healthcare system, especially in situations of AI-related errors or ethical breaches. Tailored AI education for medical professionals will help them navigate such issues. Therefore, tackling gaps in AI literacy is not only critical for keeping up with technological breakthroughs but also for ensuring the integrity and equity of healthcare delivery.

Designing Effective AI Education Programs for Medical Professionals

Educational programs should be specifically tailored to satisfy the needs of medical professionals in order to be effective. They have to be designed practically, comprehensively, and flexibly to overcome the various challenges medical professionals face in the assimilation of these technologies into their busy workflow.

Competency-Based Education

Medical professionals should be able to apply the knowledge and skills they acquire in competency-based education to real-world situations. This involves studying the principles of machine learning, gaining a solid knowledge of data literacy, and evaluating the ethical implications of AI. Programs should be designed to prepare professionals to critically evaluate AI outputs, identify biases in the AI tools being used, and apply those tools to patient care.

Take a Multidisciplinary Approach

Since AI is a multidisciplinary topic, it becomes important to include perspectives from numerous academic disciplines, including data science, ethics, law, and clinical medicine. Adopting a multidisciplinary approach can help medical practitioners become more aware of the general and technical implications for data security, patient care, and regulatory compliance. For example, courses on medical ethics might be taught alongside courses on AI training to highlight concerns about algorithmic bias and patient consent.

Implement a Longitudinal and Integrated Curriculum

A longitudinal curriculum that encompasses AI education across a medical professional's career timeline would be an excellent foundation for this emerging domain. Basic AI principles must be presented early in schooling, whereas advanced ones should be covered progressively to promote successful learning. An integrated approach can enable medical students and professionals to use their AI skills in a variety of clinical settings, potentially improving learning and strengthening their ability to deploy AI solutions in practice.

Make Use of Innovative Instructional Techniques

Innovative teaching methods, such as simulation and interactive workshops, as well as the use of case studies, have the potential to significantly improve learning outcomes. They offer hands-on training and practical insights into the use of AI in healthcare. Simulations, for example, may produce clinical scenarios in which AI tools aid in diagnosis, allowing medical professionals to practice and enhance their abilities in a controlled environment.

An Example of Innovative AI Education for Medical Professionals

Innovative AI education is becoming essential for medical professionals due to the rapid advancements in artificial intelligence and its increasing role in healthcare. Integrating AI into medical training is crucial to enhance patient care, improve efficiency, and drive medical advancements while ensuring ethical and effective AI usage in healthcare. An example of Innovative AI Education for Medical Professional is 'Doctors AI'. Doctors AI from India is a fast-growing online community advocating for AI education among medical professionals. It is an emerging network showcasing what customized education could do to spark AI literacy among medical professionals, along with how this learning could be put into practice.

Besides monthly webinars, journal club meetings, and constant community support, "Doctors AI workshops," which are designed to be both hands-on and online, are one of the main highlights. This past year, the community organized three such workshops focused on real-world use cases relevant to medical professionals. The participants' overwhelming favorable responses validated the sessions' success. Several medical professionals who attended these sessions began utilizing AI tools in their daily lives and even created modest AI-based initiatives, demonstrating the practical value of tailored education.

"Doctors AI" is now developing further workshops at the basic and advanced levels, along with workshops geared to specific target groups, such as medical students. This will not only improve the comprehension of current practitioners but will also prepare future medical professionals for AI from the start of their careers.

Address Barriers to Implementation

Despite the numerous benefits of AI education for medical professionals, various barriers may prevent its widespread implementation. Apprehension of being replaced at work, time constraints, a lack of competent teachers, and restricted funding are all prevalent issues. Collaborations with industry experts and academic institutions can provide the experience and finances required to create high-quality instructional materials, overcoming such limitations. Collaboration among medical professionals, data scientists, and AI engineers can also increase the practical value of the instructional content.

The Role of Stakeholders in Fostering AI Literacy

AI literacy efforts in healthcare are multifaceted and involve a variety of stakeholders, all of whom contribute to the ultimate goal of preparing future physicians to use AI technologies efficiently and ethically. These include:

- **Medical Schools and Institutions**: They must play an active role in promoting AI literacy by incorporating AI education into their medical curricula. They should place AI at the core of training by providing both theoretical knowledge and practical experience to students. It involves funding for the training of educators, AI labs, and simulation centers with teams of data science and AI specialists. Medical schools can prepare future medical professionals for the effective use of AI technologies in clinical settings by cultivating innovative cultures and interdisciplinary collaborations.
- **Professional Societies**: They play an important role in establishing standards and providing ongoing learning for medical professionals. They can help develop guidelines and best practices for the ethical use of AI, including issues related to data privacy and bias. These bodies can also develop continuing education resources to include workshops, seminars, and certification programs at different levels of expertise. They can organize conferences and put up forums where one can share ideas with others on the best way to remain abreast of the latest AI developments and best practices.
- **Policymakers**: They must set up the regulatory and policy framework that will guide AI in health care to facilitate its adoption. They can contribute to the development of supportive policies on legal and ethical boundaries for the use of AI in general, particularly in terms of data protection laws and clinical validation standards. For the public to trust AI technologies, ethical and regulatory issues such as algorithmic bias and data security must be addressed. Policymakers can further encourage AI research and education by providing funding opportunities for the development of medical training tools.
- **Technology Developers**: They should aim to create AI solutions that can help meet real-world healthcare needs while adhering to ethical requirements. They should involve medical professionals in the design and development stages to guarantee that the technologies generated are practical, user-friendly, and suitable for clinical applications. Developers must prioritize usability and accessibility for their product's end users by creating straightforward interfaces that medical professionals can utilize. To ensure trustworthy and successful AI systems, ethical aspects such as openness in AI decision-making and bias reduction must be addressed.

■ **Patients**: They are at the epicenter of the entire healthcare ecosystem. They can stand up for the ethical use of AI and demand transparency, throwing their weight behind regulations that support a patient's right to privacy and ensure fair treatment. By providing feedback and taking part in the evaluation of the AI tools, patients can encourage further development of these technologies for better customization according to human needs and expectations.

AI can only be successfully integrated and advanced into healthcare if medical education is tailored to meet such needs. Gaining a comprehensive understanding of AI tools is crucial for health professionals, as it is part of a broader approach to integrating AI technologies into medical practice, encompassing diagnosis and treatment planning. AI literacy necessitates more than just fundamental operating knowledge; it also necessitates critical evaluation of AI systems, as well as education on ethical problems and how to incorporate technology into healthcare processes. The value of tailored education in obtaining this skill cannot be emphasized.

Innovative initiatives like Doctors AI workshops exemplify how creative and practical education programs may help bridge the gap between AI technology and clinical practice. Hands-on training, webinars, and continuing community support ensure that medical professionals are both competent and confident in employing AI technology in real-world circumstances.

Structured interdisciplinary approaches may provide medical professionals with the fundamental understanding, practical skills, and ethical awareness required to navigate the complexities of AI. The involvement of various stakeholders is thus critical for making the AI education ecosystem more inclusive and comprehensive. Every group contributes differently to the process, from producing curricula and standards to creating supporting regulatory frameworks and encouraging ethical conversation. Collaboration among them enables a consistent and well-rounded approach to AI education while also encouraging ethical technology use.

Finally, AI literacy will be essential not just for keeping up with technological advancements, but also for determining the future of healthcare delivery. Empowering medical practitioners with the skills needed to properly employ AI enhances the likelihood of better patient outcomes, enhanced efficiency across health systems, and assurance that patients are treated fairly and ethically. As AI continues to grow rapidly in healthcare, providing such tailored education to medical professionals may prove to be the key to realizing its full potential. This proactive effort, in addition to enhancing medical practice, will help to establish a more efficient, equitable, and patient-centered healthcare system.

Bibliography

Charow, R., Jeyakumar, T., Younus, S., Dolatabadi, E., Salhia, M., Al-Mouaswas, D., Anderson, M., Balakumar, S., Clare, M., Dhalla, A., Gillan, C., Haghzare, S., Jackson, E., Lalani, N., Mattson, J., Peteanu, W., Tripp, T., Waldorf, J., Williams, S., … Wiljer, D. "Artificial intelligence education programs for health care professionals: scoping review." *JMIR Medical Education*, vol. 7, no. 4, 2021, e31043. 10.2196/31043

Kimiafar, K., Sarbaz, M., Tabatabaei, S.M., Ghaddaripouri, K., Mousavi, A.S., Mehneh, M.R., & Baigi, S.F.M. "Artificial intelligence literacy among medical professionals and students: a systematic review." *Frontiers in Health Informatics*, vol. 12, 2023, 168. 10.30699/fhi.v12i0.524

Krive, J., Isola, M., Chang, L., Patel, T., Anderson, M., & Sreedhar, R. "Grounded in reality: artificial intelligence in medical education." *JAMIA Open*, vol. 6, no. 2, 2023. 10.1093/jamiaopen/ooad037

Lomis, K., Jeffries, P., Palatta, A., Sage, M., Sheikh, J., Sheperis, C., & Whelan, A. "Artificial intelligence for health professions educators." *NAM Perspectives*, 2021. 10.31478/202109a

Malerbi, F.K., Nakayama, L.F., Dychiao, R.G., Ribeiro, L.Z., Villanueva, C., Celi, L.A., & Regatieri, C.V. "Digital education for the deployment of artificial intelligence in health care." *Journal of Medical Internet Research*, vol. 25, 2023, e43333. 10.2196/43333

Ötleş, E., James, C.A., Lomis, K.D., & Woolliscroft, J.O. "Teaching artificial intelligence as a fundamental toolset of medicine." *Cell Reports Medicine*, vol. 3, no. 12, 2022, 100824. 10.1016/j.xcrm.2022.100824

Pauling, L. (1986). *A lifelong quest for peace: A dialogue.* W.W. Norton & Company.

Tahseen, S., Channar, H.B., Bhatti, U., Laghari, T.A., Areej, S., & Kamran, S.M. "Unveiling healthcare practitioners' knowledge and acceptance of artificial intelligence in healthcare." *Journal of Health and Rehabilitation Research*, vol. 4, no. 2, 2024, 859–864. 10.61919/jhrr.v4i2.889

Wu, M., Huang, X., Jiang, B., Li, Z., Zhang, Y., & Gao, B. "AI in medical education: the moderating role of the chilling effect and STARA awareness." *BMC Medical Education*, vol. 24, no. 1, 2024. 10.1186/s12909-024-05627-4

Chapter 6

Communicate and Eliminate Barriers

Cross-communication is essential to promote innovation. By stripping virtual or physical barriers to communication, ideas have a better chance of being realized.

Transparency is key to effective relationships, which are required for innovation to thrive. The depth and width you share will determine the size of your success. Look for every opportunity and platform to share while actively eliminating barriers to communication. Effective communication will make or break innovation. If active or passive resistance rises, so must your communication. While technology provides great tools to reach many, do not neglect the power of in-person eyeball-to-eyeball dialogue.

COMMUNICATE AND ELIMINATE BARRIERS | HOW TO USE ARTIFICIAL INTELLIGENCE TO IMPROVE PATIENT SAFETY CULTURE AND PRACTICES IN HEALTH SYSTEMS | *BY KUMAR SUBRAMANIAM*

Summary

Hospitals are complex adaptive environments. Patients admitted to hospitals suffer harm from a variety of medical errors. For many reasons, including poor safety culture, stigma, overwork, and burnout, patient safety events are vastly underreported. Safety management systems have seen limited success

DOI: 10.4324/9781032715155-6

because they were largely focused on single events based on deterministic approaches – structured follow-ups, root cause analyses, FMEA analyses, etc. – that are best suited for mechanistic rather than complex adaptive systems (CASs).

A prudent approach to learning how a CAS operates is to observe it and the decisions that system participants make. This shift in approach requires implementing processes and analytics tools that allow for radically open and transparent communications. Artificial intelligence-based approaches, augmented by a culture of safety and appropriate policies, can radically improve an organization's ability to communicate freely and collaborate on managing safety events. This in turn can improve patient safety practices, to keep patients safer in healthcare environments.

Keeping Patients Safe in a Complex Adaptive System

Hospitals are complex adaptive environments. A CAS is one where a variety of actors with diverse skills, experience, and knowledge follow simple rules of engagement to learn and innovate in unpredictable ways based on unit and system-level feedback loops. A CAS is one where people are densely interconnected by virtue of their varied roles in managing patients. Many diverse skills and departments are brought together at volume and at high velocity to provide care to patients, and these skills are applied using a dizzying array of technologies. The many caregivers across independent departments make thousands of individual decisions each day. The decisions these individuals make can interact with each other in unpredictable and sometimes maladaptive ways depending on how the hospital environment is structured[2]. The external forces they face are somewhat unpredictable and may surprise even well-defined processes. In the US, external forces have led to financial pressures faced by health systems, leading to mergers and acquisition transactions, bankruptcies. These transactions could be traumatic 'life events' for the two merging systems.

The impacts of such dizzying complexity in the health system industry on patient safety are not hard to find. The World Health Organization has estimated that 1 in 10 patients were harmed in inpatient settings and suggested that as many as 4 in 10 patients are harmed in ambulatory settings. The WHO also observed that close to 50% of such harms were preventable[3]. Adverse events that could be avoided include medication errors, unsafe surgical procedures, healthcare-associated infections, diagnostic errors, patient falls, pressure ulcers, patient misidentification, and unsafe blood transfusion. Medical errors also have wide-ranging impacts on staff that are involved with and experience safety events. A majority of health-care professionals have reported suffering at least one physical or emotional 'second victim' distress from an adverse event involving patients[1].

Raising Awareness on Medical Errors and Safety Events

The Institute of Medicine published *To Err is Human* in 1999, followed by *Crossing the Quality Chasm* (Institute of Medicine, 2001), to raise awareness of the impact of medical errors on patients. Over time, State and Federal governments mandated a wide range of mandatory reporting requirements around patient safety events. Patient Safety Organizations (PSOs) were formed with the laudable goal of helping with improvements based on knowledge sharing. Systems and leaders responded with improvement initiatives and achieved limited success. These initiatives were largely based on using deterministic approaches – structured follow-ups, root cause analyses, FMEA analyses, etc. – on single events that are best suited for mechanistic rather than for CASs[4].

However, efforts to take advantage of those opportunities and to implement improvements were hampered by common barriers to reporting, barriers that discouraged potential reporters from speaking up and reduced the opportunities for learning and improvement. Barriers included system functionality (e.g. time-consuming or complex reporting processes), organizational structures to support safety and quality initiatives, organizational culture (e.g. fear of retribution), factors related to staff awareness (e.g. an insufficient understanding of the process or its importance), and poorly designed digital solutions, to name a few.

Key Barriers to Improving Safety Management

The first automated reporting systems were rudimentary systems that replaced processes using paper forms. Over time, these digital systems evolved from using Excel spreadsheets toward leveraging low-code, no-code platforms that users could build and customize. Customers bore the burden of designing and customizing their own safety event management system, with the technology vendor facilitating the process with tools and training. Quite often, the solutions customers created using the apparent freedom afforded by these early solutions lacked cohesion of purpose and an overarching architecture of purpose. Safety forms and datasets proliferated within organizations as a result, and the job of the hapless administrator was reduced to helplessly watching a mountain of poor-quality data emerge around them with no way to separate the signal from the noise.

The job of the chief safety and quality officer in a health system is complicated and therefore difficult. They remain busy playing whack-a-mole with administering the management of safety practices and workflows. They remain inundated with patient care and organizational decisions that need to be made under conditions of uncertainty and therefore have limited opportunities to create a learning ecosystem to help manage and mitigate the impacts of patient safety events. Poorly designed solutions and a variety of other reasons, including poor safety culture, stigma, overworked staff, and burnout, contribute to patient safety events being vastly underreported. When staff do report events, they are required to follow guidelines to largely focus on serious safety events. Reporting cultures can have a chilling effect on how and when safety events are recorded.

The authors assert that poorly designed system and process communication channels and stunted feedback loops have a lasting adverse impact on the ability of safety staff to capture and act on safety events. Software vendors have developed deterministic solutions that oversimplify patient safety events. As an example, safety event reporting tools routinely limit users to selecting a single category to be assigned per event. In reality, events usually involve multiple factors and concerns. Frontline staff are also asked to assign a 'harm score' to events. Research has since shown that harm scores reported by frontline staff are only moderately reliable and helpful in triaging and prioritizing safety events. System design limitations lead staff to spend tremendous amounts of time creating workarounds to help them manage their safety practices – time that would be better spent working on the safety concerns embedded in these events.

The amount of time it takes for frontline workers to submit a patient safety event report is known to be one of the top barriers to reporting[5]. Despite safety culture improvement initiatives, clinicians remain skeptical that they can report safety events without repercussions. It is telling that safety events voluntarily reported by physicians accounted for only about 5% of all reports in a major hospital system. When staff do report safety events, rarely do they receive any feedback or requests for additional information. They might not know who acted on their reported event and whether leaders were working on improving the system or process. This lack of transparency makes frontline staff believe that their opinions don't matter.

In their effort to simplify, vendors treated safety events like 'incident tickets' that lent themselves to being 'opened', 'reviewed', and 'closed' with operational metrics that favored measuring process efficiency rather than measuring improvement in safety practices. Their approaches favored stripping context from free text narratives with the goal of capturing discrete data elements for 'reportability'. Popular data visualization tools are used to create quantitative dashboards. The reliance on quantitative methods to the exclusion of qualitative approaches has limited the ability of safety reviewers and analysts to glean actionable insights using contextual information related to safety events. These limitations have had the effect of creating an artificial distance between safety and quality disciplines in a health system. "Safety Theatre" was born.

Safety and Quality

Health systems understand the value of improving their patient safety culture. There is a direct link between safety event management practices, safety culture, and care quality. Agency for Healthcare Research and Quality (AHRQ) surveys on patient safety culture SOP surveys measure safety culture at an organization. Hospital units with better scores on the SOPS scores demonstrate better performance on clinical measures of quality. A just culture of safety, a dynamic safety event reporting taxonomy, an inclusive and collaborative approach to safety event reviews, and the right analytics tools are necessary building blocks for setting up insights-driven event management practices such as structured follow-up and investigations like RCAs, ACAs, and CRPs that can help bridge between safety and quality practices.

Safety analytics tools can help health systems identify signals in the safety data. Even though SOP survey scores and key healthcare delivery outcome measures are significantly related, setting up for and acting on SOP survey results can be burdensome for organizations without the right analytic tools and assessments. Using a mix of statistical and machine learning methods, organizations can glean rich insights for use in the *Communication about Error* area of the SOP survey, the *Communication Openness* area of the SOP survey, facilitate seamless, transparent, and secure collaboration on patient safety events and the subsequent investigations to help with the *Response to Error* area of the SOPS, and explore insights on the frequency and the quality of the collaborations that occur and are measured on the *Teamwork* area of the SOPS survey.

Communication as an Engine of Innovation

Communication within departments and across all levels of an organization can be the rails on which the engine of innovation rides. This is true of deterministic systems but assumes even greater importance in CASs like a health system. Because relationships between decisions in a CAS can be non-linear and because behaviors can emerge in unpredictable ways in such systems, establishing communication pathways begins with learning how a CAS operates by observing the system, the decisions that people make, and the spontaneous collaborations that blossom when people align on shared objectives. From a patient safety perspective, healthy horizontal and vertical communication channels are necessary to allow safe reporting, transparency in feedback and reporting, and a collaborative approach to resolving root causes.

Structures and systems, including digital and other tools that support these foundational characteristics of a healthy safety management practice, are needed. These systems and tools need to be designed around the users' workflows rather than the other way around. This inside–out approach to innovation is healthy and sustainable when it includes elements of inclusivity, equity, and diversity in the design process and embraces a paradigm shift toward objectives-driven design.

Objectives-driven design acknowledges the contextual needs of an organization rather than retrofitting the needs to existing designs. An example of retrofitting is the overreliance on quantitative metrics rather than a willingness to use qualitative approaches and the tools that can support such approaches to enhance users' workflows. From a patient safety perspective, this means being open to the idea of open and dynamic safety taxonomies that can flex as the organization flexes over time; processes adapt as event trends shift over time, people transition in and out of roles, and new ideas and skills are brought to bear. An objectives-driven system can adapt to such changes because it anticipates them.

This adaptability protects precious collaboration channels within the system. From a safety event management perspective, examples of productive communication include:

■ Reporters have the ability to follow events they submitted – even when the submission is confidential – and to be able to continue communicating without fear of reprisal with reviewers.
■ A chat-like experience that is familiar to staff from their use of social media channels and enables free and fair dialogue and collaboration on risks identified within event reports and on mitigation strategies being implemented.
■ Follow-up owners for events are automatically and transparently assigned for increased accountability.

■ Self-selection capabilities on notification preferences that users can configure and manage to receive notifications directly in their email inboxes.

Using Artificial Intelligence (AI) in Safety

AI has a foundational role to play in the creation of robust communication channels, especially in patient safety management practices. Starting with voluntary event reporting, objectives-driven design methods can use AI tools to elicit insights from the context-rich information in the event reports. This avoids the problem of information stripping used in retrofit approaches to safety surveillance design. AI-driven approaches allow for a fuller representation of each event and its complexity. AI tools can help identify groups of similar events to cluster them in terms of those needing a shared approach to investigating root causes. This, in turn, allows organizations to communicate and activate processes necessary to address the issues surrounding an adverse event.

AI-driven approaches can support objective-oriented solution design to reduce perceived barriers to reporting and engaging in the life cycle of events. Event submission forms can be reduced dramatically to reduce the learning burden on staff. Submission forms can be shortened to shorten the amount of time it takes to report an event. Users can do what they do best when harm score updates are left to those who have the skills and the experience to capture them accurately. Safety events can be automatically categorized and routed to appropriate reviewers. Users can interact with the categorization engine so that it can retrain. Large amounts of qualitative data can be harnessed for a variety of ends, including the use of near-miss events to predict event trends. Most importantly, however, using AI-driven approaches allows solution designers to create unprecedented value by making it easy for customers to quickly separate the key safety signals from the noise in their proliferating safety data.

AI-driven approaches augmented by policies and a Just Culture initiative can yield dramatic improvements in safety culture through improved communications. Feedback rates to reporters can improve, leading to positive dialogue among reporters and reviewers about specific safety concerns. AI-driven solutions can enable safety analysts to see problems across units and entities that would not otherwise be readily visible. Communications change from being all about 'what happened?' to 'what's going on to cause this issue across departments?'. The organization begins shifting its mindset from thinking about events to thinking about risks. The focus of the conversation shifts to learning about organizational blind spots and identifying opportunities to mitigate risks.

Conclusion

It has been 20+ years since *To Err is Human* was published. Patients continue to be harmed at unacceptable rates. Safety event management practices have improved over the years. There is an increased awareness and action taken toward preventing adverse events from occurring. However, more needs to be done.

AI techniques can enable radical new solution designs that can make safety event reporting and communications robust, transparent, and effective. Approaches to patient safety that can pair safety staff with artificial intelligence-driven solutions can help widen their lens, give them richer insights, and help them make informed decisions to make their complex adaptive environment an increasingly safer place for patients.

COMMUNICATE AND ELIMINATE BARRIERS | AI-ENHANCED OUTREACH STRATEGIES – STRENGTHENING CONNECTIONS AND IMPACT | *BY THOM BALES, ANUPRIYA RAMRAJ, AND DEEPAK GOYAL*

The potential and promise of AI – for early healthcare diagnostics, patient outreach, and communication – have been unfolding for a while now. It started long before AI became a strategic imperative for every organization, and today it has grown in prominence such that the absence of its mention in investor earnings calls raises eyebrows.

While there have been advances in healthcare that shine a light on the potent force of AI, effective health outcomes seem elusive to the population at large. This translates into an escalating cost of delivering healthcare. For perspective, chronic diseases are the leading drivers of the US$4.1 trillion spent in the US on healthcare. They are also the leading cause of disability and death. Providing care for people with diabetes, a chronic disease, alone accounts for 25% of the healthcare costs.

AI has offered ways to detect and intervene early for chronic diseases and other ailments. For instance, since 2018, when the FDA permitted the marketing of the first medical device to use AI to detect diabetic retinopathy, an eye disease in adults with diabetes, companies have sold hundreds of eye exam devices to practices. These devices capture retina images and upload them to the cloud to be analyzed by AI using ML algorithms and generate reports for clinicians. Not only does the eye exam (that can be conducted in the absence of the doctor) give immediate results on the onset of the disease, but it also translates into dollars saved and the convenience of not having to make an additional appointment, a win-win for payers, patients, and providers.

The technology has demonstrated a consequential benefit for those diagnosed with the disease that can lead to vision impairment and blindness – better follow-up rates. Research suggests that when the test results are delivered to the patients immediately instead of after weeks or months, patients are more likely to act on it.

Health disparities caused by the social, economic, lifestyle, and environmental factors experienced by certain groups are a key focus area for policymakers and healthcare professionals. In an acutely stressed healthcare system, the use of AI can be transformative. The case in point here is using AI to identify the drivers of health inequities in vulnerable communities and to address the gaps to deliver equitable care.

The exponential growth in the digitization of the healthcare industry spurred by the pandemic has led to troves of clinical and non-clinical data being generated at a rapid pace. Between data from Electronic Health Records (EHR), pharmacies, clinical trials, and wearable devices, the industry is favorably placed to leverage AI to tackle some of its most unrelenting challenges.

Combining medical and non-medical data (social determinants of health), AI can identify and examine patterns that cause health disparities. These findings can then be used to guide public health policy, targeted communications, and fuel scientific studies focused on eradicating health inequities.

Predict Before the Predator Strikes

Enhanced risk assessment and *personalized care* are the foundation of early diagnosis, stage prediction, and management of chronic diseases. AI algorithms trained on historical medical data in conjunction with social determinants of health can pin down the drivers of specific health conditions. These insights can then be applied to real-time data, such as patients' unique medical records, to create their personalized risk profiles. Based on these assessments, physicians can craft personalized care plans and trigger targeted and timely interventions.

For instance, cigarette smoking, a key risk factor, causes at least one disease in more than 16 million Americans. Based on the personalized risk profiles, if smokers could be helped to quit and youth deterred from starting to smoke, a whopping US$240 billion in healthcare spending could be saved every year.

The shift from reactive to proactive care is the key to arresting disease progression, particularly for chronic diseases such as diabetes, hepatitis, and heart failure. The identification of vulnerable groups also enables more efficient resource allocation.

Real World Illustration – Potent Force of Data and AI in Early Diagnosis

An open source medical imaging and data repository platform created by the efforts of the Open Source Imaging Consortium (OSIC) and supported by PwC and Microsoft has enabled more timely and accurate diagnosis and treatment for Idiopathic Pulmonary Fibrosis (IPF), a rare lung disease that takes more than two years (median time) to diagnose and leaves the patient with three to five years of life expectancy. OSIC, a not-for-profit cooperative, collaborates with clinicians and researchers who share High-Resolution Computed Tomography (HRCT) scans to create a rich repository of multi-ethnic, real-world clinical and imaging data. With the help of a central repository and AI technology, OSIC is trying to enable more accurate and timely prognosis, diagnosis, and response to therapy for other rare diseases too.

Overcoming Communication Barriers

Once the at-risk population segments have been identified, health professionals face the 'last-mile' challenge of communicating with the target groups clearly and inclusively. For personalized care plans to work, patient engagement is paramount. The targeted educational resources and behavior change campaigns must be contextualized to specific population segments. Through the usage of generative AI, personalized communication campaigns can be developed that adapt to the linguistics, historical, and cultural context of the target audience. In addition to content creation and curation, AI can also help determine the most effective channels and the frequency to engage with the communities, leading to more efficient intervention.

Real World Illustration – Potent Force of Data and AI in Outreach and Personalized Patient Care

During the pandemic, when physical interaction with physicians was limited, the WHO introduced virtual health worker Florence that leverages AI to help people quit smoking. The digital health worker/counselor uses AI to help people develop a personalized plan to quit tobacco through a series of questions based on the user's medical history and habits. Unlike a typical chatbot, Florence uses facial expressions and provides real-time empathic responses. The digital counselor can respond to audio, visual, and textual information provided by users and interact in multiple languages.

Along these lines, this year WHO launched Smart AI Resource Assistant for Health (S.A.R.A.H, aka Sarah), a prototype of a digital health promoter. Sarah offers multilingual, 24x7 support via video and text on multiple devices. The digital assistant can provide information on a multitude of topics, such as mental health, heart and lung diseases, and diabetes.

Using AI, the WHO is not only amplifying its reach to educate people and enhance public health but also plugging in the gaps arising from the shortage of skilled healthcare professionals. In a study conducted by Forrester, creating personalized interactions (for individuals or populations) is the most common business value (76% of respondents) driving interest in AI at health and life sciences companies.

Real World Illustration – Potent Force of Data and AI in Enhancing Patient Experience

To meet CMS mandates for patient access and provider directory APIs, a regional health insurance carrier leveraged advanced analytics and AI to optimize its value-based care programs and provider performance, hence elevating its digital presence. The carrier was able to increase trust in the member community while empowering members to manage their information across the insurer's programs and applications.

Challenges in Realizing the True Promise of AI

The true promise of AI can only be realized by ascertaining the quality, completeness, and accuracy of the data underlying the models. This is in addition to operating within the constructs of laws and regulations that protect patient data and privacy. Healthcare systems as they stand today have data strewn across multiple sources, and they exist in silos.

A good starting point is to develop an enterprise-wide data governance strategy that aims at integrating the data from disparate sources leveraging the cloud. With the intended purpose of analysis as the North Star, qualify the sources that will form the basis of all insights. Not all organizations have the internal skills and expertise to adopt AI, and that's why partnering with a trusted AI vendor becomes crucial. Given the sensitive nature of data being dealt with, it is paramount to use AI responsibly by establishing the guardrails that help build trust and mitigate the associated risks.

COMMUNICATE AND ELIMINATE BARRIERS | OVER 1 BILLION BRAIN CELLS SERVED YEARLY | *BY RICHARD ONG, DR. SUSANA BOWLING, AND KIMBERLY SZYMCZAK*

Introduction

Passion, Drive, and Communication help bring innovation and improved patient outcomes to Ohio stroke patients. Beating the national average with 20 minutes of faster care, the stroke team at Summa helps to save an additional 40 million brain cells per patient against the national average. As medical director Dr. Bowling shared, having a vision and healthy stubbornness to serve our patients led to a state-leading stroke program. Over the past 15 years, Summa Health System (Akron, Ohio) has earned designation as #1 Stroke Care in the State, #1 Cranial Neurosurgery in the State, and #1 Neurosciences in the State (Healthgrades 2024). It is a nationally recognized Comprehensive Stroke Certification (CSC), further designated as an AHA Gold Plus Target Stroke Elite Plus and Honor Roll Advanced Therapy.

Communicating 'The Why' : The Original State and Developing the Vision

For stroke patients, a primary goal is to achieve the best level of function after their stroke. It's those first moments and hours after the stroke that are most critical.

Achieving CSC began more than 15 years ago with Summa's first designation as Stroke-certified Center. The basics of diagnosing include understanding the patient's past history, medications, and medical condition – (immediate prior) quality of life issues. Treatments and more testing are guided by time. The use of CT and, back then, an 'evolving AI' could help to better see perfusion and support clinical decision-making.

Summa sought to innovate its program and be able to offer the most advanced care it could, and so the vision to clearly understand its goals and the complexity of stroke care delivery, its stakeholders, and programmatic objectives began. The neuroscience institute also knew it would require the growth of a common and shared vision as it strived to improve care and optimize quality metrics.

The program would face questions on how to provide continuous availability when staffed for traditional hours. Doctors had to go home, but could they consider robots, automation, or technology? The focus was also on trying to keep complex patients in-house instead of transferring them out. Hiring decisions, budgets, and neurocritical care specialists would also be big decisions as they tried to allow for better coordination of services.

Developments with IT

The crisis led to innovation and a new era for the neuroscience institute. With an abrupt staffing change to some of its doctors in November 2014, Summa needed to respond with newly staffed physician coverage in six weeks. By January 2015, the institute engaged with OSU to help provide external support by strategically sourcing. This introduction of telemedicine came as a momentum builder for the program. Telehealth for stroke helped to eliminate the distance between the patient and the expert. The neuroscience program worked vigorously with IT on the needed technology, networking, and encryption in order to maintain this program. The program also worked to standardize and build upon order sets.

IT was further supporting neurology cases for large vessel occlusions. IT supported candidates for these thrombectomy procedures with communication software that enables data to go directly to the neurologist's cell phone within minutes so they can support clinical decision-making for the surgeon, as it also collaborated with radiologists who were using an integrated PACS.

Challenges and the Creative Destruction Phase

Summa's Neuroscience Institute's journey took years. It was not just going to be about thrombolytic treatment. Dr. Bowling as the medical director's vision continued to strive for growth and scale. She had further built the program with administrative support and got some awards which demonstrated credibility and achievement. The program's reputation grew. Continuous work included breaking down processes and approaching them with inquisitiveness. They would further review changes as they may have an impact on other upstream or downstream workflows. The program was truly exhibiting a culture of continuous process improvement. It would also encounter additional issues to face when it came to enhanced costs and quality measures. In some cases, data was hard to synthesize, and as the program grew, staffing was still catching up. The ability to analyze data was challenging.

Competing priorities and scarce healthcare dollars also impact access to budgets and staffing needs. Over the past 15 years, the organization faced several challenges, including securing additional, highly trained physicians, especially those in neurology subspecialties. This was particularly challenging for neurovascular, which is highly specialized. But Summa continues to shine with its growing reputation, and it has become more attractive and desirable for those with these subspecialties to join. The program would also learn that recruiting the proper team required them to be a good fit – someone who was suited for the continuous process improvement culture and journey.

Factors in Success

Familiarity with your field is required. Dr. Bowling and her colleagues see over 1,000 strokes per year. She also got additional training at MIT (SB) for AI in stroke management topic. There is also a need for interdependency with radiology in their cooperation – to help support one another in delivering care to stroke patients. Getting the right people with the right skills builds a collaborative effort and leads to the growth of the program. This was primarily accomplished with the achievement of neurocritical care board certifications for two main leaders. Summa's Dr. Hepburn, who became the director of the neurocritical care program, has been attributed as instrumental in the care of complex brain patients requiring neurosurgery and interventions.

Demming's adage holds true, and quality is driven by metrics. A multidisciplinary team would be needed to define and deliver different workstreams and metrics. Common measures include time to be seen by a physician, door-to-groin times, and/or door-to-needle time. Summa not only measures these but also asks itself where we can improve or where we fall short in comparison to other standards or benchmarks. If there are errors, can we predict if it is likely to happen again, and more so, can we remove these risks?

The performance improvement process was introduced to the Institute from the get-go, and it has been a key part of the organization's growth. It contributes and has relied on metrics as a part of its growth strategy. The primary stroke level initially had eight quality metrics, but now it has 18 due to the collaboration of critical care and other services.

Summa's neuroscience institute also cites the recent and future growth of its multidisciplinary research department. The program hired a research director two years ago, primarily for the neuroscience department. The research director is responsible for supporting the department in pursuing more clinical research and supporting national opportunities and internal Summa-directed research – primarily researching its data or industry data. The focus on research has been instrumental in securing national opportunities and Summa-directed research.

Keeping up with the industry is also vital. Surgical technology, such as the recent acquisition of a new surgical technique called NICO by neurosurgeons, improves patient outcomes. This is primarily used for brain tumors and deep brain bleeds. The technology can debulk and remove blood hematomas, making it a valuable tool for the treatment of these conditions. It is further cited that monitoring the field of multiple AI technologies for neuroscience helps in understanding more opportunities for diagnosis and collaboration as well as building on a vision for comprehensiveness and simplification. Ensuring that the team is also watching industry standards and potential changes is vital; this was evident in the expansion of the thrombectomy treatment window from six to 24 hours, which had more people meeting the expanded time criteria. And of course, multidepartmental collaboration remains a key focus. Greater awareness, contribution, goal alignment, and education help build and achieve opportunities for improved stroke care.

Lessons Learned | Summary

Summa's Neuroscience Institute's continuous improvement remains strong. It will continue to evaluate and develop the utilization of AI as a clinical decision-support tool. The program will also continue to build on its culture of improvement and accountability as it grows and scales its offerings. The team will continue to rally around accelerating its growth and improvement and recognize if it slips into a reactive versus proactive mode.

Recognition begets growth. With the accolades and recognitions, especially as a certified stroke center (CSC), the Institute's volumes have grown. Aneurysm volumes have doubled in the last two years due to comprehensive procedures and transfers from outside facilities. The subspecialty has seen improved patient outcomes. Summa also learned that some volume changes occurred during COVID-19 with the reduction of available ICU beds and a resulting lack of transfers. More recently, the volumes have returned and increased after CSC designation.

Summa's Neuroscience Institute's future remains bright. Future opportunities will include the development of neuroscience dashboards and analytics efforts to lessen the data collection burden and abstraction efficiency. And goals to grow volumes and improve quality remain intact.

About Summa Health System

Summa Health (Akron, Ohio) is one of the largest integrated healthcare delivery systems in the state. Currently a nonprofit system with 8,200+ employees and nearly 1,000 credentialed physicians. It is comprised of two main hospital campuses and an additional rehab hospital. Summa Health also operates 15 medical centers, and four emergency locations. Summa has approximately 1,000+ licensed beds, with approximate patient volumes of 42k (inpatient), 129k (ED), 450k (outpatient), and 20k (surgeries). Related, SummaCare is also a provider-owned regional health insurance company that covers approximately 63k members.

Appendix/Data

Figure 6.1 shows the evolution of the Stroke Evaluation Program, Figure 6.2 shows the recognitions earned by the Summa Neuroscience Institute, Figure 6.3 shows how the 'ACH ED Door to Drug Times' measured against the goal of < 60 minutes over a period of 2017–2023, and Figure 6.4 shows how 'Summa Thrombolytic Administrations' are measured against goals over a period of 2019–2023 within three different time ranges.

Figure 6.1   Stroke Program Evaluation.

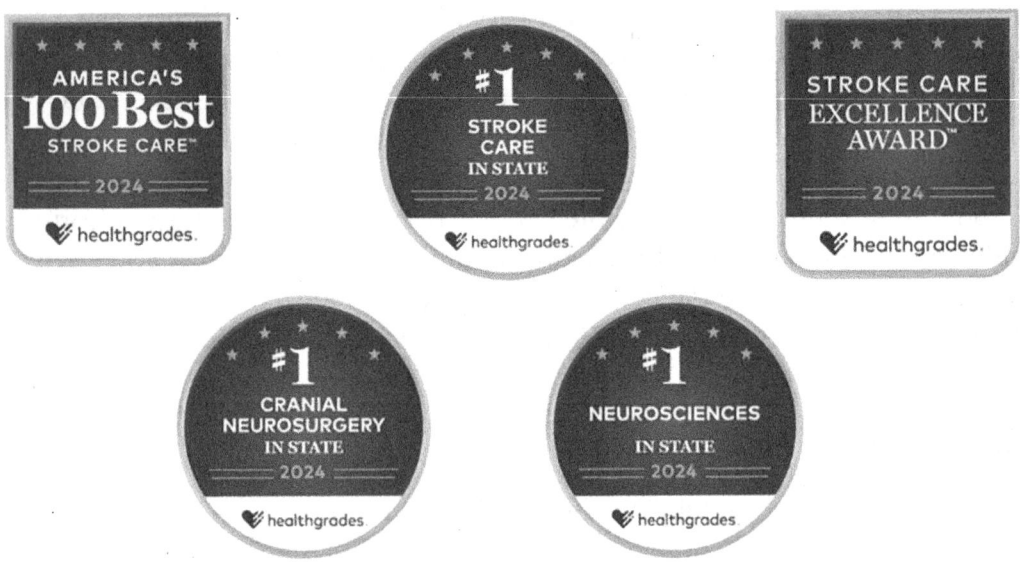

Figure 6.2   Summa Neuroscience Institute Recognitions.

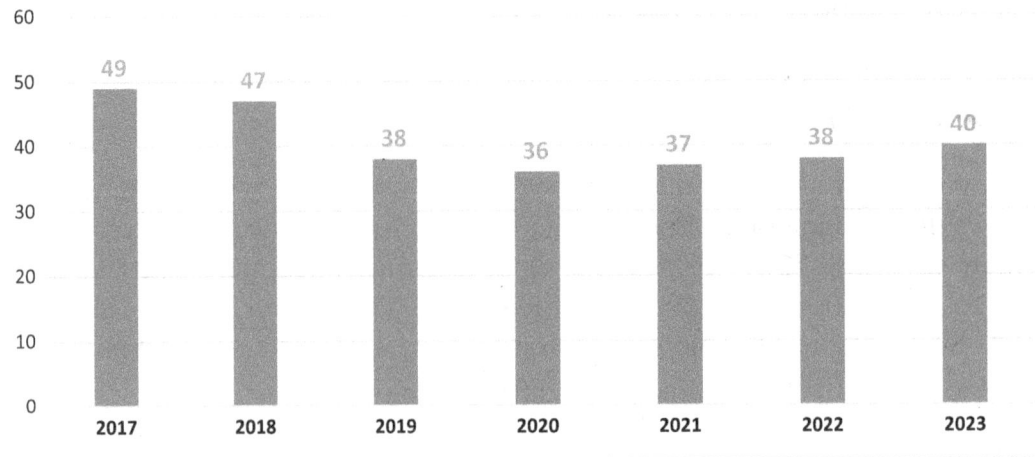

Figure 6.3   ACH ED Door to Drug Times (Goal < 60 minutes).

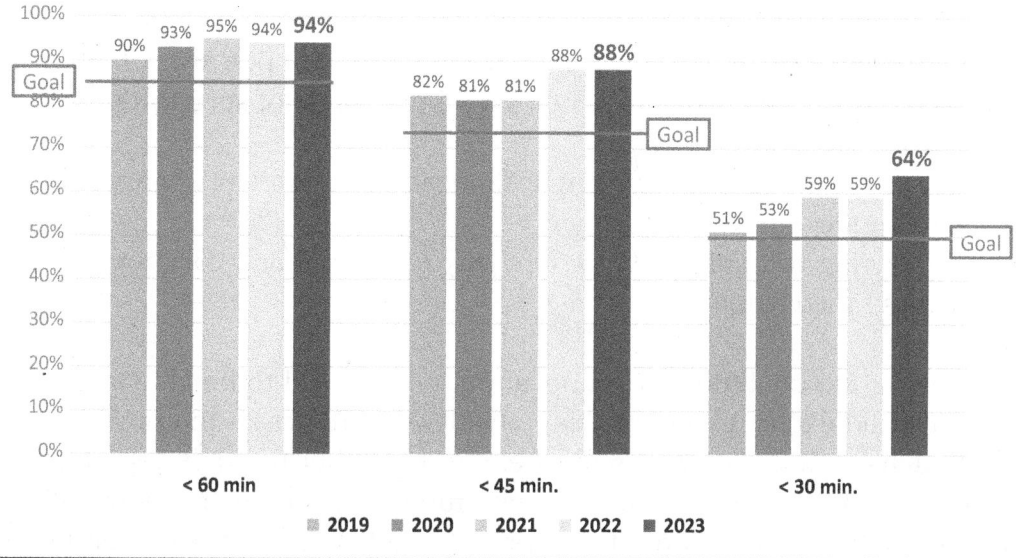

Figure 6.4 Summa Thrombolytic Administrations - Final 2023.

COMMUNICATE AND ELIMINATE BARRIERS | BRIDGING SILOS TO CONNECT INNOVATION AND OPERATIONAL TEAMS | *BY GRACE CURRIE AND JIAN LIU*

Many hospitals globally have some degree of digital innovation as part of their strategic agenda. Despite this, recent results from the 2022 HIMSS State of Healthcare report found that 80% of health systems are stuck in the planning phase of digital innovation. Many government-funded healthcare organizations have difficulty progressing innovation programs for multiple reasons, such as:

- The requirement to operate at lower budgets means that teams are often understaffed to support innovation.
- Managing multiple competing priorities, particularly in clinical operations, requires a large portion of time to be dedicated to maintaining legacy IT systems, leaving little time for new projects.

- Healthcare is more culturally risk-averse compared to other industries, and there is often hesitation to financially invest in perceived 'high-risk, high-reward ideas', that may not have a guarantee of successful outcomes.
- The nature of healthcare being CAS means that constant change over time can lead to change fatigue.
- Underlying cultural resistance that may limit work and collaboration across siloed teams.

To promote the conditions for innovation, teams need to be able to communicate and exchange new ideas, as well as work across the organization to achieve innovation at scale. Team silos, either through departments or units, attempt to define and delineate functions and key accountabilities within the organization. This approach tends to work well when the work itself is clearly defined and there are no requirements to adapt in the context of VUCA (Volatility, Uncertainty, Complexity, and Ambiguity) environments. This is clearly not the case for healthcare, as clinician burnout, increasing population demand for services, and increased complexity of disease presentations are some of the major challenges facing health services globally. There is no question that innovation in healthcare is required; health systems are becoming unsustainable in their current operational working models and will need to change to become smarter, more efficient, and with more capability to learn, or they risk being left behind.

The siloed nature of many healthcare organizations presents a challenge to innovation. Although silos by themselves are not inherently an issue, rather it is the silo mentality they can promote if teams are not given a framework of how to step outside these psychological boundaries.[2] Resistance to working across silos (i.e. horizontal spanning), can be due to not historically having the opportunity to collaborate, and therefore the default approach is not to initiate or seek information on projects other teams are working on. Resistance can also result from a lack of role autonomy, where staff from lower hierarchical structures are not empowered to approach other teams or up the management hierarchy with opportunities for innovation (i.e. vertical spanning). Other times, cultural resistance to collaboration can result from the interaction of teams with political agendas who may be competing for resources within the organization. In this case, silos can promote a mentality where teams do not share information, with the primary focus becoming how to maximize the performance of the silo rather than the organization.[3]

To accelerate innovation, many hospitals are partnering with academia and industry teams by creating cross-functional innovation teams. Rather than focusing on maintaining the status quo, these teams are specifically tasked with redesigning and building new digital infrastructure or tools to support clinicians and other hospital staff in their work. Newly integrated innovation teams in organizations that do not have existing collaborative networks, may find difficulty gaining traction with other operational teams in the hospital, particularly when teams are historically reluctant toward or not used to collaborating across silos.

Boundary spanning is the capacity for teams to cross silos and work with one another to achieve organization-wide strategic goals. Innovation programs, particularly at scale, require this important skill to improve learning, collaboration, and stakeholder buy-in, facilitating the conditions for successful integration within hospital operations.

Our Context

The Sydney Children's Hospitals Network (SCHN) in Sydney, Australia, is the largest pediatric tertiary health service in the southern hemisphere, caring for up to 170,000 children per year through over 100,000 emergency presentations, 60,000 hospital admissions, and over 1 million occasions of service for non-admitted patients. The Network comprises two large pediatric hospitals: Sydney Children's Hospital, and Children's Hospital Westmead, as well as several pediatric service units across New South Wales. The Learning Health Initiative (LHI) is a partnership program between SCHN and the University of Sydney, aiming to transform the hospital network into a learning health system. A cross-functional team was established, consisting of clinician researchers, data engineers, data scientists, UX designers, and operational staff, to build a cloud-based data analytics pipeline that improves access, organization, and analysis of routinely captured eHR data.

Large-scale innovation programs in complex system settings such as ours may require systems-thinking approaches to strategically redesign the environment, with the aim that creating the right conditions may influence the likelihood of a particular outcome occurring. In the following sections, we outline how we have approached the integration of our cross-functional innovation team, as well as shifting organizational culture to support innovation.

Creating the Environment: Opportunities for Breaking Down Barriers

1. Create opportunities to build trust

    Environmental intervention: Set up the innovation team within the operational hospital structure

    Successful innovation involves both individual and collective risk, vulnerability, and facing the unknown. Trust between individuals, teams, and partner organizations is a key enabler in facilitating an open exchange of ideas and the generation of new approaches that go beyond business as usual.[4] Additionally, stakeholders need to trust the vision of the innovation program and the potential value that will make the journey worthwhile.[4] We began leading our innovation program as an external university-based team with affiliate status; however, we experienced initial difficulty in infiltrating and integrating this team within the hospital. We found that hospital staff did not perceive the innovation team as part of the hospital, and there was some apprehension toward allowing university staff access to certain IT systems needed to complete the digital infrastructure build. The program was also perceived as an external 'research project', and we found the program was not being prioritized by staff who saw clinical care and research as separate functions of the organization. Recognizing this, we attempted to shift these perceptions by creating a new operational team, the Learning Health Unit, within the hospital. Although it was the same team and program, the formal embedding of this team helped to shift the perception toward innovation being led by the hospital. Since making this change, we have noticed improved engagement and trust, particularly with other clinical and operational teams.

2. Create opportunities for better awareness and understanding

    Environmental intervention: Organize a workshop to present the innovation program to each silo to improve awareness and understanding

    Our hospital network has over 16,000 employees and is a very large and dynamic ecosystem with constant pressure and change. Generally, across many large organizations, including ours, there is often poor visibility and awareness of what is happening across the organization, including specific projects, but also skills and capability. To improve awareness of the innovation program across our IT portfolio, we planned a workshop to create opportunities for operational staff to meet the innovation team and understand the goals, objectives, and activities being conducted. These types of workshops may also help to improve understanding of the underlying 'mental models' of the system, work, and innovation culture from the perspective of each team in the silo or across departments. Understanding mental models and the differences in mental models between teams may help bring barriers to the surface, identify environmental interventions, or strategically assist the innovation team to find commonalities between team perspectives.

3. Create opportunities for buy-in and learning

> *Environmental intervention: Organize an 'innovation development program' seminar series and/or strategic retreats to have siloed teams interact and problem-solve together*

Innovation requires an environment where learning and risk-taking are valued and supported. Where maladaptive competition exists between teams, it may be difficult to achieve the necessary buy-in and support for the innovation program. A digital innovation development program, designed as a seminar series, focuses on inviting external guest speakers from other hospitals and healthcare organizations to share their digital innovation projects. The aim is to create a non-confrontational way for diverse stakeholders to participate, including those who may have barriers or resistance to collaboration. The other advantage here is that this approach also creates a learning culture where the outward focus of presenters can assist the teams to feel united by a common goal with examples of what may be possible through collaboration. Strategic retreats for goal setting and problem-solving may also assist in demonstrating the value of collaboration by creating opportunities to exchange ideas in overcoming shared challenges.

4. Create opportunities for rethinking roles in innovation

> *Environmental intervention: Restructure roles and responsibilities, either informally through service delivery models or formally through job descriptions and titles*

Innovation requires an optimized team collaboration structure and an effective service delivery model. A significant challenge in healthcare innovation is that existing operational teams often do not view innovation as a priority or part of their role. These teams frequently become overwhelmed with daily routine activities or are diverted to other operational priorities, perceiving innovative projects as an additional burden. Consequently, their interest and engagement in innovation are typically low.

An individual's interaction with the organization is through their role (i.e. the role of individual organization interaction, as described by Irvin Borwick) [5], and so it is important to understand how people may perceive their role in innovation. In addition to the cross-team collaboration workshop to bring better awareness and understanding, we are exploring a new service delivery model that integrates operational team resources into innovation projects at an early stage. Previously, team members were often assigned technical tasks late in the project without a comprehensive understanding of the context. This approach led to poor task execution and weak collaboration between project and operational teams. The new model involves embedding key operational resources at the project's inception, allowing them to play a crucial role in planning and co-designing future solutions. These operational personnel will also serve as liaisons with the broader ICT teams across the government. This strategy not only fosters close collaboration between teams but also significantly enhances the innovative drive within the operational teams by redefining roles in innovation.

As we create new job descriptions or update existing ones, incorporating responsibilities such as fostering innovation, promoting experimentation, learning from failures, and identifying efficiency opportunities will further transform our operational teams to align with a commitment to continuous improvement.

Summary and Key Takeaways

To influence innovation at scale, a systems lens can be helpful to mediate shifts toward breaking down silos and achieving better communication and collaboration across teams. Each intervention we have designed for our environment is attempting to feed into the next at different levels, including micro/individual, team/silo, and networks of teams. This is important for dynamic and large-scale environments such as hospitals, as facilitating change at one level on its own may not achieve the desired effect to shift the overall organizational culture. Importantly, culture change may take some time without immediate feedback in real-time, which can make it difficult to assess whether a particular approach is working or needs to pivot. Change leaders should encourage regular qualitative feedback cycles (every 6 months) from stakeholders of how well teams are working together in addition to obvious innovation outputs (e.g. successful launch of new IT software). Leaders may also need to identify and design additional modifications to the environment to ensure that teams have the necessary social infrastructure in place to support innovation and collaboration.

Bibliography

Begun, J.W., & Zimmerman, B.M. Health care organizations as complex adaptive systems. In S.M. Mick & M. Wyttenbach (eds.), *2003 Advances in Health Care Organization Theory*. San Francisco: Jossey-Bass, 2003, pp. 253–288.

Borwick, I. Organizational role analysis: managing strategic change in business settings. In: *Coaching in depth: the organizational role analysis approach*. London: Routledge, 1st Edition, 2006.

De Waal, A., Weaver, M., Day, T., & van der Heijden, B. "Silo-Busting: overcoming the greatest threat to organizational performance." *Sustainability*, vol. 11, no. 23, 2019, 6860. 10.3390/su11236860

Dovey, K. "The role of trust in innovation." *The Learning Organization*, vol. 16, no. 4, 2009, 311–325. 10.1108/09696470910960400

ECRI. "Building a better safety-event-reporting system—Johns Hopkins Armstrong Institute for Patient Safety and Quality meets the challenge." *Device Evaluation*. May 17, 2023. Retrieved from: https://www.ecri.org/components/HDJournal/Pages/17th_HTE_Award_Runner-up_Johns_Hopkins.aspx?tab=2

HIMSS 2022 State of Healthcare Report. 2022 Accessed via: https://www.himss.org/SoH-Report

Institute of Medicine. (1999). *To err is human: Building a safer health system*. National Academies Press. Retrieved from https://doi.org/10.17226/9728

Institute of Medicine. (2001). *Crossing the quality chasm: A new health system for the 21st century*. National Academies Press. Retrieved from https://doi.org/10.17226/10027

Liukka, M. et al. "Action after adverse events in healthcare: an integrative literature review." *Int. J. Environ. Res. Public Health*, 17, 2020, 4717. doi:10.3390/ijerph17134717

Pisek, P. Institute of Medicine (US) Committee on Quality of Health Care in America. In: *Crossing the Quality Chasm: A New Health System for the 21st Century*. Washington (DC): National Academies Press (US), 2001. Appendix B, Redesigning Health Care with Insights from the Science of Complex Adaptive Systems. Available from: https://www.ncbi.nlm.nih.gov/books/NBK222267/

Serrat, O. Bridging organizational silos. In: *Knowledge Solutions*. Singapore: Springer, 2017. 10.1007/978-981-10-0983-9_77

Trbovich, P.L., & Shojania, K.G. "Root-cause analysis: swatting at mosquitoes versus draining the swamp." *BMJ Qual Saf*. vol. 26, no. 5, 2017, 350–353. doi:10.1136/bmjqs-2016-006229

Chapter 7

Stress Simplicity

Do not overcomplicate a solution to a problem; keep the following principle in mind: "When you have two competing theories that make exactly the same predictions, the simpler one" is better to implement.

It seems counterintuitive, but the majority of innovations are rather simple. The temptation to take a problem and create a complex solution exists in most of us. We tend to overthink an opportunity and therefore overengineer a fix. Innovation is often as basic as developing an elegant yet simple solution to a complex issue or opportunity, not the opposite way around. If the innovation can't be easily explained, start again.

STRESS SIMPLICITY | ENHANCING EMERGENCY CARE THROUGH AI-DRIVEN PROTOCOLS | *BY HARVEY CASTRO*

In the fast-paced and critical field of emergency medicine, leveraging artificial intelligence (AI) can fundamentally transform the care we provide to our patients and the operational efficiency of our practices. This essay explores the integration of AI in emergency departments (EDs), offering a roadmap that aims to save lives and optimize the delivery of care.

DOI: 10.4324/9781032715155-7

Introduction to AI in Emergency Care

As an emergency physician, I am acutely aware of the first point of contact for patients with acute health issues, where every moment is crucial. Our EDs confront many challenges, including overcrowding, protracted wait times, and a high potential for human error during intense, high-stakes situations. Implementing AI-driven protocols promises to mitigate these issues by bolstering decision-making capabilities and enhancing patient flow, ultimately leading to improved outcomes and greater efficiency.

By integrating AI into triage systems, we can revolutionize the way we assess and prioritize patient needs. Machine learning algorithms can assist us in categorizing patients more accurately, ensuring that those requiring immediate attention are seen promptly, thus reducing wait times and potentially saving more lives.

Furthermore, AI can offer invaluable support in diagnosing complex conditions by sifting through extensive datasets and identifying patterns that may escape the human eye. For instance, AI systems can scrutinize imaging results with exceptional precision, aiding in the early detection of critical conditions, such as strokes or internal bleeding, allowing quicker and more precise treatment.

Predictive analytics also play a pivotal role in emergency care, offering the ability to forecast patient influx and manage resources more effectively. We can preemptively adjust staffing levels and prepare essential supplies by predicting peak periods, alleviating the pressure on our personnel and facilities.

In my experience, the adoption of AI in healthcare must be strategic. It's not merely about embracing new technology; it's about integrating it to enhance human expertise and guarantee a synergy that uplifts the quality of patient care. With this in mind, my roadmap for AI integration in emergency care includes thorough steps for education, ethical considerations, collaboration with AI developers, and continuous evaluation of outcomes.

In the sections that follow, I will detail specific AI applications in emergency care, discuss the ethical framework necessary for their deployment, and propose a structured approach for weaving these technologies into the fabric of ED operations, drawing from my lessons learned and the forward-thinking perspectives I've shared in my previous work.

AI-Driven Triage Systems

In my practice, I have witnessed the transformative potential of automated triage systems within emergency care. Harnessing the power of AI to evaluate incoming patients based on their symptoms, vital signs, and medical history is instrumental in prioritizing care efficiently. When we consider the deployment of an AI triage system, like the one at Toronto's Humber River Hospital, which reportedly reduced initial assessment time by half, we see a clear indicator of the substantial improvements in patient flow and resource allocation that can be achieved.

This kind of AI integration is more than just a technological upgrade; it's a paradigm shift in how we approach emergency care. By utilizing sophisticated algorithms, these systems can quickly analyze complex medical information and assist in making triage decisions that could be life-saving. They act as a force multiplier for the triage nurses, allowing for a more rapid response to critical cases while ensuring that less urgent cases are managed appropriately.

Moreover, beyond immediate triage, AI systems can be programmed to learn and improve continuously. As more data is collected, these systems can refine their algorithms for even better accuracy in patient assessment. This means that the more we use AI-driven triage systems, the more efficient they become, providing us with an ever-improving tool to deliver optimal emergency care.

However, it's crucial to approach such systems' implementation carefully. As a proponent of AI in healthcare, I advocate for a holistic approach that involves training staff to work effectively with AI, ensuring the technology adheres to the highest patient privacy and data security standards, and maintaining a human touch in patient interactions. After all, AI should augment and not replace the invaluable human element in healthcare.

The next sections will delve deeper into how we can successfully integrate AI-driven triage systems into EDs, ensure their alignment with clinical goals, and address potential challenges such as ethical considerations and user acceptance, all while drawing from my experiences and the collective wisdom of the healthcare community.

Diagnostic Enhancements through AI

Through my exploration of AI's impact on healthcare, I have become a strong advocate for its ability to augment diagnostic capabilities. AI algorithms can interpret complex medical data at speeds and with a level of detail that is simply unattainable by human clinicians alone. A prime example of this can be seen at Beth Israel Deaconess Medical Center in Boston, where AI-powered tools assist radiologists in analyzing CT scans, enabling them to identify critical conditions such as strokes with greater speed and accuracy than ever before.

Integrating AI into diagnostic processes is not just about improving speed; it's about enhancing the precision and reliability of diagnoses. AI can detect subtle patterns in imaging that may indicate disease, often long before they would be noticeable to the human eye. This can lead to earlier interventions, which can be critical for conditions where time is of the essence.

However, as with any technological advancement, the adoption of AI in diagnostics comes with its learning curves. It requires a recalibration of workflow processes, additional training for medical professionals, and an unwavering commitment to continuous improvement. The ethical considerations around patient data privacy and the potential for AI to influence clinical decision-making must also be at the forefront of any integration strategy.

In this section, I aim to explore these implementations in greater depth, highlighting the successes we've seen and the challenges we've faced. I hope that sharing these experiences can pave the way for more informed and effective use of AI in emergency diagnostics, ultimately leading to better patient outcomes and a more robust healthcare system.

As we delve into the specifics of how AI is reshaping diagnostic practices, it's important to remember that these technologies are tools designed to support and elevate the expertise of medical professionals. By working in tandem with AI, we can unlock new potentials in patient care, making the most of the invaluable data at our disposal and ensuring that every patient receives the best possible diagnosis and treatment plan.

Streamlining Patient Management

In my continuous pursuit of excellence in emergency care, I have recognized the indispensability of AI-driven management systems in optimizing our operational workflows. These advanced systems are designed to forecast patient inflow and resource requirements with high accuracy, which is paramount for allocating beds and scheduling staff effectively. By predicting the ebbs and flows of patient admissions, we can better prepare for surges and avoid the pitfalls of overcrowding and understaffing.

These AI systems go beyond mere predictions; they enable us to monitor our patients in real-time with impressive precision. By integrating various data streams, such as vital signs and lab results, these systems can alert healthcare providers at the earliest signs of a patient's condition worsening. This is crucial in the ED, where seconds can mean the difference between life and death. It allows for prompt interventions, mitigating risks and improving the chances of a favorable outcome.

Additionally, using AI in patient management can dramatically reduce administrative burdens on our staff. By automating routine tasks and streamlining documentation processes, we can free up our healthcare providers to focus on what they do best—caring for patients. This enhances the quality of care and contributes to higher job satisfaction among staff, which is integral to maintaining a dedicated and motivated workforce.

In this section, I plan to delve into the specifics of how AI-driven management systems are integrated into the ED's operations, the impact they have on patient care, and the strategies we use to ensure they complement rather than complicate our healthcare delivery. I will also discuss the importance of training and change management, as the human component in implementing AI solutions is as critical as the technology itself.

The goal is to provide a comprehensive overview of how AI can streamline patient management in the ED, drawing from my experiences and best practices developed across the healthcare industry. With a thoughtful approach to integration, AI can be a powerful ally in our mission to deliver efficient, high-quality emergency care.

Ethical Considerations and Patient Safety

Reflecting on integrating AI into healthcare, I am acutely aware of the profound ethical considerations it brings to the forefront. The issues of data privacy, algorithmic transparency, and the potential for inherent biases within AI systems are matters that we, as healthcare providers, must navigate with the utmost care and diligence. We must adhere to ethical guidelines, such as those proposed by the American Medical Association, which advocate for patient-centered care, transparency, and accountability in the usage of AI.

Patient safety and trust are the cornerstones of effective healthcare delivery. As such, we must ensure that the AI technologies we integrate into our systems enhance care without compromising these fundamental principles. This means rigorously safeguarding patient data to maintain privacy and confidentiality in compliance with HIPAA and other relevant regulations. It also means demanding transparency in the AI tools we use, understanding how they arrive at their conclusions, and ensuring that these conclusions are free from biases that could lead to disparities in patient care.

In my practice, I have been committed to ensuring that AI serves as a tool for improving patient outcomes while upholding ethical standards. This involves continuously evaluating and re-evaluating AI applications to identify and eliminate any biases related to race, gender, socioeconomic status, or any other factor. It also means engaging in open dialogues with patients about the role of AI in their care, obtaining informed consent, and providing reassurance that their data is treated with the highest level of security and respect.

In this section, I aim to explore the ethical challenges posed by AI in more depth and discuss the measures we must take to address these concerns effectively. By maintaining high moral standards and placing patient safety at the forefront of AI adoption, we can harness the full potential of these technologies to revolutionize healthcare while preserving the trust and confidence of those we serve.

Collaborative Innovations

In my experience, the most successful AI implementations are born from a collaborative ethos, embracing the expertise of both healthcare institutions and technology companies. I have seen firsthand how partnerships focusing on developing AI for health record analysis, such as the one between Stanford Hospital and Google Health, can yield groundbreaking innovations. These collaborations are integral in creating AI solutions that are not only technologically advanced but also finely tuned to the unique demands of healthcare delivery.

Such cooperative ventures enable us to leverage tech giants' vast data repositories and computational prowess while infusing the nuanced understanding and clinical expertise that only experienced healthcare professionals can provide. It is through this melding of strengths that we can develop AI tools that are truly transformative, enhancing patient outcomes and streamlining processes in ways previously thought impossible.

Moreover, these partnerships serve as a model for how diverse teams can work together to tackle some of the most pressing challenges in healthcare. They foster an environment of shared learning, where insights from different fields converge to push the boundaries of what AI can achieve. I am convinced that by continuing to engage in such synergistic relationships, we will pave the way for innovations that advance medical practice and uphold the highest standards of patient care.

In this section, I will delve into the dynamics of successful collaborations between healthcare providers and tech companies. I'll share insights on how these partnerships can be structured to drive innovation, the challenges they may encounter, and the strategies for overcoming these challenges to achieve shared goals. Through this discussion, I hope to draw a roadmap for others in the healthcare sector looking to embark on similar collaborative journeys with AI at the helm.

Conclusion and Future Directions

As we stand at the cusp of a new era in emergency care, marked by the rapid evolution of AI technology, I am humbled and excited by the possibilities. Our strategies for implementing AI in emergency medicine must be dynamic and ever-evolving, anticipating the needs of tomorrow's healthcare landscape. Future innovations could revolutionize how we manage patient admissions, particularly during peak times such as flu season or in response to large-scale emergencies.

I envision a future where predictive analytics streamlines patient flow and aids in disaster response planning, ensuring that we are always prepared for the unexpected. The potential for AI to improve patient outcomes and efficiency in emergency care is boundless, but it requires a commitment to continuous research and development. We must foster an environment where interdisciplinary collaboration is the norm, drawing on the strengths of various specialties to innovate and refine AI applications in healthcare.

Moreover, as we forge ahead, we must uphold the highest ethical standards in every AI solution we develop and implement. We must ensure that patient safety, privacy, and trust remain at the forefront of our efforts. Only by adhering to these principles can we build a future where AI not only enhances the capabilities of emergency medicine but does so with the utmost respect for the rights and dignity of every patient we serve.

The journey toward integrating AI into emergency care is ongoing and filled with challenges and opportunities. It is a path that I am committed to navigating with vigilance and optimism, ever mindful of AI's potential to transform our field. By embracing innovation, prioritizing interdisciplinary collaboration, and maintaining a steadfast focus on ethics, we can realize the full potential of AI in emergency medicine and set a new standard for patient care in the years to come.

Call to Action

As a healthcare leader and advocate for integrating AI into our medical practices, I urge my colleagues and fellow leaders in the field to actively invest in AI research and pilot projects. These initiatives are not mere experiments; they are critical steps toward refining AI technologies in clinical settings, ensuring that they meet the highest efficacy and safety standards.

The rapid pace of AI development necessitates that we evolve in tandem with these advancements. To do so, we must prioritize the continued education of our medical staff on the latest AI tools and techniques. This ongoing training is vital for maintaining excellence in patient care and fostering innovation within our institutions.

I call on my peers to champion these efforts, support the teams at the forefront of AI development, and create policies that encourage the ethical use of AI. Together, we have the opportunity to lead a healthcare revolution—one that is powered by intelligence, both artificial and human, and one that promises a future of improved patient outcomes and optimized emergency care.

Let us embrace this moment with the knowledge that our actions today will shape the landscape of emergency medicine for generations to come. It is our collective responsibility and privilege to ensure that this future is as bright and beneficial as possible.

STRESS SIMPLICITY | HOW EMBRACING SIMPLICITY SAVED OUR AI HEALTHCARE TRIAGE INITIATIVE | *BY EDWARD W. MARX*

> That's been one of my mantras - focus and simplicity. Simple can be harder than complex: You have to work hard to get your thinking clean to make it simple. But it's worth it in the end because once you get there, you can move mountains.
>
> *Steve Jobs (2011)*

I served as the lead on a co-development project between HealthNxt (a Tech Mahindra Health and Life Sciences spinout) and a large integrated health system based out of Oklahoma. HealthNxt is a virtual care platform that integrates multiple applications, giving the patient and clinician a single pane of glass from which to manage all things virtual care. It takes disparate and often complex systems into a single user interface, making their virtual care experience optimal.

One area that caused the combined team significant frustration and delay was the AI-enabled health triage capability. A significant portion of the ROI and user experience was predicated on the use of AI to assess and prioritize healthcare needs, directing patients to the most appropriate levels of care in a highly personalized process while reducing workloads on an already overburdened clinical and administrative staff. Objectives and key results included improved access to care, reduction in operational costs, experience scores, and quality outcomes.

The system included the following capabilities, some of which led to frustration and halted the entire project until we were able to simplify our approach.

1. **Symptom Checkers and Chatbots**: AI-powered chatbots interacted with patients, asking about their symptoms and medical history. Based on the information provided, the chatbot offered preliminary assessments and advice on the next steps, which might include self-care recommendations, scheduling a doctor's appointment, or seeking immediate medical attention.

2. **Clinical Decision Support**: The system analyzed patient data, including electronic health records (EHRs), lab results, and imaging, to help clinicians diagnose conditions more accurately and quickly. The system also suggested treatment options based on the latest medical research and guidelines, leveraging a well-documented large language model.

3. **Resource Allocation**: The system algorithms prioritized patients based on the severity of their condition, helping to ensure that the most critical cases were seen first. This can improve patient outcomes and reduce wait times.

4. **Telemedicine**: The system could suggest enhanced telemedicine services by providing initial triage for patients before they connect with a healthcare provider. This can help ensure that patients receive timely care and that healthcare resources are used efficiently.

5. **Population Health Management**: In future releases, the system would analyze data across a population to identify individuals at high risk for certain conditions. This would enable proactive outreach and interventions to prevent the onset of diseases or manage chronic conditions more effectively.

6. **Remote Patient Monitoring**: In future releases, we would incorporate the data we were collecting from the remote monitoring module to analyze data from wearable devices and remote monitoring

equipment to detect early signs of deterioration in a patient's condition. This would trigger alerts to both the patient and healthcare providers, allowing for timely interventions.

7. **Language Processing**: In future releases, we would incorporate AI-enabled natural language processing (NLP) capabilities to understand and interpret patient descriptions of their symptoms, making the triage process more accessible and efficient, especially for non-native speakers or those with limited medical knowledge.

The team's initial excitement began to wane significantly as more clinical leaders became involved. While everyone was supportive of introducing advanced technologies, leaders became concerned with a variety of aspects, including loss of control, fear of clinical error, and lack of internal agreement on standard protocols. As the initiative unraveled, it appeared even among the medical staff that there was little agreement in terms of evidence-based protocols versus their specific clinical practice. We spent significant time moderating debates among high-performing clinicians, each with their own way of handling common cases. Many were reluctant to give up perceived control to an automated solution. Over weeks we found ourselves chasing many tangents while executive support faltered.

With the initiative all but dead, the project team came back together and began to focus on the basics. We found common ground and built a new campaign around gaining support from the clinical staff. We needed to take all of these complex challenges and simplify them in a way they were easier to address. In the end, the triage capability was adopted, and the objectives and key results were attained.

Here is how we stressed simplicity to reach our shared goals with our customers.

1. **Education**. We realized that AI is pretty new, and while everyone had intellectual knowledge of the capabilities, very few truly understood even the basics. We took a week to really focus on developing educational materials that would give everyone a baseline knowledge of capabilities. We sought out other successful examples of AI-enabled triage from around the world. This not only helped gain support but excitement as well.

2. **Training**. We made early prototypes available for clinicians to download and use. Filled with training data, they began to personally see the potential and how it would help patients and their staff. Everything is easy to use.

3. **Doc Whisper**. We had the documents on our team become the main interface with other clinicians, so there was instant trust and respect. They also led the workshops where we invited interested clinicians to engage and develop all the protocols for the triage.

4. **Storytelling**. We stopped using any technical jargon, including the word AI, and just shared stories via likely scenarios and what we experienced from other similar applications. In one case, we invited a clinician from a different organization using automated triage to share success stories.

5. **Genius Desk**. Borrowing from Apple, we set up "pop-up" Genius Desks wherever clinicians congregated for any period of time. The medical staff lounge, the OR lounge, and at any medical staff-related meetings. For those who weren't able to join a workshop, we would go to them. We always stressed the easy experience.

Here is how we stressed simplicity to reach our shared goals with our internal team.

1. **Human-Centered Design**. We doubled down on the triage design to make it as user-friendly as possible, eliminating unnecessary attributes and incorporating highly intuitive features. We stripped down almost 50% of the features and functions to save for redesign and future releases. We conducted focus groups for additional inputs and design guidance, which ultimately made the triage easier to interact with.

2. **Reminder Quotes**. We assigned a different team member each week to start off our meetings with a simple quote with an example of how they were trying to actualize it in our project. Here are some examples.

    a. **"Simplicity is the ultimate sophistication." —Leonardo da Vinci**: It seems contradictory; sophistication is defined as being less natural, less naïve, and more worldly. But if you think about it, it makes sense. Simplicity is grounded in truth, transparency, and honesty.

    b. **"Simplicity is the glory of expression." —Walt Whitman**: A glance at the marketing materials of most businesses shows a propensity to try to say as much as possible as often as possible to as many people as possible. Less truly is more if you want people to register and remember your most compelling selling points.

    c. **"Progress is man's ability to complicate simplicity."—Thor Heyerdahl**: You may find new business opportunities by complicating—or expanding or enlarging upon—someone else's business, product, or service concept. Adopt an attitude of continuous improvement and look for ways to improve on your own business as well as opportunities to improve upon those of others.

d. **"Everything should be made as simple as possible, but not simpler."—Albert Einstein**: There's a fine line between simple and boring!

e. **"Don't make the process harder than it is."—Jack Welch**: Marketing 101: Make it as easy as possible for customers to find you and to buy from you! When you have the opportunity to eliminate or diminish complexity in the customer experience or buying process, do so.

In hindsight, we learned, or should I admit, relearned, core principles from other initiatives requiring heavy change management emphasis. As excited as the team was with our "killer app," we took our customers for granted and assumed they would be as energized and emboldened as we were. We mistakenly believed they would already understand and accept the underlying technologies involved, even though they were not yet widely utilized. The bottom line is that we forgot the customer in all of our technology euphoria. We must never forget it is our job as leaders to not force our customers to deal with the complexities of all the underlying technologies used to deliver care today.

Steve Jobs was right. Thankfully, our team rebounded, and the clinicians were forgiving.

Author's Note: Our triage adoption was limited despite the emphasis on simplicity. Changes in leadership and focus and continuing concerns with clinical risk. While most generally available AI-enabled healthcare triage systems now embrace simplicity, there are many published scientific articles which question the clinical effectiveness of such systems. As this field matures continuously, I would encourage greater study before adopting.

STRESS SIMPLICITY | STRIKING THE BALANCE: EFFECTIVE AI IMPLEMENTATION IN HEALTHCARE SYSTEMS | *BY ALEX GORYACHEV*

Implementing AI in healthcare IT can lead to significant challenges, such as resource misallocation and excessive innovation, which often overshadow potential benefits. It is critical to have both careful and balanced AI implementation with clear metrics, gradual integration, and thorough engagement of all stakeholders to avoid adverse effects.

Implementing innovative AI technology as part of an IT healthcare program is fraught with risks and potential problems. The lack of financial and programming resources. Improper planning. Possible issues concerning the technology itself—bad fit, too early to market, and so on.

But those are just a few of the major potential problems. The biggest one, unfortunately, is one that many organizations and healthcare IT leaders never see coming.

Sometimes, There Is Too Much Innovation

On the surface, this might seem improbable, but it's not. The common reasoning when implementing new or better IT tech for critical cutting-edge industries like healthcare often goes something like this: given technology's tremendous potential and the improvements that can be realized, there's no such thing as too much.

Unfortunately, sometimes there is too much innovation, and it's a more common problem than most IT leaders think. It keeps many healthcare organizations from realizing true value, and some of those organizations end up going backward instead of forward. Given how common this issue is, it's worthwhile to identify and explore the causes, examine how they take root, and determine what organizations can do to keep negative tech innovation outcomes from occurring.

The Biggest Danger of Excess Innovation: Where Are Your Resources Focused?

Much of the wasteful spending associated with over-innovating is about resources—time, people, and money. Given that there is a limited amount of these resources in every organization, resource allocation is the first issue that must be considered when adding new technology. Specifically, the relevant resources must be focused on enhancing patient outcomes rather than just emphasizing the innovative technological benefits they can provide.

Having considered this question, it makes sense to step back and take a broader view of where else resources should be focused in an

IT implementation. There are several of them; what follows is a rundown of a few of the more important ones.

Sometimes, instituting a broad improvement in patient care systems can lead to much more significant improvements in patient welfare and outcomes across the board.

For some organizations, it might be enhancing their EHRs to make them more usable. Or maybe there's a significant need to focus more on cybersecurity improvements to protect vital patient data that has become compromised over time due to a lack of attention and effective system updates.

Closely Examine the Hidden Costs of New Technology

In healthcare, especially, wasteful innovation can be beyond costly. Expenses are already high in most healthcare organizations, to the point where one of the frequently heard phrases in this particular field is "health care is broken." Adding excessive technological innovations without knowing the explicit economic ramifications can ramp up those cost factors even further.

Cost issues aren't limited to the numbers found on a healthcare balance sheet. Opportunity costs can be a significant issue as well, as organizations can tie their resources to innovative initiatives that have no practical value.

Burnout is another opportunity cost that can affect existing employees, given that continuous learning and adaptation are almost always a significant part of a constantly changing technology stack. Because of this, usability and efficiency are definitely something you should consider. If the implemented system doesn't make workflow more efficient and help employees become more adept at solving patient problems, it's worth a look to see if it's even worth installing it in the first place.

Finally, there's the time factor, which may be the most expensive opportunity cost. Adding hours to cover the required time for innovation is expensive, and so is adding hours to the workload of already stretched IT professionals. The amount of available time is finite, obviously, and in many instances, it represents the cost of other opportunities, which are especially difficult to pin down.

To prevent these problems from occurring, a different kind of strategic approach is required to implement IT innovation in healthcare. Specifically, investments in IT technology must be directly tied to a clear and pragmatic core objective, for example, improving patient outcomes, enhancing workflow and employee efficiency, and securing patient data. This impact on these areas must be provable, and it has to be based on careful and thorough data analysis. Long-term sustainability must also be considered as well, and the overarching goal must be based on the idea of increasing the vitality and well-being of the healthcare ecosystem.

Adding AI to the Innovation Portfolio Poses New and Different Risks and Potential Problems

Adding AI to the technology innovation portfolio in healthcare is especially tempting and promising, and it also comes with formidable challenges. On the positive side, AI can potentially transform the entire healthcare delivery system while improving patient outcomes, and the new healthcare analytics have the potential to be revolutionary.

But a judicious approach to adding AI is essential, and it must also be tightly focused to avoid common pitfalls. What follows is a summary of some of the major ones:

1. **The Decision Debacle**: AI can analyze huge amounts of both specific and broad-scope data much faster and more accurately than humans, and if this is done properly, it can lead to better patient diagnoses, treatment plans that are both targeted and personalized, and predictive healthcare analytics that can be life-changing for both patients and their doctors. If the AI focus is aligned with core healthcare services and needs, this kind of technology can optimize processes, reduce costs, and improve patient care, and it also has the potential to enhance the entire healthcare ecosystem in a given organization.

2. **Cost Efficiency**: If AI is used properly to increase cost efficiency, the benefits can be both direct and measurable. AI systems can streamline operations, reduce redundancies, and automate routine costs, and this powerful combination can be used to lower healthcare costs across the board. The key to doing this effectively is to assess AI technologies that provide tangible, measurable metrics that feed into long-term savings and efficiencies.

3. **Reduce Wasteful Spending**: AI solutions tend to be very promising and attractive, and they often promise large, broad-scale positive results. Many IT leaders in healthcare tend to assume that those results will be easier to realize than they actually are, which can cause them to gloss over or even ignore the strategic fit of new AI healthcare technology.

It's also important to remember that AI, like any new innovative technology, often comes with cost factors that can quickly spiral, especially early on. To avoid wasteful spending, the impact of the technology needs to be carefully evaluated with a focus on improving delivery and outcomes. That evaluation should also be tightly focused on implementing the *right* AI that works as a solution, rather than just adding AI because it's necessary to keep up.

4. **The Workforce Impact of AI**: Adding any new technology tends to take a toll on workers, especially early on during the initial phases of implementation, and AI is no exception. This is even more true in the current media climate—both mainstream journalism and tech news sources are full of stories that exaggerate the potential of AI without realistically considering the timelines involved or the possible difficulties, downside, and risks.

   How does this typically play out in healthcare? In a poor AI implementation, it's all too easy for healthcare staff to experience stress and the sense of being overwhelmed, along with resistance to change, and then finally burnout. The immediate solution is to focus on integrating AI into the clinical workflow in a way that's focused on minimizing stress, and beyond that, it's essential to respect the established, successful standards for patient care along with the healthcare professional practices that are linked to those standards.

5. **AI, Privacy, and Ethics**: AI has raised privacy and ethics issues in virtually every industry where it has been implemented, and these considerations are critical in heavily regulated industries like healthcare. Patient data is incredibly sensitive by nature, which means data security must be airtight when AI is implemented. Moreover, the decisions made by the mechanisms of AI technology must be as transparent as possible, particularly when it comes to diagnostics and treatment plans. The tendency to underestimate the impact of too much AI can create ethical dilemmas throughout a given healthcare system, so it's important to lay out an ethical framework in advance that completely explains how these issues will be handled.

6. **Opportunity Costs and Strategic Focus**: Unfortunately, the race to add effective AI to healthcare can detract from ongoing efforts to improve the infrastructure of a given healthcare system as a whole, not to mention staff training and patient support services. While improvements in these areas might be seen as mundane, they often form an essential part of the backbone of the healthcare system, so new AI must be carefully aligned to support that system at all levels.

Adding AI Best Practices to Avoid Excess Innovation

Taken as a whole, these issues make it abundantly clear that there are many challenges that come with adding new AI technology to a given healthcare system. The overarching solution is to take a balanced approach that covers ethical issues and emphasizes positive patient outcomes, cost-effectiveness, and the well-being of the healthcare workforce. To do this, it's essential to have a comprehensive set of best practices in place when adding new AI technology, so let's take a more in-depth look at what those best practices need to look like.

The first initial steps are among the most important ones. Here are the pieces that need to be put in place:

- Set clear transformation goals before and after adding AI technology to your healthcare environment.
- Assemble a team with the right business and technical transformation expertise, and make sure the leader of the team is aware of and aligned with the existing structure and procedures of the healthcare ecosystem.
- Put robust stakeholder engagement and altered management practices in place to ensure AI buy-in and engagement across your entire healthcare organization before AI is added and best practices are put in place.

Once these pieces are in place, attention can be focused on specific best practices:

1. **Set Clear Metrics**: Innovation metrics can be hard to track, and that tends to be especially difficult with any new technology. To keep from getting sidetracked, key metrics must be set up in advance that form a baseline foundation for a successful implementation, and it's important to make sure those metrics line up with patient services, outcomes, and overall organizational goals. In addition, both those metrics and the outcomes they're designed to produce must be fully understood by both employees and stakeholders, and regular meetings and check-points should be set up to make sure that a high level of understanding continues to hold.
2. **Always put business processes first**: Many healthcare organizations go into an AI implementation with the idea they're going to be adding the proverbial shiny new IT toy that will have a huge impact across the

healthcare environment and accelerate a complete business transformation throughout the entire organization. That viewpoint misses the mark. Any AI implementation should be driving specific outcomes and executing clear strategies to get to those outcomes in measurable milestones.

3. **Drive transparency**: Get everyone on board and on the same page. In every organization, there's a natural tendency for employees to think and execute in silos, and this is especially true in healthcare given how different many of the fundamental business functions truly are. To get scalable innovation with AI, all voices across the organization must be heard, and their input, changes, and possible solutions must lead to a path that produces a solution that prevents the possible formation of silos. Project objectives, challenges, and opportunities must be clearly defined, and everyone must be given a voice.

4. **Slow down and think big picture**: With AI, there's a natural tendency to want to accelerate the technology to achieve the maximum benefits, but often the best course of action is the opposite of that. Slowing the process down and looking carefully at the larger picture of an AI implementation allows IT leaders to evaluate vendors in this rapidly developing field, understand regulations, and ultimately align the technology with established healthcare objectives. A comprehensive communication strategy that emphasizes constant, active listening must also be put in place.

5. **Execute innovation steps in small, measurable milestones**: Given the almost unlimited potential of AI, there's another natural tendency to think in terms of advances in terms of leaps and bounds. Small, measurable milestones are far easier to execute, and they create momentum as the project progresses. Also, they give the organization as a whole the opportunity to pivot when necessary, which is especially necessary in healthcare given the accelerated pace of change in general. AI is evolving and changing very quickly, and dividing an implementation into smaller steps makes it easier to mitigate the risks and keep up with those rapid advances.

6. **Communicate**: It's easy to talk about the importance of communication during AI deployment, especially in the current media climate. Such communication must always include transparency and the willingness to ask for advice when necessary. Be transparent, measure success, and make sure active listening is a key component of any healthcare communication mechanism. These mechanisms must

address a variety of workforce issues, including resistance to AI, concern about job security, and the attitude within or across the workforce that management isn't being completely transparent about the impact and ongoing implementation of AI.

Conclusion

Excessive innovation is a common and often under-recognized problem in advanced technology implementations. Recognizing it and preventing negative healthcare and patient outcomes involves careful consideration of resources, cost factors, privacy issues, and other important parameters to put an effective strategy in place. This is especially true in AI healthcare technology implementations, which require an across-the-board evaluation of all of these parameters, along with an effective set of best practices.

While the concerns that come with excessive innovation are valid and genuine with AI, the rewards of avoiding it and instituting solid best practices can be impressive indeed. They include adding more effective products, having them produce the desired results, and ending up with a happy, effective workforce that embraces AI and the innovation that comes with it rather than resisting change and opposing the process with obstacles. AI can bring with it a wide array of benefits that can benefit your organization across the board, and avoiding too much innovation and adding those best practices can be the springboard to make it happen.

Bibliography

Jobs, Steve. Quoted in Isaacson, Walter. Steve Jobs. Simon & Schuster, 2011.

Chapter 8

Recognize and Reward

Recognize or reward the efforts of stakeholders to innovate even at the smallest Levels.

To maximize innovation potential, we must not forget the power of motivation in human behavior. People will largely do what they are primarily rewarded and recognized for. For innovation to thrive, consider launching multiple reward and recognition programs to reinforce culture, enhance engagement, and encourage collaboration. Programs should reward not only those who generate ideas but also all the support teams enabling success. That which is rewarded and recognized is repeated. Innovation will multiply commensurate with the affirmation given.

RECOGNIZE AND REWARD | CREATING A NOVEL PATH AND RALLYING THE RISING STARS | *BY WAEL SAASOUH*

> AI Is Like Electricity. Just As Electricity Transformed Every Major Industry a Century Ago, *AI Is Now Poised to Do the Same*
> —**Andrew Ng**

Artificial intelligence (AI) offers transformative potential in healthcare, segmented into (1) clinical applications and (2) administrative support. Clinical applications enhance patient care through data-driven insights and

DOI: 10.4324/9781032715155-8

predictive analytics. Key opportunities include decision support systems, which recommend treatment protocols based on vast data sets, and patient triage technologies that optimize care delivery by assessing the criticality of patient conditions. The role of AI in medical imaging leverages "computer vision" for accurate diagnosis, treatment planning, and patient monitoring. Furthermore, risk prediction models identify patients at the highest risk of adverse outcomes, enabling preemptive care.

AI applications geared toward administrative support are equally noteworthy, often more so, due to the avoidance of legislative and compliance nuances. Notable efficiencies include ambient documentation, which automates the capture and translation of patient-physician interactions into medical records; and electronic medical record summarization, which can condense extensive patient histories. Task automation (e.g., handling prior authorizations) decreases the human labor needed for repetitive actions, while virtual assistants can further decrease administrative burdens. In totality, all of these opportunities allow providers to focus more of their attention on where they add the most value, direct patient care.

An important aspect of providing clinical care, however, centers around the well-being of the clinical team. Clinicians, assistants, support personnel, and administrative staff all have critical roles to play. As such, it is imperative that they be provided with a healthy work environment that fosters their productivity and recognizes their contributions.

Those who have raised toddlers are familiar with the saying, "Ignore a behavior you don't want repeated". In contrast, and on a larger scale of business, management, and leadership, fostering positive team habits depends on a rewards system. This system can function as a catalyst for progress, innovation, and team morale, whether it is simple recognition or elaborate award ceremonies. Regardless of the method, anchoring leadership practices in such processes promotes team engagement, idea generation, and a sense of accomplishment and fulfillment. Through positive reinforcement, productivity can be enhanced when the process also recognizes supporting teammates.

The tech industry is ahead of its counterparts on this front. Forward-thinking leadership teams focus on employee wellness, decreasing the stress of day-to-day work, and providing outlets for minimally restricted creative input. Meetings, lunch breaks, and cubicles are transforming into outdoor walking discussions, recreational opportunities, and open-concept workspaces. This is crucial for talent attraction as well as retention but is unfortunately largely lacking in the healthcare industry.

One approach which is starting to surface within the healthcare industry, however, is to focus more on rewarding employees and inspiring healthy habits at the workplace. Direct recognition, advancement opportunities, and fostering collaboration are three main components of this multi-pronged approach. With the increasing conglomeration of practices and the decline of small private medical groups, this applies more to large-scale organizations but can be adapted to smaller practices when applicable.

Direct Recognition

A simple and direct way to acknowledge team efforts is through recognition of talent and accomplishments. A variety of methods can be employed to accomplish this.

- An increase in compensation is attached to various leadership titles, such as chief of a site and regional medical officer.
- Members of high-functioning teams have defined pathways to promotion.
- A market-wide leadership conference can be held annually to discuss and promote the vision and mission of the organization to regional leaders.
- Promoting innovative thinking by encouraging suggestions and maintaining an open-door policy without restricting communication within a team.

Advancement Opportunities

In executive-level teams, bringing in external talent of diverse backgrounds is vital to the organization's advancement, however, the situation is quite different at the local level. Effective leadership can often be found within a team. Leadership roles require a deeper understanding of team culture, practices, and conditions. Leaders who are successful are capable of anticipating their team's response to an executive decision and reconciling differences of opinion based on their previous experience. Thus, developing leaders from the active roster offers significant local benefits.

Investing in and guiding employee growth and development is a non-trivial task that must be undertaken. This can be accomplished through focused leadership courses, annual conferences, and webinars, as well as a staff newsletter. Furthermore, team leaders should identify up-and-coming leaders within their teams and provide them with guidance and encouragement.

Fostering Collaboration

This process can take two forms: actively connecting individuals and teams on common projects, and passively highlighting opportunities for those seeking collaboration and bringing to their attention venues of collaboration they might otherwise miss. Essentially, the former involves implementing an executive strategy directly. Here, top leadership must create opportunities and assign responsibilities to teammates expected to implement them.
On the other hand, teammates' voluntary efforts to advance and innovate are more crucial to the latter strategy. Although less aggressive, the latter approach can uncover hidden talents, initiative, and leadership capabilities in team members.

The following examples demonstrate how this can be accomplished.

- **Organization-Wide Town Halls**: quarterly webinars featuring executive leadership and highlighting the mission, vision, and progress of the organization as a whole, with a periodic focus on local success stories.
- **Organization-wide publications**: newsletters, email blasts, and other communications that showcase employee accomplishments, providing visibility and recognition for innovative initiatives and successes. These also update clinicians on guidelines, best practices, and regulations.
- **Structured talent management programs**: with input from a variety of offices such as Operations, Clinical Operations, Clinical Quality, and Human Resources. Such a structure systematically identifies potential leaders and provides a roadmap for training and advancement. Moreover, since the process is methodical, it reduces the cost of identifying leaders in a more conventional way.

The common denominator in all of these initiatives is the mass dissemination of news and ideas. This allows the prudent innovator to identify venues for collaboration and recognize individuals who are best suited to facilitate the achievement of ideas and visions. Briefly, it offers team members who may not otherwise have the space to share ideas and communicate with each other an opportunity to network at the enterprise level.

Proposed Utilization and Expected Impact of AI

While this model could increase employee engagement and retention, it may be further optimized with the use of recent advances in AI. The wide availability of seemingly unlimited potential for AI-based technology opens the door to some innovative approaches, of which we suggest some along with their anticipated advantages and potential limitations.

It is worth mentioning that the administrative applications of AI are particularly intriguing in light of recent legislation (at the time of this writing, 2024). The updated interpretation of ACA Section 1557 by the Department of Health and Human Services (HHS) underscores the liability of the user, particularly when AI tools are deployed for clinical decision-making—where there is potential for discrimination of patients based on protected categories (race, gender, etc.). This legal framework necessitates sophisticated auditing for any closed AI model, presenting adoption hurdles and potentially steering AI innovations into safer, lower-liability applications (Table 8.1).

An overarching theme of limitations is naturally the cost and return on investment (ROI) for the budget managers. Every solution needs a financial ROI or at least a semblance of one. With healthcare margins being tight and lean models—sometimes overly lean—becoming the standard, no expenditure will be undertaken without serious consideration of financial sustainability. Put simply, projects emphasizing ROI will likely be prioritized.

A conservative approach—favoring "human-in-the-loop" and "opt-in design" paradigms—ensures practitioners can choose to integrate AI-enhanced workflows without mandatory participation. As we come to terms with both the potential and regulatory challenges, it becomes clear that the transformative power of AI can only be harnessed through strategically mindful integrations that respect both economic constraints and legislative frameworks.

Table 8.1 Practical suggestions for implementing AI at the workplace: solutions, advantages, and limitations

Area for advancement		Proposed AI supplementation solution	Anticipated advantage	Potential drawbacks and limitations
Direct Recognition	Personalized incentives	AI gamification of achievements	Create gamified reward systems where employees earn badges for completing tasks	May foster unhealthy competitiveness
	Work-from-home employees	Virtual and mixed-reality platforms	Organize events in realistic environments that include remote employees	Less incentive for employees to work from an office location
Employee Education Opportunities	Investment in employee education	Customized learning modules based on employee interest and areas of strength	Identify particular skill sets and leverage AI to advance and specialize them	May prove costly and also create hyper-specialization to the degree of disconnect among employees
Fostering Collaboration	Open-ended employee engagement surveys	Deeper analysis of employee responses to elucidate sentiment and direction	More targeted intervention, especially in areas of particularly low engagement or morale	Requires human oversight to ensure appropriate analysis of data, which can be daunting for large institutions
	Productivity	Chatbot/AI assistants	Real-time feedback on performance and problem-solving powered by institution-specific training modules and potential formation of connections among like-minded employees	Over-reliance on virtual assistants and loss of personal skills
	Team work	Identification of key team players from project updates	Identifies high-functioning collaborators and utilize their methods to raise the level of collaboration across the institution	AI may misrepresent personalities and recommend "the loudest speaker" regardless of actual productivity

Research and Academic Advancement	Task automation	Automation of routine tasks such as scheduling, recording meeting minutes, and generation of routine documentation	Allows clinicians more time to focus on non-routine tasks which require human input	Human oversight remains necessary particularly when automation is involved in high-impact documentation (governmental grants, legal documentation, etc.)
	Academic writing	AI assistance in curating, distilling, and writing manuscripts (literature review, language editing, etc.)	Saves extended periods of time on tasks that are routine in academic research	AI hallucinations and misrepresentations may have a negative impact on the quality of academic output
	Statistical support	AI assistance in analyzing large databases and gathering insight from data points	Provides insight into complex datasets, allowing for more refined, clinically meaningful questions to be answered	Over-analysis of data may lead to erroneous but statistically plausible conclusions

RECOGNIZE AND REWARD | REWARDING THE WAY INTO AI INNOVATION | *BY SAKSHIKA DHINGRA*

Introduction

Innovation in healthcare, particularly through the use of AI, has the potential to revolutionize patient care, improve outcomes, and increase efficiency. However, fostering a culture of innovation requires more than just technological investment; it necessitates recognizing and rewarding the individuals and teams who drive these advancements. This essay explores the importance of recognition and rewards in promoting AI innovation in healthcare, using the example of the Mayo Clinic's AI-driven initiatives to illustrate these concepts in practice.

The Importance of Recognizing and Rewarding Innovation

Recognition and rewards play a crucial role in motivating individuals and teams to pursue innovation. In the context of healthcare, where the stakes are high and the challenges are complex, these motivational tools can drive the development and adoption of AI technologies. Here are several reasons why recognizing and rewarding innovation is essential:

1. **Fostering a Culture of Innovation**: Recognition and rewards signal to employees that their innovative efforts are valued. This creates an organizational culture that encourages experimentation and risk-taking, which are essential for innovation. When employees feel appreciated and see that their contributions are making a difference, they are more likely to engage in creative problem-solving and pursue new ideas.

2. **Attracting and Retaining Talent**: In the competitive field of healthcare AI, attracting and retaining top talent is crucial. Recognizing and rewarding innovative contributions helps organizations attract skilled professionals who are motivated by the opportunity to make a meaningful impact. It also helps retain existing employees by providing them with a sense of accomplishment and career satisfaction.

3. **Enhancing Collaboration and Teamwork**: Innovation often requires collaboration across different disciplines and departments. By recognizing and rewarding collaborative efforts, organizations can break down

silos and foster teamwork. This is particularly important in healthcare, where interdisciplinary collaboration is often necessary to develop and implement AI solutions effectively.

4. **Accelerating Implementation and Adoption**: Recognizing and rewarding innovation can accelerate the implementation and adoption of AI technologies. When employees see that their innovative ideas are being taken seriously and rewarded, they are more likely to invest the time and effort needed to bring these ideas to fruition. This can lead to faster development and deployment of AI solutions that improve patient care and operational efficiency.

Case Study: Optum

Optum is a prime example of a healthcare organization that has successfully leveraged recognition and rewards to drive AI innovation. This case study examines the strategies employed by Optum to foster an innovative culture, attract and retain top talent, and enhance patient care through AI advancements. By focusing on recognition and rewards, Optum has been able to position itself as a leader in the healthcare AI industry.

Overview of Optum

Optum aims to transform healthcare by harnessing the power of AI to improve patient outcomes and operational efficiency. The company offers AI-driven solutions for a range of applications, including diagnostics, treatment recommendations, clinical trial matching, and population health management. Optum's innovations are grounded in advanced machine learning, natural language processing, and data analytics.

Strategies for Recognizing and Rewarding AI Innovation

Optum has implemented a variety of strategies to recognize and reward innovation, encouraging employees to contribute to the development and deployment of AI technologies.

1. **Innovation Awards and Competitions**: Optum hosts annual innovation awards and competitions to recognize outstanding contributions to AI advancements. These events provide a platform for employees to

showcase their innovative projects and solutions. The awards include categories such as Best AI Algorithm, Most Impactful Clinical Application, and Best Collaborative Project. Winners receive monetary rewards, public recognition, and opportunities for professional development.

2. **Monetary Incentives and Grants**: Optum offers monetary incentives, such as bonuses and grants, to employees and teams who demonstrate significant innovation. These incentives are tied to specific milestones, such as the successful development of a new AI tool or the implementation of an AI solution that improves patient care. Research grants are also provided to support innovative projects, enabling employees to pursue groundbreaking work without financial constraints.

3. **Career Advancement Opportunities**: Recognizing that career growth is a powerful motivator, Optum provides career advancement opportunities to employees who contribute to AI innovation. This includes promotions, leadership roles in innovative projects, and access to specialized training and development programs. By linking innovation to career progression, the organization encourages employees to invest in creative problem-solving and continuous improvement.

4. **Innovation Labs and Collaboration Hubs**: Optum has established dedicated innovation labs and collaboration hubs where employees can work on AI projects. These spaces are equipped with cutting-edge technology and provide a collaborative environment that fosters creativity and cross-disciplinary teamwork. Regular innovation workshops and hackathons are held to encourage idea generation and rapid prototyping.

5. **Non-monetary Recognition**: In addition to monetary rewards, Optum emphasizes non-monetary recognition. This includes public acknowledgment of innovative contributions through internal communications, company newsletters, and social media. Personalized thank-you notes from leadership and certificates of recognition are also used to show appreciation for employees' efforts.

Impact of Recognition and Reward Strategies

The recognition and reward strategies employed by Optum have had a significant impact on its ability to drive AI innovation. These strategies have created a culture that values creativity, collaboration, and excellence, leading to the development and implementation of groundbreaking AI solutions.

Improved Patient Outcomes

AI innovations at Optum have led to substantial improvements in patient outcomes. For example, the Optum for Oncology solution uses AI to analyze vast amounts of medical literature and patient data, providing oncologists with evidence-based treatment recommendations. This has enhanced the accuracy and effectiveness of cancer treatment, leading to better patient outcomes.

Enhanced Operational Efficiency

AI-driven solutions have also improved operational efficiency at Optum. Tools for Clinical Trial Matching use AI to quickly identify suitable clinical trials for patients, reducing the time and effort required for manual matching. This has streamlined clinical trial processes and increased patient participation, accelerating the development of new treatments.

Attraction and Retention of Top Talent

Optum's commitment to recognizing and rewarding innovation has attracted top talent from various fields, including data science, medicine, and engineering. The organization's reputation for fostering a culture of innovation and providing opportunities for career growth has made it an attractive employer for professionals seeking to make a meaningful impact in healthcare.

Strengthened Industry Leadership

By continuously investing in AI innovation and recognizing the contributions of its employees, Optum has solidified its position as a leader in the healthcare AI industry. The company's success has attracted partnerships with leading healthcare providers, research institutions, and technology companies, further enhancing its ability to drive AI advancements.

Challenges and Considerations

While Optum's recognition and reward strategies have been successful, there are challenges and considerations that other organizations can learn from.

Ensuring Fairness and Equity

To ensure fairness and equity in recognition and reward programs, Optum has established clear criteria and transparent processes. This includes setting objective benchmarks for innovation and regularly reviewing the impact of rewards to avoid biases.

Balancing Short-Term and Long-Term Goals

Optum balances short-term achievements with long-term strategic goals by supporting both immediate innovations and projects with long-term potential. This approach ensures that the organization continues to make incremental improvements while also investing in transformative innovations.

Managing Resource Allocation

Resource allocation for recognition and reward programs is carefully managed to ensure sustainability. Optum prioritizes high-impact projects and uses a combination of monetary and non-monetary rewards to maintain motivation and engagement without overextending resources.

Conclusion

Recognizing and rewarding innovation is essential to driving AI advancements in healthcare. Optum's success in leveraging these strategies demonstrates the powerful impact that recognition and rewards can have on fostering a culture of innovation, attracting and retaining top talent, and improving patient care and operational efficiency. As AI continues to transform healthcare, organizations must prioritize recognizing and rewarding the individuals and teams who drive these advancements, creating an environment that encourages continuous innovation and ultimately leads to better outcomes for patients and the healthcare system as a whole.

The Mayo Clinic, a leading healthcare organization, provides another exemplary model of how recognizing and rewarding innovation can drive AI advancements. The Mayo Clinic has been at the forefront of integrating AI into healthcare, leveraging its potential to enhance diagnostics, treatment, and operational efficiency.

Innovation at Mayo Clinic

The Mayo Clinic has implemented several AI-driven initiatives aimed at improving patient care. These include AI algorithms for early detection of diseases, predictive analytics for patient outcomes, and AI-powered tools for personalized treatment plans. The success of these initiatives can be attributed in part to the organization's commitment to recognizing and rewarding innovation.

Recognition and Reward Strategies at Mayo Clinic

1. **Mayo Clinic Innovation Exchange**: The Mayo Clinic Innovation Exchange is a platform that fosters collaboration and innovation among clinicians, researchers, and entrepreneurs. This initiative provides resources and support for innovative projects, including access to funding, mentorship, and state-of-the-art facilities. The Innovation Exchange also recognizes and rewards innovative contributions through regular showcases and events.
2. **Annual Innovation Awards**: Mayo Clinic hosts annual innovation awards to recognize outstanding contributions to healthcare innovation. These awards include categories for individual and team achievements, highlighting significant advancements in AI and other technologies. The awards ceremony is a high-profile event that celebrates the innovative spirit of the Mayo Clinic community.
3. **Research Grants and Funding**: Mayo Clinic provides research grants and funding opportunities for innovative projects. These grants support the development and implementation of AI-driven solutions, encouraging researchers and clinicians to pursue groundbreaking work. Funding is often tied to specific milestones, ensuring that projects progress toward tangible outcomes.
4. **Career Development Programs**: Mayo Clinic offers career development programs that recognize and reward innovative contributions.

These programs include leadership training, professional development workshops, and opportunities for career advancement. By investing in the growth and development of its employees, Mayo Clinic ensures a continuous pipeline of talent committed to driving AI innovation.

5. **Public Recognition and Communication**: Mayo Clinic regularly communicates its innovative achievements through internal and external channels. This includes press releases, academic publications, and presentations at industry conferences. By publicly recognizing the contributions of its employees, Mayo Clinic enhances its reputation as a leader in healthcare innovation and motivates others to contribute to its success.

Impact of Recognition and Reward Strategies

The recognition and reward strategies employed by Mayo Clinic have had a significant impact on its ability to drive AI innovation. These strategies have fostered a culture of innovation, attracting top talent and encouraging collaboration across disciplines. They have also accelerated the development and implementation of AI-driven solutions, leading to improved patient outcomes and operational efficiency.

Improved Patient Outcomes

AI innovations at the Mayo Clinic have led to significant improvements in patient outcomes. For example, AI algorithms for early disease detection have enabled earlier interventions, improving survival rates and reducing the burden of disease. Predictive analytics have helped clinicians identify high-risk patients and provide targeted care, reducing complications and hospital readmissions.

Enhanced Operational Efficiency

AI-driven solutions have also enhanced operational efficiency at the Mayo Clinic. For instance, AI-powered tools for scheduling and resource allocation have optimized workflows, reducing wait times and increasing patient throughput. By streamlining administrative processes, AI has allowed healthcare providers to focus more on patient care, improving overall efficiency and satisfaction.

Strengthened Reputation

Mayo Clinic's commitment to recognizing and rewarding innovation has strengthened its reputation as a leader in healthcare innovation. This reputation has attracted partnerships with industry leaders, research institutions, and technology companies, further enhancing its ability to drive AI advancements. The organization's success has also served as a model for other healthcare organizations, demonstrating the importance of recognition and rewards in fostering innovation.

Challenges and Considerations

While recognizing and rewarding innovation is essential, there are challenges and considerations that healthcare organizations must address to ensure the effectiveness of these strategies.

Ensuring Fairness and Equity

Recognition and reward programs must be designed to ensure fairness and equity. This includes providing equal opportunities for all employees to contribute to innovation and be recognized for their efforts. Organizations should establish clear criteria for recognition and rewards, avoiding biases that could undermine the effectiveness of these programs.

Balancing Short-Term and Long-Term Goals

Organizations must balance short-term and long-term goals when recognizing and rewarding innovation. While it is important to celebrate immediate achievements, it is also crucial to recognize efforts that contribute to long-term strategic objectives. This includes supporting projects that may take time to yield results but have the potential for significant impact.

Managing Resource Allocation

Resource allocation for recognition and reward programs must be carefully managed to ensure sustainability. Organizations should consider the financial and operational implications of these programs, ensuring that they provide meaningful incentives without compromising other priorities.

Conclusion

Recognizing and rewarding innovation is crucial to driving AI advancements in healthcare. By fostering a culture of innovation, attracting and retaining talent, enhancing collaboration, and accelerating implementation, these strategies enable healthcare organizations to harness the full potential of AI. The Mayo Clinic's success in leveraging recognition and rewards to drive AI innovation serves as a powerful example of how these strategies can lead to improved patient outcomes, enhanced operational efficiency, and strengthened reputation.

As these two industry examples prove, reward and recognition programs are not optional. They really do help drive change and provide focus to complex projects. As AI continues to transform healthcare, organizations must prioritize recognizing and rewarding the individuals and teams who drive these advancements. By doing so, they can create an environment that encourages continuous innovation, ultimately leading to better care for patients and a more efficient and effective healthcare system.

Note: The author leveraged ChatGBT3 to source additional documented examples of AI in healthcare to compliment the others used in the article. We leveraged AI the same way we would search for examples using traditional methods such as Google or a public library for basic research.

RECOGNIZE AND REWARD | REWARDING THE WAY INTO AI INNOVATION | *BY THE KAROLINSKA INSTITUTE RADIOLOGY TEAM*

Karolinska Institutet is one of the world's leading medical universities. Our mission is to contribute to the improvement of human health through research and education. Karolinska Institutet accounts for over 40 percent of the medical academic research conducted in Sweden and offers the country's broadest range of education in medicine and health sciences. Since 1901, the Nobel Assembly at Karolinska Institutet has selected the Nobel laureates in Physiology or Medicine.

Karolinska Institutet was founded by King Karl XIII in 1810 as an "academy for the training of skilled army surgeons". Today, Karolinska Institutet is a modern medical university and one of the foremost in the world. With our close relationship to the clinical milieu, a well-established infrastructure, and a stable financial situation, Karolinska Institutet has excellent prerequisites for sustaining high-quality research and education.

Karolinska Institutet is known for its research in a wide range of biomedical fields, including the application of AI in healthcare. We are involved in various AI-related projects, particularly in the areas of medical imaging, diagnostics, and personalized medicine. Researchers at the institution are exploring how AI can be used to improve the detection and diagnosis of diseases, such as cancer, by analyzing medical images more efficiently and accurately than traditional methods.

Additionally, Karolinska Institutet is part of various national and international collaborations that aim to advance AI in healthcare. These collaborations often involve partnerships with other universities, research institutions, and industry players to share expertise, data, and resources.

AI

The institution's commitment to AI research is part of a broader trend in the healthcare industry, where AI is seen as a transformative technology that can enhance patient care, improve outcomes, and increase the efficiency of healthcare systems. Karolinska Institutet's contributions to AI research are significant, as they not only advance the field but also have the potential to impact clinical practice and patient care on a global scale.

One example of Karolinska Institutet's work in AI is the development of algorithms that analyze digital pathology slides and radiology images to identify patterns or anomalies that may indicate disease. These AI systems help pathologists and radiologists by providing a second opinion or by highlighting areas of interest that may require further examination. AI in radiology is a rapidly advancing field that has the potential to transform the way radiologists interpret medical images and diagnose diseases.

Our cross-functional Team was formed to accelerate the practical application of AI in our daily workflows. Team members included professionals from Research, Radiology, Technology, and Academia. We were held together by a strong project manager who kept us on task and on time. Our first use case was Lung Nodule Detection. From start to finish, our project lasted 9 months. While inspired by the vision and impact, we also took time to plan the finish, rewarding the Team and all who would come to help us on the journey.

AI Project Outcome

The project was successful and this is how we use AI Lung Nodule Detection.

1. **Data Collection**: We searched a database of thousands of CT scans of the chest, some of which show lung nodules that may be indicative of lung cancer.
2. **Algorithm Training**: Our researchers use this dataset to train a deep learning algorithm, such as a convolutional neural network (CNN), to recognize patterns associated with lung nodules. The algorithm learns from the images, adjusting its parameters to improve its accuracy in identifying nodules.
3. **Validation and Testing**: Once trained, the algorithm is validated using a separate set of CT scans to ensure its accuracy and reliability. It is important that the algorithm performs well on data it has not seen before to prevent overfitting.
4. **Integration into Workflow**: The validated AI algorithm is integrated into radiology's picture archiving and communication system (PACS). Now, when a new chest CT scan is uploaded, the AI automatically analyzes the images.
5. **Assisting Radiologists**: The AI algorithm provides a second opinion to the radiologists. It highlights areas on the CT scan that it identifies as potential lung nodules, along with a probability score indicating the likelihood of each being cancerous.
6. **Decision Support**: radiologists review the AI's findings alongside their own interpretations. The AI's analysis can help radiologists detect nodules they might have missed, especially in challenging cases or when they are dealing with a high volume of scans.
7. **Improved Diagnostic Accuracy**: With the assistance of AI, radiologists achieve higher diagnostic accuracy and faster detection of lung nodules, potentially leading to earlier treatment and better patient outcomes.
8. **Continuous Learning**: The AI system is set up to learn continuously from the feedback provided by radiologists. Each confirmed diagnosis is used to further train the algorithm, improving its performance over time.

9. **Ethical and Regulatory Considerations**: We ensure that the use of AI in radiology complies with ethical guidelines and regulatory standards, including patient privacy and data security.

10. **Reporting**: The final radiology report includes the radiologist's interpretation, which may be informed by the AI's analysis. The report is then sent to the referring physician for further clinical management.

This Lung Nodule Detection example illustrates how AI is a powerful tool in radiology, enhancing the capabilities of radiologists and potentially improving patient care. However, it's important to note that AI is not meant to replace our radiologists but rather to augment their expertise and efficiency. The use of AI has been well accepted by our radiologists and patients.

Reward and Recognition

The Team brainstormed a variety of reward and recognition ideas. Given the requirements of the project and its success, we did not want to neglect all those who gave so much time and energy to enable the outcomes. At the same time, we wanted to be sure to personalize the approach for each member, understanding that one size does not fill all.

1. **Recognition**: We worked with our internal marketing department, who developed wonderful summaries that were shared inside the organization. We wanted everyone to feel appreciated but not force them to get dressed up and walk up on a stage. The overall project was also widely shared as a sterling example of the best of our Institutet.

2. **Reward**: We had set aside funds that might normally be used for a lavish dinner and plaque but instead invited everyone to a popular shopping center. We met first in a coffee shop. Everyone was given a gift card to use with a commitment to meet 90 minutes later back at the coffee shop. Most of the Team had completed their purchases and were happy to reveal them to one another. Some purchased shoes, others clothing, and some toys related to their hobby. Everyone had something they wanted. One of our leads needed more time and promised to show pictures when purchased. That was fine.

The Team really resonated with this approach. Highly personalized and just the Team celebrating with one another. No having to dress up and memorize a speech.

We often forget to recognize and reward. We continue to have significant AI success and celebrate in similar ways. We believe one reason for our innovation success is this unique, tailored approach.

Note: The author leveraged ChatGBT3 to source additional documented examples of AI in healthcare to compliment the others used in the article. We leveraged AI the same way we would search for examples using traditional methods such as Google or a public library for basic research.

Chapter 9

Co-create Solutions

Appreciate the complexity of attention that innovation requires and expose the organization to demands from all stakeholders.

Innovation does not happen by innovators alone. We must be careful not to fall into the belief that innovation is reserved for one person or a special team whose primary function is to develop solutions to problems or inventions to opportunities. Innovation is primarily cultural and thrives in team-based organizations. Avoid the trap that innovation is for a select few and all others are discounted. Innovation happens best when it becomes the culture of the entire organization, and everyone has the opportunity to engage.

CO-CREATE SOLUTIONS | INNOVATION IS EVERYONE'S RESPONSIBILITY | *BY GINNY TORNO*

At Houston Methodist, you're likely to hear "Innovation is Everyone's Responsibility." Innovation is one of our organizational pillars and is ingrained into presentations, meetings, and discussions throughout our daily engagements. There is a "core" innovation team; however, the majority of the core team is made up of team members who also have other organizational responsibilities. Each member of Innovation balances their efforts between both roles. The Chief Innovation Officer is also the SVP of the

DOI: 10.4324/9781032715155-9

organization and CEO of our main hospital. My role in innovation is paired with leading the inpatient clinical IT teams. Each member of the core team leads a different area within Houston Methodist. This enables powerful advantages; each member brings operational knowledge to the group to identify needs; we can also vet potential solutions quickly to know if they may be successful and are worth pursuing.

Broadening that structure, there are several workgroups led by Innovation team members that enable larger participation, governance, and feedback. Workgroups include clinical transformation, business, ambulatory, and AI, to name a few. Those workgroups review ideas that can be brought forward by anyone in the organization. Current innovation projects within those workstreams are also reviewed with open discussion and feedback.

At the highest level of the organization is the DIOP Steering Committee. DIOP stands for Digital Innovation Obsessed People and was the nickname for the original focused innovation workgroup in the organization, formed in 2018. The name stuck and is still used today, 6 years after inception. The steering committee is comprised of executives from every area of the organization and is a final review point for new innovation projects as well as programs or initiatives that should be explored. A crucial part of our executive support is the CEO of Houston Methodist. Without support for innovation from the highest level, it would likely be much tougher to gain buy-in and succeed.

This sounds like a lot of structure, but it enables all parts of the organization to be directly involved in innovation while providing many avenues to participate.

In addition to this internal structure, there must be a co-creation mindset with our business partners that helps to enable new and innovative processes and technologies. "Partner" is intentionally used, because the successful model is to work side by side as one team and create something together that benefits all organizations involved. There is often a desire to partner with younger organizations who have a product(s) but need to work with a healthcare organization to try it out. This is often a bread-and-butter situation for Houston Methodist. We can mold technology to meet our needs while in turn providing a more complete and robust product for our partners to implement with other partners. We brag about them when we present at conferences around the country. Sweetening the pot, we also like to partner and co-create with other healthcare organizations to make an even stronger group, sharing ideas and feedback to collaborate and help each other grow. These concepts will be illustrated with examples of successful initiatives at Houston Methodist.

Using Data and Analytics to Improve Patient Care – Virtual ICU

The first innovation project at Houston Methodist started with a small pilot in an effort to alleviate shortages of clinical personnel working in the ICU, especially during the night shift. We worked with a partner to implement a tool that streams vital signs to a central monitoring station. That system also uses predictive analytics to warn us if a patient is deteriorating before there is a code event. To implement this, we needed to co-create the requirements, design, and implementation of the solution with clinical and operational partners throughout the organization. It involved the creation of a new service line – our virtual operations center. There were security and privacy reviews needed. It included mounting cameras in patient rooms (a first for us) and additional clinical monitoring tools to allow remote monitoring and viewing of patients in this critical area of the hospital. There was a detailed staffing analysis to determine how to set up a virtual operations center and to counterbalance the bedside team.

There is no way to make a change this big without co-creating, even for a pilot. All necessary areas of the organization must be included from the beginning, from the executive level to the staff level. Similarly, the vendor partner needs dedicated resources to learn the organization and help design a successful product and workflow. The hospital and the partner need to be nimble and make adjustments quickly as needed changes surface.

This product was put in place leading up to the initial COVID-19 outbreak in the United States. The timing ended up being unintentionally perfect, as the infrastructure was in place to rapidly expand this service to all eight hospitals at the beginning of the pandemic. Rapid expansion of this technology would not have been possible without the previously mentioned broad team involved in innovation; there was already awareness and excitement about it across all hospitals before expansion. Today, this technology is still in use and has evolved as needed to add new predictive algorithms and functionality. We have curated an enormous dataset that is invaluable for research initiatives. In addition, the virtual operations center has expanded to many more service lines and now supports telesitting, telestroke, and virtual nursing as well.

Virtual Nursing

Leveraging the platform created to support our Virtual ICU program, we were able to stand up virtual nursing quickly as well (accelerated by the pandemic). This implementation is particularly interesting because it was pursued due to nursing shortages that were not solved with retention incentives, signing bonuses, or other benefits. Patient volumes continued to increase without a proportional increase in nursing. A special task force devised a plan using existing technology in our organization and worked with a pilot unit to test it out. Data and analytics came into play with time studies completed before and during the pilot to compare and gauge effectiveness.

What makes this initiative more interesting from a co-creation perspective is that while nursing, patient experience, and operational teams were involved in planning and piloting, there was initial skepticism by clinical staff from a few angles: Is my job going away? How can a virtual nurse provide the same level of care I can? Nurses were very stressed in general due to ongoing shortages and the pandemic. While there was reassurance provided from the executive level that this was an effort to help nurses and patients, healthy skepticism still existed as the program expanded across the organization.

What we found was that in a matter of days, nursing units jumped on board and loved the program. Admissions and discharges were handled by a virtual nurse who was able to spend quality time with each patient, freeing up the bedside nurse to do more emergent tasks. An unexpected effect was more robust data collection from the virtual nurse. We saw a huge improvement in data quality compared to units without the virtual nursing program, where a bedside nurse may have to skip through some data entry while they are pulled in multiple directions.

Treatment Plans and Outcomes

Another wildly successful innovation initiative uses data and analytics to analyze patient status and recommend treatment options. It does this by matching patients in our EHR to a large repository containing millions of patient records. The tool finds patients who are a close match using many factors – age, race, and diagnosis are just a few. Each type of procedure we want to analyze with this tool requires a custom build. Those builds require collaboration between physicians, nursing, IT, quality, HIM, and the vendor partner to ensure the right patients are identified, and the recommendations are accurate. Once built, tested, and implemented, this tool can show physicians what treatments and procedures similar patients have received and the outcomes! This can be powerful as it aids physicians in critical decision-making. It absolutely requires close collaboration and teamwork to succeed.

Efficiency in Operating Rooms

One of the biggest revenue generators in a hospital is OR operations. Each surgeon or operating team may do things differently, take more or less time to complete tasks, and experience varying levels of efficiency with time management across the board. We implemented a tool that introduced cameras to our ORs. These cameras learn the room, and after a period of time are able to collect data and provide analytics to recommend operational efficiencies. If the same procedure takes 45 minutes with one surgeon but 75 minutes with another on a consistent basis, why is that? What are the outcomes for those patients? Perhaps there are opportunities to evaluate what they may be doing differently and make some changes. On a simpler scale, how long is the OR empty between procedures, and how long does cleaning take? This tool recommends opportunities to compress time, introduce operational improvements, and enable more surgeries, allowing us to help more patients on a daily basis. The level of co-creation and collaboration for a tool like this is immense – surgical teams, operational leaders, IT, patient consent teams, legal, risk … multiple service lines all had to work together for this to be successful. Our vendor partner is nimble; they are part of the team and work closely with OR operations to adjust analytics based on the needs of each OR.

Conclusion

On a daily basis, it is clear that co-creation is essential to the success of innovation. From time to time, a group may start down a road with something new and then realize that other parties need to be involved. Those moments remind us why there needs to be a collective group approach. I've also observed organizations that have a separate Innovation group that is not otherwise involved, and they struggle in comparison. Another Houston Methodist innovation principle is "succeed fast, fail fast." To do this, innovation must be everyone's job and be part of "what we do here." It is also critical to scale successful initiatives across a multi-hospital organization.

CO-CREATE SOLUTIONS | AN INNOVATIVE APPROACH KU TOOK TO AI DOCUMENTATION USING THE ABRIDGE PLATFORM | *BY GREGORY ATOR AND CASEY BRYSON*

Physician burnout is a risk for our providers (Eschenroeder et al. 2021). Clinicians of all sorts are affected, but physicians are expected to work whatever hours are required to meet the demands of the role. Studies have shown that administrative tasks related to the EMR are a contributory factor (Harry et al. 2021). This concern leads our physicians, young and old, to work long hours and lose the "joy in medicine" that was the reason in many cases for becoming physicians.

This workload forces clinicians to engage in so-called "pajama time" or after-hours work. Indeed, some of our providers work into the early hours of the morning and rise again, sluggishly, to take on another day. This is not speculation and hyperbole but comes from EMR clickstream data that tells us exactly what time and hour all the work is performed. In the face of these challenges, we sought an approach to improve the efficiency and effectiveness of our providers. This data reveals that documentation is the most time-consuming activity of our office-based providers. Improving this activity based on these EMR-derived data was a key outcome of our approach.

Unfortunately, with the demands and pressures of the modern healthcare environment, we found the traditional improvement process of "going to the gemba" to work with individual providers was too labor intensive and not likely to move the improvements through the system as fast as needed.

This led us to explore partnerships with companies that would be more willing to innovate in this space and partner with us at the same time. We ultimately found a smaller company, eager for the challenge, in Abridge and, in collaboration with them, found a solution using novel technology to several of our concerns, including time spent in documentation and the general stress of getting through the day as a digital doctor. Abridge's approach is to use generative AI (GAI) to passively listen to the patient's physician's conversation and summarize that conversation accurately and in near real-time. This allows physicians to avoid having a second conversation with the computer after talking to the patient in the examination room. Additionally, while in the exam room, they can concentrate on communication and understanding the patient rather than "type talk and listen" or worse yet saving it till the end of the day when it encroaches on family time. Our data show that physicians are much happier with this approach.

In selecting the partner to develop solutions to help physicians deal with the EMR burden in documentation, we focus first on the key deliverable, the product. Several characteristics of the product were identified. First, we looked at trust and transparency. In healthcare, trust is a key component. Patients and their caregivers require it, and important ancillary tools like an AI-aided documentation tool must be delivered. Trust is particularly important at this stage of the evolution of these products, as the capabilities are developing rapidly and we had several new areas we wanted to co-create in. We quickly identified areas to develop and innovate around but needed to be sure that the company put the customer first. We early on structured our rollouts to allow for large-scale, unmoderated communications mechanisms staffed by our team, the user physicians, and Abridge. This was so that all our physicians would have unfettered, real-time access to the experts developing the product to hear the good, the bad, and the ugly of product development with as little friction as possible between company leaders and customers. This has been proven to facilitate an agile production approach where almost daily improvements are made and released and then opened for feedback. The financial approach was mutually respectful, allowing for a win-win approach for product development technically but also one that allowed for the voice of the customer to be clearly heard.

One of the key enablers of this relationship with Abridge was the partnership at the top between company management and KU technical and physician informatics leaders across both organizations. It was most helpful to have a physician leader at the helm of Abridge and an even better one that still practices, that they understand first-hand where medicine is, and even live it on occasion. Not because they have to, but because they want to have real empathy for the practicing physician's experience. Burnout is not a topic for discussion, it's a fresh lived experience. Additionally, I think this experience leads to certain technical decisions that are improved by regular use of the product first-hand, just like a real customer would.

Having a unified understanding of the purpose and goal of the product led to developing a mutual roadmap meeting the business drivers of both companies. This led to a reduction in much friction typically seen in these types of relationships because of misaligned incentives. Through these roadmap sessions, we identified capabilities following basic documentation. A platform approach heavily dependent on deep integration with the transactional EMR system was considered. This physician-to-physician partnership quickly identified the next bane of physician practice: that of a billing inquiry. These had never been real-time and typically come days to weeks after the patient has left the doctor's mind. They involve arcane conversations about terminology and details necessary for optimal coding. The rub for the physician is that they have moved on; they have seen tens if not hundreds of patients since the index patient, and so they must go back to the record and spend "free time" going through the record to identify details to answer the query. The teams quickly started to develop an AI-based real-time coding query that, while the note was being created, asked for the details to satisfy good billing.

An additional feature of mutual interest was enhanced patient communication. Abridge had long had a consumer-facing product that facilitated patient physician communication. A common experience, particularly at a quaternary care center like KU, is the scene of the patient leaving the exam room and asking their partner "what did she say" about diagnosis, treatment, and next steps. So, simultaneous production of a patient-friendly summary in an actionable format was seen as a huge value add. Given the relationship developed in the process of co-creating innovative solutions, rolling out such a product just happened without a contract addendum or discussion.

The AI documentation product relies on a smartphone app that is placed in a convenient location in the exam room. As a point of integration, the provider's schedule is available for patient selection. With one click, the session is started and records the ambient conversation. This interaction can be supplemented with the standard tools available in the EMR to the physician for documentation with modification. What is not required is interaction with the keyboard on a routine basis. After the recording phase, the physician goes to an Abridge web page and pulls up the conversation. The audio recording is available for reference in a synced display with the transcript and finally the summarization. Clinicians have control over the pronouns used, the verbosity, and other structural elements of the output. If a summary statement is questioned when it is highlighted, the evidence in the transcript is summarized in an overlay to the transcript. [ED: Screenshots x 2 - basic layout, evidence if desired] At the bottom of every note is a feedback widget. A 1–5 star overall rating is available. Additionally, a full textual capability is present to encourage feedback to the development team. After review, which is strongly encouraged, the clinician closes out this phase by asserting a complete click. This is then made available to the EMR. The user then returns to the EMR screen and, with a refresh, brings this completed information into the EMR in the appropriate location. It can be edited there as well but is discouraged as no feedback is available currently to the team at Abridge.

Finally, the patient-facing conversation is available in the Abridge portal as a Patient Visit Summary, which condenses the conversation to a consumable document that can be used by the clinician in perhaps the patient instruction part of the record. It has a summary of the visit, a plan where the diagnosis is expanded, and a treatment plan described, followed by detailed succinct instructions.

Several aspects of the above clinician interaction are important. Adoption is enhanced by designing this tool to be an adjunct to the many, in some cases, highly developed tools. Clinicians don't have to completely replace years of workflow and can add this tool where appropriate. Some don't use legacy tools; others mix and match, so the user has a choice. Transparency and trust are enhanced because the user can see exactly what was produced. This is important to the question of hallucination, which is an important concept in GAI, of course. Many hallucinations can be attributed to poor audio quality and mishearing of what was said. Being able to see this by referencing the transcript and even the audio establishes the validity of the tool, as needed by the user, rather than on someone else's word. Also, it is important, and something not typically appreciated perhaps, is that the question of "Did I really say that?" By listening to the recording, you can either verify or not believe what really happened. Again, something that is lost when attention is directed to the keyboard rather than the patient's words.

All of this is built on a concept of deep integration with the transactional EMR system, where doctors take care of patients, make recommendations, and suggest treatments. In this case, KU contributed a deep understanding of this system and brought a partnership with the EMR vendor, in this case Epic, to the table. In order to be maximally effective and efficient for providers, deep integration in and out of the EMR is beneficial. This type of coordinated interaction involving three major corporations is only possible with alignment and transparency as to goals and outcomes and mutual respect of capabilities and judgment.

Once alignment was achieved on goals and strategy, we proceeded to jointly develop a rollout plan. Partnership with physician informatics leadership was critical to understanding where and how to deploy the solution. Many factors were considered in the rollout process. Specialties with strong physician informatics champions were prioritized to help with change management and troubleshooting needs.

To validate the solution, our KU innovation physician informatics expert was initially provisioned for the solution. He was able to thoroughly test it and make sure that it was performing as expected. Extensive feedback was collected and continuous feedback was given to the team at Abridge during the rollout.

After we had determined basic functional integrity and consistently well-received performance, we extended our rollout to other users. The second group of users were not, for the most part, members of the physician informatics team. They were mostly a variety of specialties, but most were chosen because of their willingness to support an early-stage product and tolerance for being "experimented on" with technology. Their feedback was a critical part of the exercise. The product was deployed and used on a production basis for approximately three months to validate that the product was continuing to meet expectations and particularly responsiveness in return for finished summary text.

Once the product function was verified with this group of diverse users and feedback was good, we proceeded with a rapid development effort with our EMR vendor Epic to integrate the output of the product into the established workflows of our users. Prior to this development, users were expected to copy and paste the output from the product from a web page into the appropriate places in the documentation encounter. This was tedious, and fortunately, due to a collaborative process with the EMR vendor and excellent technical help on both teams, it was a short-lasting inconvenience.

Our next step after concluding this three-month deployment of the product was to evaluate the capability of the company to scale up to the second wave of users, which was mutually agreed would be a total of 200 users. We had extensive conversations with the company on topics such as scalability, culture, and commitments made and kept on both sides. After successful evaluation of the partnership based on these criteria, we decided to continue the rollout. Specialties and pace of enrollment were coordinated in a mutual fashion to ensure a successful experience for both parties. Throughout this time we had, and continue to have, our open feedback customer company interaction channel to promote honest feedback with a low friction process for users. At the conclusion of the 2nd wave rollout, which is taking place as this is written, we plan to undertake a survey of users and compare subjective and objective measures of the success of the product. Outcomes, including time in chart, ability to close charts soon, and potential for more productivity, will be assessed in partnership with Abridge.

As we continue to have a mutually beneficial experience in rolling out this innovative product, we are considering and now executing a mutual research effort addressing the key issues with physician workflows and, in particular, looking at outcomes that directly address these concerns. Evaluations of both the patient and physician experience are being undertaken as of this writing.

An advisory council is being formed at this writing to help the customer and vendor remain aligned throughout the relationship. Topics will include outcomes, adoption, product enhancements, and roadmap discussion.

In summary, a co-creation paradigm as described here is an excellent framework for innovation. The primary accelerant is the alignment that is worked on in advance of the ideation phase. Such that business alignment and alignment to mutually agreed upon goals are already in place, and thus all decision-makers are aware of the parameters of engagement. To be specific, the alignment details should involve incentives, culture, and a mutually respectful working relationship. In this atmosphere of alignment, innovative ideas rise to the fore and suddenly are mature concepts, and from there into production.

CO-CREATE SOLUTIONS | CO-CREATION FOR DATA RESOLUTION | *BY DEBRA GRAVES*

The Organization

Commonwealth Care Alliance (CCA) is an organization with a unique model that delivers better health outcomes through seamless integration, a community focus, and an emphasis on the behavioral health needs and social factors that account for so many critical gaps. The model is based on our deep, data-powered understanding of what puts people at risk, together with our unique ability to find and engage hard-to-reach individuals. CCA is a multi-state organization with a presence in Massachusetts, Rhode Island, and Michigan. Our members have significant health challenges. As a multi-state organization, we are accountable not only to our members but also to various state and federal regulatory agencies for medical claims adjudication. These regulations are in place to protect the member/patient and providers. They govern this important process of evaluating and processing insurance claims submitted by healthcare providers in the healthcare industry.

The Process

The medical claims adjudication process involves insurance payers reviewing and determining the amount owed to healthcare providers for services they rendered. There are three possible outcomes. The claim can be paid in full. Which is when the insurance payer approves the claim without discrepancies, and the healthcare provider receives the full payment amount agreed upon. The other is a reduced payment, which occurs if discrepancies or inconsistencies are found (e.g., improper coding or lack of documentation), then the payment amount may be reduced. If a claim does not meet the criteria, it may be denied.

Most states mandate that medical bills be submitted within 180 days of the date of service. Physicians generally have up to 365 days to submit claims. Insurance companies typically have a 90-day or 120-day deadline for submitting claims. Claims submitted after this deadline may be automatically denied by the review system. If a claim is denied, the appeals process has specific time limits. To appeal a decision, an appellant must file a request within 120 days from the date of receiving the initial audit determination. An appeal must be filed within 30 days of the demand letter to stop recoupment.

For CCA, as a smaller organization, a vendor adjudicates our medical claims. Physicians and institutions submit their medical claims to our vendor, who processes the claims based on established criteria. Once the claims are adjudicated, a file with the adjudicated claims is sent to the payment vendor. This vendor issues payments, ACH, or checks, to the physicians and institutions.

Data is everything to a healthcare organization. It drives everything from quality-of-care measures to the timely processing of claims and benefit statements to our members and providers. Access to quality data and notification are necessary to ensure the fair and accurate processing of medical claims, which benefits both patients and healthcare providers.

The Challenge

The issue for our Claims Operations Team was the absence of accurate data that they needed to monitor the adjudication of claims, payments to providers, and explanation of benefits statements (EoBs). EoB statements are sent to the member after they have had an encounter with their primary care provider or a hospital stay. The statement details any procedures that were conducted and the payment responsibility, if any, to the member.

It was not just a data issue; it involved processing and notification to the Claims Operation Team and other involved parties that a problem existed. Claims were being adjudicated, but because of process glitches, payments were not being distributed to providers and EoB statements were not being sent to the members. CMS regulations state that providers must be paid within a set amount of time and that EoB statements to members must be delivered within 30 days after the month's end. The data and process issues and errors resulted in delays in statements to members and payments to providers.

The Claims Operation team is not the only area that depends on this data. Several teams and departments also rely on the data. The encounters team uses claims data for reporting, and our Quality Measures department utilizes the claims data for managing our members' healthcare.

Solutions and Prevention

Co-creating solutions involves collaborative efforts to address challenges, innovate, and develop effective answers. Here are the steps we took to facilitate co-creation:

To address this problem, we needed several departments to collaborate, think creatively, and develop effective answers. This is the very definition of co-creating. The problem and the solution needed to be clearly defined. For that, we needed to involve the major stakeholders. The major stakeholders in this case were our Business Process, Claims Operations, and IT teams.

A Business Process team works within an organization to optimize and streamline various operational processes. Our Business Process team examined the existing adjudication workflows, identified the inefficiencies, and noted areas that required improvement. Standardized procedures were created that allowed process consistency going forward. Within our organization, our claims department is responsible for compliance with state, federal regulations, and industry standards. As a stakeholder in this process, they were the ones to explain the guidelines and the compliance issues that had to be met for our organization to avoid penalization for non-compliance with the claim adjudication timelines.

The Business Process team recommended a system of notification between the vendors and our organization. The purpose of these notifications was to make certain that the correct people/organizations and departments were aware when a file failed processing and payments were in jeopardy. The notifications were automated based on the timing of file exchanges. Files were normally exchanged between organizations within a few hours. The new process was set up to send acknowledgment when a file was received and send a notification if a file was not received within the standard amount of time. Additionally, if there was a data error that resulted in a file failure, the adjudication vendor would receive a notification alerting them to the failure and providing them with the details that caused the failure. Given this information, the adjudication vendor was required to resolve the error and resubmit the file within a predetermined amount of time.

The next step in the process involved engaging the Claims Operation Team for validation and approval. This was accomplished through a series of meetings and other correspondence. The claims team provided the timing guidelines and regulations required for processing claim payments. Through creativity and the sharing of ideas, the Business Process and Claims Operations teams developed the requirements for data sharing and the notification process. The IT team was involved with this process from the start. IT made suggestions based on system configuration and future system changes. Once the requirements were agreed upon and documented, the IT team sized and prioritized the work needed. Given the urgency of the issue, IT engaged resources from other projects to obtain a quick resolution. Once development was complete, the notification system had to be tested. Testing involved coordination between all the teams, both within CCA and with the vendors. The testing revealed that some refinement was needed. The notifications required more error detail so that the vendors could take the appropriate actions to process payments to our providers and institutions and issue benefit statements to our members. The process was placed into production and has resulted in a significant reduction in file failures and an increase in communication with our members.

The collaboration between CCA departments and their vendors resulted in a process that not only addressed the current issue but provided an example of what could be accomplished when people connect and exchange ideas to reach a solution. This solution promoted accountability between departments within CCA and with our vendors, resulting in the timely transmission of claims data and payments. Each team contributed ideas to the solution, thereby making a repeatable process for resolving other issues that affect the organization. The notification process is just one example of co-creation in our organization, an organization that promotes diversity, innovative thinking, and communication to reach solutions that benefit the health and well-being of our members.

CO-CREATE SOLUTIONS | AI IN HEALTHCARE – USING LARGE LANGUAGE MODELS TO REVOLUTIONIZE LONGITUDINAL CARE MANAGEMENT | *BY ROHIT MAHAJAN*

Large Language Models (LLMs) like ChatGPT are one of the most exciting recent developments in AI. These LLMs, which have the ability to generate human-like text, have opened up a new world of possibilities for natural language processing and other associated applications across all industries and almost every touchpoint where we interact with AI.

Simply put, LLMs are incredibly smart computer programs that have been trained with an enormous amount of human-generated text from all available internet sources as well as direct input by their developers. This training helps LLMs understand human language extremely well and generate quite meaningful and relevant responses in very human-like speech.

LLMs and GAI are having a profoundly transformative impact across many industries, but perhaps no more so than in healthcare, where LLMs are being leveraged to assist doctors, researchers, and patients.

LLMs are poised to create huge efficiencies for clinicians as well as facility administrators by liberating them from their keyboards. LLMs could also prove to be very good at checking in with patients with chronic conditions during the time between conventional encounters with caregivers, writing notes in patients' records, and summarizing patients' issues. All of this could make care much faster and may even allow physicians to spend more quality time engaging with their patients.

Such musings are far from academic. In September 2023, Oracle Computer announced that it is poised to market an AI-powered voice- and screen-based Clinical Digital Assistant that can conduct administrative tasks in response to conversational voice commands. In June 2024, Oracle launched its Clinical Digital Assistant and early adopting clinicians have quoted being able to save 10-12 minutes per patient. Major GAI players, including Google, IBM, Microsoft, and NVIDIA, have all been focused on healthcare of late.

GAI and LLM solutions properly leveraged and deployed are revolutionizing healthcare in terms of enhanced clinical decision-making, medical research/drug discovery, and remarkable improvements in patient communication and engagement.

Longitudinal Care Management and GAI

Longitudinal care management (LCM) is a relatively new concept in healthcare based on proactive care management to prevent hospitalizations and minimize the burden of complex illnesses. The basic mission of any company providing LCM is to have patients in their organization spend more time at home and less time in the hospital. As you might imagine, to be as effective and game-changing as it can be, LCM requires an enormous level of individualization to develop intense personal care plans and achieve that goal.

This is where GAI solutions driven by LLM's come in.

Vivid Health is one of the nation's leading innovators in providing solutions for LCM. They recognized that GAI could fulfill the promise of LCM by improving efficiency, reducing administrative burdens, making up for staff shortages, and improving patient engagement.

They partnered with Cambridge, MA-based BigRio to develop an LLM-driven end-to-end solution, that today can assess a patient's status on any combination of more than 100 chronic conditions across 16 specialties, generating personalized care plans at scale in under 30 seconds. That's over 75 million possible care plan combinations in a fraction of the time it typically takes to pull together individualized plans.

Vivid approached BigRio with the challenge to create a multi-tenant patient care application that could do the following:

- Comprehend patient assessments across 16 specialties and 100 conditions to assess a patient's medical status and provide care accordingly.
- Capture patient assessment responses via mobile and desktop devices, 24 hours a day, seven days a week.
- Collaborate with providers to provide personalized care plans for each patient that the doctors and nurses could adjust and approve rather than having to build themselves.
- Increase the speed and scale of data analysis and care plan creation significantly, thus reducing provider time in front of the computer.
- Provide a seamless tracking solution for patient follow-up based on the needs of each patient.

BigRio and Vivid Health worked in collaboration to design and implement a novel multi-tenant system that leverages GAI and LLMs to provide a better, more comprehensive patient care journey that benefits both the patient and the care team. Together, the two AI innovators created a system that utilizes an LLM to extract pertinent information and generate actionable recommendations that guide healthcare professionals in developing the best plan of action for patients.

In a press release announcing the launch of the AI platform co-created with BigRio, Patrick Mobley (American Medical Association, 2023), CEO of Vivid Health, said,

> When we are facing provider burnout, a nursing shortage, and a growing patient population with multiple conditions, it would be ethically wrong not to try and fix this problem in the time it takes for a patient to walk to the doctor's office. We fundamentally believe there should be a single, enterprise platform that integrates into any EMR to guide patients on the right journey, no matter if they're facing pre/post-surgery, chronic care, oncology, women's health, mental health issues or any unique combination of these conditions.

Additionally, to create a customized LLM solution for their healthcare clients', BigRio has launched its proprietary GAI tool, Odyssey Accelerator. The first-of-its-kind platform, Odyssey Accelerator, enables healthcare operations of all sizes and developers of healthcare IT to use GAI to transform the way they search or query enterprise data, design workflows, derive enterprise analytics, generate reports, and build a proof-of-concept model before scaling it enterprise-wide. Critically, the tool keeps all such queried data 100% private, which allows employees and other stakeholders of the organization to connect to all enterprise knowledge, search, chat, and query without having to expose or compromise their data to the public domain.

Retrieval-Augmented Generation

BigRio's Odyssey Accelerator relies on a recent breakthrough in GAI technology – Retrieval-augmented generation, or RAG. RAG excels at enhancing report generation, creating user-friendly dashboards, and the analysis of complex information by intelligently integrating relevant, up-to-date data into coherent outputs. RAG's ability to dynamically pull and synthesize information from vast data sources ensures that decision-makers have access to the most accurate and current insights, making it indispensable for informed decision-making and strategic planning.

Odyssey Accelerator serves as the foundational framework for deploying tailored RAG solutions and integrating with EMR/EHR systems like Epic and others.

LLMs Are Transforming Healthcare, But Challenges Remain

The American Medical Association (AMA) is in full support of LLM solutions like Vivid Health's AI-driven LCM solution. The organization has found about 20% of US-based practices are already using AI. The AMA's President, Jesse Ehrenfeld, MD, MPH, (American Medical Association, 2023) says "AI should be leveraged first to unburden physicians." In other words, "use the AI to detether us from our computers, help bring us back to our patients and restore the patient-physician relationship," Ehrenfeld noted.

However, in a recent report, the AMA also outlined some of the issues with GAI and the challenges that remain. The report *The Emerging Landscape of Augmented Intelligence in Health Care* by Patrick Mobley (American Medical Association, 2023) explores key terms and definitions, potential applications and use cases, and other opportunities and risks that current and future AI tools present.

The report emphasized that GAI and LLM applications, such as real-time clinical transcription, answering patient questions via chatbot, and drafting personalized patient education materials, have immense potential to improve efficiency and patient engagement across all medical specialties today.

However, alongside these opportunities, the AMA underscores the many challenges and risks healthcare organizations face when pursuing AI implementation. Bias, explainability, transparency, model hallucination, coding and payment, privacy, regulation, and liability are the primary challenges that providers must reckon with prior to, during, and following the deployment of GAI tools.

Odyssey Accelerator was specifically designed to help mitigate these concerns. Retrieval-augmented generation strategies can be specifically targeted to minimize these risks by exercising greater discretion in the selection of training data, thorough auditing of GAI outputs, maintaining total data privacy, and taking corrective steps to minimize any biases identified. Odyssey's ability to provide a proof-of-concept model before enterprise-wide deployment provides an ideal arena to detect and solve such issues prior to large-scale launch.

Where Will This Take Us?

Over the past decade, we've seen a proliferation of innovation hit the healthcare market. Then, suddenly, in the past 12 months, the world was introduced to the single most powerful efficiency tool ever created: GAI. The underpinning of success for most clinical organizations has always relied on staff efficiency plus patient and provider engagement.

Creating an engaging customer experience has always been a particular challenge in healthcare. A constant complaint among healthcare consumers is "feeling like a number" and dealing with hospitals and healthcare providers that seem to lack a personal touch in a setting where that should be the rule rather than the exception.

Vivid/BigRio's GAI-driven LCM solution is just one example of how LLMs can change all that with their unique ability to craft deeply individualized customer care plans and doctor-patient exchanges. Drawing from past data and leveraging the power and security of RAG technology, GAI tools can create bespoke emails and responses, bypassing the old "one-size-fits-all" approach. In tandem with this, the technology's predictive prowess can foresee a patient's future needs, desires, and actions. This foresight lets care providers be much more proactive, offering solutions even before the patient voices their requirements.

Right now, the healthcare sector is experiencing a tectonic shift with the integration of GAI. What was theoretical only a few months ago is now being used in real-world applications across the clinical landscape, reshaping how caregivers provide services and how healthcare organizations manage operations.

Vivid Health's AI-driven LCM platform is currently the most powerful on the market. Its successful development and deployment stand as a testament to GAI's potential to enhance the quality and efficiency of healthcare delivery. As these technologies continue to evolve, they will likely address more complex healthcare challenges, paving the way for a future where AI-driven solutions are integral to every aspect of healthcare.

The eventual large-scale adoption of these kinds of technologies will bring us that much closer to an efficient, effective, and patient-centered healthcare system, where clinicians and other healthcare suppliers can not only provide more effective and efficient care but revolutionize the entire patient experience.

Conclusion

What follows is less of a summary and more of an admonishment. My hope is that this is not just another book with some good stories but a catalyst for you and me. A catalyst for our industry. A catalyst to push harder and more thoughtfully along this healthcare technology journey. The beauty of the innovation pathway is its simplicity. The processes are proven, and the framework is widely adopted. While I do not believe there is a formula for innovation, this framework provides a solid process and pathway from which to innovate. We must do everything possible to propagate repeatable processes with bonafide examples that might inspire others to innovate with AI.

Simply put, organizations that embrace AI have a higher likelihood of success in an increasingly competitive marketplace. Survival of the Digitalist.

This is how you do it.

Blending cultures is a key place to start. You must make sure you have organizational buy-in and commitment. In cases where this is not possible, start small, gain experience, establish credibility, and doors may open. I admit that occasionally, you just need to create a skunk's works of sorts, demonstrate value, and ask for forgiveness later.

While it is critical to leverage technology, never start there. We are in the people business. You have to strike that perfect balance in your organization between people, processes, and technology. Win the confidence and hearts of people, and everything else will fall into place.

Some may think planning is an innovation inhibitor, but our contributors have shown otherwise. Innovation success is often multiplied when you use sound planning principles and create roadmaps. Sometimes innovation just happens as needs arise, but roadmaps have a stronger track record.

John Maxwell says that "one is too small a number for greatness." I agree. Very few innovations come from a single person. They come from a team of teams or an agile environment where collaboration and communication dominate the culture. I do not recall any innovation that I have been involved with that emanated from just one person.

One of the key tasks of a leader is to eliminate barriers. Some of the contributors highlighted roadblocks to innovation and how they overcame them. Whenever you pioneer, you naturally encounter barriers. Accept this fact, and do not be discouraged. Rather, see barriers as signs you are on the right path. Then relentlessly eliminate them.

A primary key to Apple's success has been the diligent pursuit of simplicity. Too often we complicate matters, which in turn reduces our opportunity for success. Always seek to simplify the complex. The more focus, the sharper the solution. Innovation dies with complexity.

It's human nature to be driven by recognition and reward. We have a propensity to repeat those things which are rewarded. Create programs and incentives for innovation. It will eventually become the fabric of you and your organization. Celebrate failure. Especially failure.

Just as you seek to collaborate within your organization, consider including other key partners. Many of the examples in this book were instances of supplier and provider collaboration. Member and patient collaboration is powerful as well. Often, a collaborator will have the missing piece for you to complete or enhance your innovation.

Now that you have completely read this book, I want to leave you with what I believe is the single biggest key to successful innovation: You.

To be innovative, you must be innovative.

You can take the innovation pathways framework and adopt it in your organization. As the stories demonstrate, when the framework is adopted well, it will work. If you want to get to the next level, work on yourself. Seek to be an innovative person if you are not already. Too often, I speak with people who are frustrated because of a lack of innovation in their organization. The first question I ask them is how they make sure they are personally innovative. If they are still using kiosks at the airport, probably not innovative. If they still have a printer in their office, probably not innovative. If they are still going to their local bank or grocery store, probably not innovative. If they have the same hobbies as they did ten years ago, the same clothing and music styles ... probably not innovative. If they don't routinely read and study inside and outside of their expertise, they are probably not innovative. Same phone forever? Same glasses? Same drink? Basically, if you are limiting your experiences, you are unable to take advantage of all the diversity in science, nature, tech, the arts, and philosophy. It is the combinations of these inputs that make one innovative.

So, if you are not innovative, you will struggle to innovate.

The solution is simple and pragmatic. Do new things. Constantly introduce change into your life. Consume diverse news and listen to contrarian viewpoints. Activate Twitter, Snapchat, and Instagram. Download new music. Learn a new dance or hobby. Go back to school. Use all the tech in your car. Grab a mentor who is a generation or two younger. If you are a technologist, learn art or learn music. If your background is in the arts, dive into a tech certification. I guarantee that as you become innovative, everything else will follow. And we will change the world.

AI has already demonstrated great the value and it is up to leaders like us to continue the relentless pursuit of new discoveries that ultimately help save lives.

Bibliography

American Medical Association. (2023, June 15). ChatGPT, AI in health care and the future of medicine with AMA President Jesse Ehrenfeld, MD, MPH. https://www.ama-assn.org/practice-management/digital/chatgpt-ai-health-care-and-future-medicine-ama-president-jesse

American Medical Association, & Manatt Health. (2023). *The emerging landscape of augmented intelligence in health care.* American Medical Association. https://www.ama-assn.org/system/files/future-health-augmented-intelligence-health-care.pdf

Eschenroeder, H.C., Jr, Manzione, L.C., Adler-Milstein, J., Bice, C., Cash, R., Duda, C., Joseph, C., et al. "Associations of Physician Burnout with Organizational Electronic Health Record Support and After-Hours Charting." *Journal of the American Medical Informatics Association*, vol. 28, no. 5, 2021, 960–966. 10.1093/jamia/ocab053

Harry, E., Sinsky, C., Dyrbye, L.N., Makowski, M.S., Trockel, M., Tutty, M., Carlasare, L.E., West, C.P., & Shanafelt, T.D. https://www.linkedin.com/pulse/vivid-healths-ai-platform-revolutionizes-longitudinal-patrick-mobley/ "Physician task load and the risk of burnout among US physicians in a national survey." *Joint Commission Journal on Quality and Patient Safety*, vol. 47, no. 2, 2021, 76–85. 10.1016/j.jcjq.2020.09.011

Index

Pages in *italics* refer to figures and pages in **bold** refer to tables.

For Product Safety Concerns and Information,
please contact our EU representative GPSR@taylorandfrancis.com
Taylor & Francis Verlag GmbH, Kaufingerstraße 24,
80331 München, Germany

Printed by Integrated Books International,
United States of America